University-Business Partnerships

ISSUES IN ACADEMIC ETHICS

General Editor: Steven M. Cahn

Campus Rules and Moral Community: In Place of *In Loco Parentis*
by David A. Hoekema, Calvin College

University-Business Partnerships: An Assessment
by Norman E. Bowie, University of Minnesota, Twin Cities

A Professor's Duties: Ethical Issues in College Teaching
by Peter J. Markie, University of Missouri–Columbia

Neutrality and the Academic Ethic
by Robert L. Simon, Hamilton College

University-Business Partnerships

An Assessment

NORMAN E. BOWIE

Rowman & Littlefield Publishers, Inc.

ROWMAN & LITTLEFIELD PUBLISHERS, INC.

Published in the United States of America
by Rowman & Littlefield Publishers, Inc.
4720 Boston Way, Lanham, Maryland 20706

3 Henrietta Street, London WC2E 8LU, England

British Cataloging in Publication Information Available

Library of Congress Cataloging-in-Publication Data

Bowie, Norman E., 1942–
University-business partnerships : an assessment / Norman E. Bowie.
p.   cm. — (Issues in academic ethics)
Includes bibliographical references and index.
1. Research—United States.   2. Research—Finance—United States.
3. Universities and colleges—Research—United States.
4. Engineering—Research—United States.   5. Industry and
education—United States.   6. Partnership—United States.   I. Title.
II. Series.
Q180.U5B68   1994   607'.2—dc20   93–45481 CIP

ISBN 0–8476–7896–2 (cloth : alk. paper)
ISBN 0–8476–7897–0 (pbk. : alk. paper)

Printed in the United States of America

Contents

ISSUES IN ACADEMIC ETHICS

Foreword
by Steven M. Cahn, general editor

Academic life generates a variety of moral issues. These may be faced by students, staff, administrators, or trustees, but most often revolve around the rights and responsibilities of the faculty. In my 1986 book *Saints and Scamps: Ethics in Academia* (Rowman & Littlefield), I set out to enumerate, explain, and emphasize the most fundamental of these professorial obligations. To do justice to the complexities of academic ethics, however, requires the work of many scholars focused on numerous areas of investigation. The results of such an effort are embodied in this series.

Each volume concentrates on one set of connected issues and combines a single-authored monograph with reprinted sources chosen by the author to exemplify or amplify materials in the text. This format is intended to guide readers while encouraging them to develop and defend their own beliefs.

In recent years philosophers have examined the appropriate standards of conduct for physicians, nurses, lawyers, journalists, business managers, and government policymakers but have not given equal attention to formulating guidelines for their own profession. The time has come to observe the Delphic motto "Know thyself." Granted, the issues in need of critical examination are not exotic, but as the history of philosophy demonstrates, self-knowledge is often the most important to seek and the most difficult to attain.

Preface

This study of university-business partnerships evolved from an earlier paper on the subject published in Professor Steven Cahn's *Morality, Responsibility and the University* (Temple University Press, 1990). Research on the project began in 1990 shortly after my arrival at the University of Minnesota. I was fortunate from the beginning to have philosophy Ph.D. student Paul Jeffries as my research assistant. Paul did the bibliographical work, secured the various documents from universities, government agencies, and corporations, and critically evaluated the early drafts of the manuscript. Throughout our association, we had many conversations based on ideas and suggestions Paul provided. Many of the suggestions undoubtedly have been incorporated into the manuscript but at this point it is difficult to specify those arguments for which Paul deserves credit. Suffice it to say that this is a much better book than it would have been without Paul's input.

During the past year I have benefited greatly from the assistance of another Ph.D. student in philosophy, Denis Arnold. Denis has read and critically evaluated the two most recent drafts of the manuscript, providing editorial assistance and substantive suggestions for strengthening old arguments as well as providing new ones. Yet a third philosophy Ph.D. student, Bryan Frances, has been responsible for the permissions. I am also grateful for the suggestions provided by my colleagues in Strategic Management and Organization in response to a presentation based on the manuscript. Finally I acknowledge the support of Steve Cahn who provided the opportunity for the project and the encouragement to see it through to completion.

In the previously published article, I maintained a fairly positive evaluation of university-business partnerships. At the time I believed that the problems associated with them were not essentially different in kind or scope from problems in academia generally. If university-business partnerships raised conflict-of-commitment problems, so, for example, did traditional consulting and professional service. This book is far more skeptical and critical. There are more negative data available. The University of Minnesota has had serious problems with some of its partnerships in the medical area. (A couple of these problems are briefly discussed in the book, but this is not a book about problems in University of Minnesota university-business partnerships.) Finally Paul Jeffries and Denis Arnold came to the issue with a more skeptical view than I. Their challenging questions have made a mark. Ultimately, however, I am responsible for the assessments made here. Suffice it to say that opinion in the 1990s will probably be more balanced and cautious regarding university-business partnerships.

Minneapolis, November 1993

Acknowledgments

The following readings in Part Three are reprinted with permission, as noted.

"The Evolution of Research and Development Policy in a Corporation: A Case Study" by W. G. Simeral is reprinted from *Partners in the Research Enterprise: University Corporate Relations in Science and Technology,* Thomas W. Langfitt, Sheldon Hackney, Alfred P. Fishman, and Albert V. Glowasky, eds., with the permission of the University of Pennsylvania Press and the author.

"The Commercialized University" by Derek Bok is reprinted from "Universities: Their Temptations and Tensions," *Journal of College and University Law,* 1991, with the permission of the National Association of College and University Attorneys and the author.

"The Erosion of the Academic Ethos: The Case of Biology" from the background paper by Nicholas Wade in *The Science Business: Report of the Twentieth Century Fund Task Force on the Commercialization of Scientific Research* (New York: Priority Press, 1984). Reprinted by permission of the Twentieth Century Fund.

"Pajaro Dunes Conference—Draft Statement" reprinted with permission of the National Association of College and University Attorneys.

"Government-University-Industry Research Roundtable: Model Agreements for University-Industry Cooperative Research" is reprinted from "Simplified and Standardized Model Agreements for University-Industry Cooperative Research" with the permission of the National Academy Press.

"National Science Foundation Program Announcement: Industry/University Cooperative Research Centers Program" is reprinted by permission of the National Science Foundation.

"Government-University-Industry Research Roundtable: New Alliances and Partnerships in American Science and Engineering" Academy Industry Program. Reprinted with permission from *New Alliances and Partnerships in American Science and Engineering.* Copyright 1986 by the National Academy of Sciences. Courtesy of the National Academy Press, Washington, D.C.

"Government-University-Industry Research Roundtable: Industrial Perspectives on Innovation and Interactions with Universities" is reprinted from "Summary of Interviews with Senior Industrial Officials" with the permission of the National Academy Press.

"Corporate Funding of Academic Research (AAUP Report)" is reprinted from "Academic Freedom and Tenure: Corporate Funding of Academic Research," *Academe,* November–December 1983, by permission of *Academe.*

"The University of Minnesota: Disclosure of Conflict of Interest" is reprinted by permission of the University of Minnesota Board of Regents.

"Guidelines for Technology Licensing to 'Start-up' Companies in Which Stanford Faculty Are Involved" is reprinted by permission of Stanford University.

"Massachusetts Institute of Technology: Conflict of Interest" is reprinted from "Guide to the Ownership, Distribution and Commercial Development of M.I.T. Technology," M.I.T. Technology—Policies and Procedures, 1989, by permission of the Massachusetts Institute of Technology.

Introduction

The decade of the 1980s was one of experimentation, growth, and dynamism in American business. Mergers and acquisitions grew exponentially in size and number. In part they were made possible by junk-bond financing and government deregulation. These in turn were made possible because of a fundamental shift in American values. High levels of debt became acceptable and our attention focused on competitiveness. Government regulation was seen as a problem rather than a cure for our economic ills.

In the 1990s a reassessment of eighties' attitudes and values is underway. Hostile takeovers create social harm. High levels of debt are bad; low levels of debt are good. Junk-bond financing is what the name implies: junk. Government regulation is sometimes necessary to prevent the excesses that can result from private greed.

During the "go-go" years of the 1980s another business phenomenon exploded on the scene yet passed virtually unnoticed in the popular consciousness. Business entered into strategic partnerships with universities. Not only were these partnerships permitted by government, they were positively encouraged. What remains to be seen is whether this development will fall into disfavor, as has happened with hostile takeovers and junk-bond deficit financing. However, as we shall see, the early 1990s present concrete evidence that a critical reassessment has indeed begun.

This monograph tells the story of the explosive growth of university-business partnerships during the 1980s. The story begins in the early part of the twentieth century when such partnerships began to emerge. It continues with an account of how recent studies in biotechnology fueled desires for income by both parties and how government encouraged this goal by passing legislation that made university-business

1

partnerships administratively easier and more likely to bear fruit. In the 1980s government aid for education decreased sharply and some university officials sought to soften the blow by entering into partnerships with business. State governments enacted legislation that provided financial support for university-business partnerships in the hope that these partnerships would strengthen the state's competitive position by encouraging businesses to develop and remain within the state. The most pressing question about these partnerships is whether greater involvement with business will make higher education better or worse. Thus this monograph concludes with an extensive evaluation of the costs and benefits business partnerships bring to American higher education.

Before beginning our story, it is necessary to point out that there are many types of university-business cooperative arrangements and that only a few of them—those that raise the most questions—can be covered by this research. Of special interest are cooperative research centers or industrial associates programs. Many of these centers are administered by universities with the purpose of applying academic research to the solution of business problems, especially problems of technology transfer. Receiving less attention will be personnel exchanges; individual consulting arrangements (numerically the largest of the university-business cooperative arrangements); and industry support for seminars, speakers, and publications. (For a representative list of different types of university-business cooperative research, see the report by the Business–Higher Education Forum, *Beyond the Rhetoric*, 1988.)

PART ONE

An Assessment of University-Business Partnerships

SECTION ONE

A History of the Development of University-Business Partnerships, 1920–1980

Our story begins at the University of Wisconsin in the 1920s. In 1924 Professor Henry Steenbock published research demonstrating that Vitamin D could be activated by irradiating food. (This discovery eventually enabled the United States to eliminate rickets as a childhood disease.) Steenbock did more than publish his research; he sought to patent his discovery. He was motivated to take this unusual step in part because he did not want his work abused by careless manufacturers and also because he had a genuine desire that the University of Wisconsin share in the benefits of his research (Blumenthal, Epstein, and Maxwell, 1986, 1621). When Steenbock offered the university the rights to the invention, the university's Board of Regents turned him down on the grounds that there was no guarantee of a return (Bremer, 1978). Private industry was not so reticent. The Quaker Oats Company offered Steenbock $900,000 for exclusive rights (Blumenthal, Epstein, and Maxwell, 1986).

In 1925 the Wisconsin Regents made another decision that definitely would not be seen in the 1980s. They voted not to accept any funds from private business or from private philanthropic organizations. Progressives in the Republican party had objected to a gift from John D. Rockefeller. Since the Regents had removed the University as a possible recipient of funds, the founding of a foundation was necessary if interested faculty and donors were to achieve their goal of receiving funds from private businesspersons like Rockefeller. At that point the dean of the graduate school found nine alumni to donate $100 each to start a foundation. That foundation was to become the Wisconsin Alumni Research Foundation (WARF).

5

The Wisconsin Alumni Research Foundation was a nonprofit organization and technically separate from the university. As such it could
receive private funds from business. It also became the owner of
patents of products invented by faculty working in cooperation with
industry, including Steenbock's patent for the irradiation of food to
activate Vitamin D. Steenbock's patent brought the Wisconsin Alumni
Research Foundation great success. During its first fifty years, WARF
issued 650 licenses, about 400 of which were under the Steenbock
patent. There were 1,702 invention disclosures during this fifty-year
period. Forty-three, or about 2.5 percent, resulted in income-producing
inventions. Of these forty-three inventions, fourteen have produced
between $10,000 and $100,000, nine have produced between $100,000
and $1,000,000, and four have produced in excess of $1,000,000 (Bremer).

It should be noted that Wisconsin faculty participation in WARF has
always been voluntary. The WARF royalty policy has consistently
awarded 15 percent to the inventors and the remaining 85 percent to
WARF's annual research grant to the university. In addition WARF
does not ask for a delay in publication, even if publication would mean
that no products from the invention would be developed (Bremer).

Nonetheless, the early experience of the Wisconsin Alumni Research Foundation provided two crucial examples of the kinds of
problems university-business partnerships could create. The first problem focused on WARF's licensing policies and the legal defense of its
patents. In addition to his concern for the University of Wisconsin,
Steenbock was also concerned about the health of the dairy industry
and was worried that it would suffer undue hardship if the manufacturers of oleomargarine could benefit by using his irradiation process.
Oleomargarine is a competitor of butter, and the presence of Vitamin
D in butter but not in oleomargarine would give the dairy industry a
competitive advantage. As a result, WARF withheld a Vitamin D
irradiation license from the oleomargarine industry for many years
(Edsall and Bearman, 1979).

In the 1940s the foundation's attempt to pursue two patent infringement suits on the Steenbock Vitamin D irradiation process resulted in
antitrust charges by the federal government. In a stunning defeat for
WARF the Ninth Circuit Court ruled that the creation of Vitamin D by
sunlight was certainly not patentable, and that others had preceded
Steenbock in using artificial irradiation as the cure for rickets. The
court rebuked the foundation for withholding a license from the manufacturers of oleomargarine. In 1946, the final chapter in the fight over

Steenbock's discovery was concluded. Since the principal patent was soon due to expire, the foundation surrendered the Vitamin D patent to the public rather than fight the matter in court. The foundation was sued again in 1965 and in 1970, and again the foundation surrendered its patents (Blumenthal, Epstein, and Maxwell, 1986).

In 1948, WARF's withholding of the irradiation license for oleomargarine and other licensing restrictions were the subject of a *Reader's Digest* exposé entitled "Combination in Restraint of Health" (Maisel, 1948). Among the charges made in that article were the following:

1. The licenses were narrowly restricted. One firm could irradiate evaporated milk alone while another could only irradiate fluid milk.
2. Licensees were restricted to selling their food product only to food manufacturers licensed by and paying royalties to the foundation.
3. By not granting a license to the makers of oleomargarine, the poor were deprived of a source of Vitamin D to protect them from rickets.
4. Food producers were restricted in the amount of Vitamin D they could put into their food products. This forced patients who needed Vitamin D to pay exorbitant rates for pharmaceutical products. The manufacturers of these pharmaceuticals had licensing agreements with the foundation that in effect fixed prices.
5. Licensing agreements with the pharmaceutical companies had rigid controls on both the potency of the dosage and the size of the packages.
6. When General Mills developed a different way to manufacture a Vitamin D pharmaceutical, the foundation commissioned a study to test the efficacy of the two products (General Mills and Steenbock's). When the study concluded there was no essential difference between the two, the foundation attempted to prevent publication of the research.

Ironically, the government could do nothing until the foundation sued for patent infringement. Then the Department of Justice was able to bring the antitrust implications of WARF's licensing policies before the court. The *Reader's Digest* article contended that a Vitamin D treatment for arthritis cost $25 before the patent was surrendered and $4.50 thereafter. If these numbers are correct, research dollars for University of Wisconsin faculty were obtained in part from the sufferers of arthritis.

The fact that the Wisconsin Alumni Research Foundation managed contracts, license arrangements, and patents had forced this academic research foundation to act like a business. It had to protect its patent rights in court. A patent for a treatment for secondary anemia was successfully defended in court in 1936. Not surprisingly, in WARF's first report, published in the year of its patent victory, the authors acknowledged that a "business" built on patents must have the financial reserves to protect them. The report stated, "If a patent becomes valuable, one may rest assured that the most strenuous efforts will be made to void it. Even if this isn't accomplished, infringers are sure to arise." Thus many of the criticisms of the university-business partnerships of the 1980s arose in the early part of the century. Patents had to be defended and such defenses are costly. There was a danger that licensing arrangements would be manipulated in ways that violate the university's commitment to the free flow of knowledge. As universities became involved in business activities, there was a danger that they would behave unethically or illegally. The unfolding of events surrounding the irradiation of Vitamin D patent was amazingly prescient.

The second difficulty concerned distributional inequities caused by the policy of the foundation of supporting only research in the natural sciences. In the 1950s and 1960s arts and social science faculty pressed the foundation for support. By the mid-1960s the foundation relented and agreed to share some of its funds with nonscience faculty. The issue of distributional inequities, like the others mentioned above, is prominent in contemporary discussions of university-business partnerships. Many contend that the profits from university-business partnerships should be shared across all the university's programs so that the humanities and social sciences do not become impoverished relative to the biological and natural sciences.

WARF represents an example of a foundation independent of the university although closely allied with it. Another early example of university-business partnerships is found at the Massachusetts Institute of Technology, where the notion of such partnerships has enjoyed widespread institutional support. MIT was founded in 1862, the same year that Congress passed the Morrill Act establishing land-grant universities. MIT was designed as an alternative to the classical education of the time, which had little room for science and no room for applied science focused on practical problems. In the first quarter of the twentieth century MIT established the most prestigious department of electrical engineering in the world. That achievement was due in large part to Dugald Jackson, who had come to MIT in 1907. He had been the chief engineer for the Edison GE Company (Chicago office) and had established the first department of electrical engineering at the University of Wisconsin. With the approval of the Electrical Engineering Department's Visiting and Advisory Committee, Jackson actively sought financial support from industry for research that had commercial application. For over ten years he received annual support from AT&T. When AT&T funding ended in 1925, GE provided funding on an annual basis (Noble, 1977, 139–40).

Seeking industrial support for research with commercial applications was not limited to MIT's Department of Electrical Engineering. By the turn of the century MIT had developed a most distinguished chemistry department. Most of its faculty were originally MIT undergraduates who had studied at German universities (Servos, 1980). The faculty had two conflicting philosophies regarding the future of research at MIT. Arthur Noyes led one faction, which believed MIT should be converted from an engineering school to a science-based university with a graduate school that emphasized basic research. Rather than teach students applied engineering science, Noyes and his followers believed they should be educated in the principles of the physical sciences. In 1903 this group of faculty, with the support of like-minded alumni and trustees convinced the administration to create a Research Laboratory of Physical Chemistry that would be devoted to basic research in chemistry. The laboratory was financed by MIT, the Carnegie Institution of Washington, and by Noyes himself. Within a few years, it had gained an international reputation as the premier research institute in chemistry (Servos, 1980).

The other faction, led by William Walker and engineering consultant alumnus Arthur D. Little, argued that MIT should be faithful to its tradition of training applied scientists. This faction was particularly successful at organizing the undergraduate curriculum so that applied procedures were its focus. Since the equipment and materials used in illustrating basic operations on an industrial scale were expensive and prone to rapid obsolescence, Walker and his supporters established what amounted to a cooperative extension program that enabled MIT faculty and undergraduates to study industrial processes on site at selected industrial plants (Servos, 1980). In 1908 the Research Laboratory of Applied Chemistry was created with Walker as its director.

Both Noyes's and Walker's labs were created as semiautonomous units with the bulk of their income drawn from research contracts with industrial companies and trade associations (Servos, 1980). Walker, however, wanted his laboratory to be of assistance to American industry as it competed with Germany as well as other European industrial firms. But the focus of competition was Germany. The Germans had developed university-business partnerships in the nineteenth century and Walker wanted his MIT laboratory to be a model for similar research laboratories in other American universities.

Thus MIT had two semiautonomous laboratories with competing research philosophies. Noyes's emphasized basic research in chemistry; Walker's emphasized applied research in chemical engineering. MIT did not choose between them but as the twentieth century wore on, Walker's laboratory prospered at the expense of Noyes's. Walker won the battle for undergraduate enrollments. In 1905–1909, the majority of MIT undergraduates majored in chemistry rather than chemical engineering. In 1910–1914, undergraduate majors in chemical engineering outnumbered majors in chemistry by a ratio of better than two to one. The numerical advantage increased to the point where in 1920–1924 only fifty-two undergraduate degrees were awarded in chemistry while 419 degrees were awarded in chemical engineering. The funding of MIT shifted in Walker's direction as well. Before 1910, the old Boston elite funded the school. After 1910, such outsiders as George Eastman (Rochester, N.Y.) and Pierre du Pont (Wilmington, Del.) provided MIT with grants that exceeded the value of MIT's endowment and plant in 1910 by a factor of three. Individuals like Eastman and Du Pont were not engaging in noblesse-oblige thinking; they wanted to build a relationship with MIT so that they could have access to MIT's chemical engineering graduates.

As Walker gained influence, some of Noyes's allies on the faculty left for the University of California at Berkeley. Noyes tried a number of tactics to restore the balance. Walker forced MIT President R. C. Maclaurin's hand. In April 1919 Maclaurin asked Noyes to withdraw from an active role in the chemistry department; Noyes resigned (Servos, 1980).

In the battle between basic research and applied research, applied research by 1920 was the apparent winner. Walker was appointed director of the newly established Division of Industrial Cooperation and Research. This entity was an attempt by MIT to solve a financial crisis precipitated by a series of adverse political events. The Massachusetts Supreme Court voided a cooperative arrangement with Harvard that deprived MIT of funds that Harvard gave it to provide engineering education to Harvard students, and in 1920 the Massachusetts legislature failed to renew its appropriation for MIT (Noble, 1977, 142).

In the Division of Industrial Cooperation and Research, cooperation took the following form: Industrial firms paid MIT an annual retaining fee, and MIT provided consulting services and access to alumni records. Walker lined up $400,000 worth of contracts in the first year. Compare that to MIT's 1920–21 budget of $1.7 million (Servos, 1980). Just as in the 1980s, a university-business partnership was created in large part as a response to declining government support.

MIT's plan attracted wide attention and was described at length in the March 1920 *Scientific American*. The idea of university-business cooperative relationships caught on quickly at universities with a heavy emphasis in technical training. Cooperative relationships during this time were established at the universities of Rochester, Pittsburgh, Cincinnati, Dayton, Akron, and Lehigh, as well as at Case Institute and the Drexel Institute of Technology (Noble, 1977, 145).

However, the dangers of the Walker approach quickly became apparent. At its apogee, Walker's laboratory made a number of decisions that gave considerable ammunition to its critics. Walker's sales tactics resulted in such criticism, that the administration forbade Walker from using them. On January 1, 1921, Walker resigned. His "victory" over Noyes had lasted only a year.

Although the laboratory survived Walker's departure its activities were severely criticized. Industry was interested in narrowly defined questions (e.g., Vacuum Oil Company wanted a better method of manufacturing oil barrels so that the barrels would not leak during shipment) (Servos, 1980). Academic readers might expect such narrowly focused applied reseach to be turned down, but since the lab needed outside funding, the administrators of the lab did not turn down the more specific proposals they received. The acceptance of some assignments as specific as improved oil barrels might have been tolerated if research topics of interest to an entire industry had been forthcoming, but alas they were not. One of the concerns about university-business partnerships in the 1980s was that the pressure to obtain funding would skew research away from basic research to applied research and even more ominously from basic research to specific product development. MIT's early successful partnership was criticized on just these grounds.

Some research projects created other problems. Humble Oil Company refused to allow laboratory staff to publish its discovery of a better method for the vacuum distillation of lubricating oil. Under the terms of its contract with the lab, Humble Oil had every legal right to do so. Another research discovery was suppressed by the National Lime Association (Servos, 1980). Critics complained that laboratory staff were more like commercial consultants than members of an educational research center. Some members of the laboratory staff concurred. Restrictions on publication and the suppression of research are concerns of many critics of contemporary university-business partnerships.

Finally, there were difficulties in the consistency of funding. Most of the contracts were signed on a year-to-year basis. When economic conditions worsened, the number of contracts decreased. As a result, there was a perception that it was difficult to attract and even more difficult to retain the best people. As John Servos (1980) concluded in his research on the early MIT experiments:

> The depression underlined in dramatic fashion the dangers inherent in a policy of relying upon industrial patronage for the support of research at educational institutions. What had appeared initially as a natural and beneficial alliance of businessmen and applied scientists revealed itself in the 1930's to be a temporary and unstable partnership. Contributions to the support of applied research at MIT and other American educational institutions were marginal expenses to most businesses; when the need to economize became urgent, they were among the first costs to be cut. Those who had depended upon industrial support, at MIT as at other schools, were quick to suffer the consequences.

It is still too early to tell whether the 1980s strategy of developing university-business partnerships will provide increased rather than decreased financial stability in the years ahead. The recent negative report, to be discussed in detail later, from some business participants in university-business partnerships is certainly a cause for concern.

As a result of these difficulties and the more theoretical interests of engineers, MIT began to correct the imbalance that had developed between basic and applied research. Declining financial support resulted in the termination of the Research Laboratory of Applied Chemistry in 1934. The mission and organization of the Division of Industrial Cooperation and Research were redefined. If projects could be handled by private consultants, these projects could not be accepted. Firms that wanted to keep the results of the research confidential suffered heavy financial penalties. Creative research was to be the foremost criterion for promotion. Consulting activities counted for little, and too much consulting actually hurt a professor's chances for promotion. A tax of 50 percent was placed on consulting fees. Karl Compton, president of MIT during the 1930s adopted Noyes's vision of MIT as a science-based university. The traditional emphasis was restored.

What message from these historical case studies should we bring to our project? In the 1990s American universities are experiencing serious financial problems as well as a crisis of public confidence. It is too early to tell whether those universities that have sought to solve their financial and public relations problems by developing partnerships with businesses will be successful in the long run. However, the historical case studies examined here show that such partnerships can bring problems of their own.

Government Assistance For University-Business Partnerships

The vast increase in the number and configuration of university-business partnerships in the 1980s has many explanations, but surely a necessary condition for the extent of their development was a policy decision by government to promote them. The development of university-business partnerships has been a matter of public policy at both the federal and state level. This governmental support has been extremely popular. At the federal level, the effort began with the Nixon administration in the 1970s. Two prominent programs, the Industry-University Cooperative Research Projects Program and the Industry-University Cooperative Research Centers Program, have been administered by the National Science Foundation. Because the Projects Program resembles traditional consulting relationships and is usually limited to two-year projects, we shall focus on the Centers Program.

The Centers Program began as a series of pilot projects in 1972. These projects were sufficiently successful so that an expanded program began in 1978. These centers are administered by a university that coordinates a number of interrelated research projects. Each research project typically involves an interdisciplinary team of university faculty and representatives of several businesses. Initial funding is provided by the government with contributions from the university and industry. University funding often consists of a waiver of the overhead for industrial support of the center. Industrial funding is often arranged through a consortium of sponsor businesses that pay an annual membership fee. Since it is the intent of the program to make these centers self-supporting, NSF support is limited to a one-year planning grant and a five-year decreasing operational grant. This program is still in place. The most recent Program Announcement describes the goals of the program:

1. Develop industry, state, and other support for industry/university interaction on industrially relevant fundamental research projects.

2. Promote university research to provide a knowledge base for industrial and technological advancement while training students.

3. Promote research centers that become self-sustaining with industry, state, and other funding within a five-year period.

Under this program at the end of fiscal 1989, forty-one centers were operational and twenty-two of those were self-sustaining. Among the centers that have been established are those at Alfred University (New York), the University of Arizona, Brown University, the University of Rhode Island, the University of California at Berkeley, the University of California at San Diego, San Diego State University, the University of California at Los Angeles, the University of Southern California, Carnegie Mellon University, Case Western Reserve University, the University of Colorado, the Colorado School of Mines, the University of Florida and Purdue University (joint), Georgia Institute of Technology, another at Georgia Tech in conjunction with the University of Arizona, the University of Iowa, Iowa State University, Lehigh University (Pennsylvania), the University of Maryland, the University of Massachusetts, New Jersey Institute of Technology, New Mexico Institute of Mining and Technology, the University of New Mexico, the University of North Carolina, Duke University, North Carolina State University, North Carolina State University in conjunction with Virginia Polytechnic Institute, Northeastern University, Northwestern University, Ohio State University, Oklahoma State University, Pennsylvania State University, the University of Pittsburgh, Rensselaer Polytechnic Institute, Rutgers University, the State University of New York at Buffalo, the University of Tennessee, the University of Texas at Arlington, the University of Texas Health Science Center, the University of Washington, and the University of Washington in conjunction with Washington State University.

Interestingly, only two of the centers specialize in biotechnology—the research interest that supposedly launched the explosion of university-business partnerships. The vast majority of the centers focus on applied industrial processes (e.g., industrial welding and aseptic processing and packaging). Several centers specialize in computer software or information systems.

A second program under NSF provides specifically for Engineering Research Centers (Centers for Cross Disciplinary Research in Engineering). The program began in 1985; eighteen centers had been established by fiscal year 1989. Persons submitting a proposal for this program are told to include a section on Industrial Collaboration and Knowledge/Technology Transfer. These engineering centers may receive NSF support for up to eleven years. There is an on-site, third-year and sixth-year review procedure that results in a decision either to renew or to phase down.

As we enter the 1990s, the NSF Centers Program is being enlarged still further. A 1990 Initiative Announcement from NSF alerts interested parties of NSF's intention to support a number of State/Industry University Cooperative Research Centers modeled after the 1970s Industry/University Cooperative Research Centers Program. This decision resulted from an agreement between NSF and the Science and Technology Council of the National Governors' Association of the States. These new centers would combine some of the features of the NSF-supported Industry/University Cooperative Centers and some of the features of the state-supported centers (discussed below). The Initiative Announcement characterizes the difference between the two as follows:

> Consistent with the Federal goals, the NSF Industry/University Cooperative Research Centers perform generic, fundamental research, which is industrially relevant and underlies technological advances.
>
> State sponsored centers have generally given greater emphasis to development, including proprietary research and product development— research which might lead to greater local and regional economic development.

The NSF wants to support hybrid centers that would "involve improved coupling across basic and applied research and promote technological advances, technology transfer, and subsequent commercialization." The announcement distinguishes between the core and noncore activities of centers. Core research activities are those associated with the Centers program (i.e., generic, fundamental research relevant to industrial needs). Core activities also include measures to promote the implementation and use of technology. Noncore programs are those associated with state-sponsored centers that support or that have the potential to support proprietary projects.

The financing of these centers will be complex. The NSF, states, and industry will share in the funding of core research activities. The technology transfer activities will be supported by industry and the states. Existing centers under state programs or the federal NSF Industry/University Cooperative Research Centers may apply under this program. A state can only support two proposals for center awards under this program.

What is significant here is that in all programs the NSF has given all the potential economic benefits to the centers. Basically, the traditional centers may retain patent rights to the inventions and they may also retain all income from copyrightable material including software. Industrial sponsors may obtain royalty-free, nonexclusive licenses on center patents. In the hybrid centers, industry sponsors are permitted royalty-free nonexclusive patent rights for core research projects. Noncore-sponsored projects provide for the possibility of exclusive licenses. In the hybrid centers all patents belong to the university and royalties and fees are split according to the following formula: 25 percent to the inventor (or in accordance with the university royalty-sharing schedule), 25 percent to the university, and 50 percent to the center.

It should be noted that changes in university patent policies in the 1970s helped pave the way for these cooperative relationships. Harvard, for example, changed its policy in 1974, which made it possible for the university to assign patents to industry. These cooperative arrangements were helped even more by changes in federal patent policy. Allowing universities, industry, and individuals economic gain on projects that were partially supported by public funds represents a departure from earlier government policy. The change in government thinking began with changes in the patent laws. A bit of history is in order. Government contracts to fund research and development became significant during World War II and continued with extensive funding of medical research in the 1950s. During this time there was no standard federal policy. Different agencies chose some variation between two extremes.

Under a title policy, the government acquired title to all contract-generated inventions and patents issued on them. Under a license policy the contractor was permitted to have title to the inventions and patents issued on them although the government was to have use of the inventions for all government purposes (Bremer, 1978). This situation prevailed into the 1960s. In 1963 a presidential memorandum, based on a philosophy of encouraging more inventions, established guidelines for a more uniform federal patent policy. Many government agencies revised their guidelines. Two important agencies in terms of support for higher education, the Department of Health, Education, and Welfare, and the National Science Foundation, adopted guidelines that enabled universities to retain patent rights (Bremer).

The next beneficial change occurred in 1980 with the passage of the Stevenson-Wydler Technological Innovation Act that provided for NSF support for the Industry-University Cooperative Research Centers already discussed. Meanwhile the passage of the Bayh-Dole Act in the same year gave universities patent rights even when government funding supported the research. In 1984, Congress passed legislation that allowed universities and other nonprofits patents on the work done in Department of Defense labs they ran. The Department of Defense tried to have the law nullified. In 1987 President Ronald Reagan issued an executive order that restricted the Department of Defense's discretion in these matters (Guterl, 1987, 45). The most recent beneficial change occurred with the Federal Technology Transfer Act of 1986, an act that amended the Stevenson-Wydler Act. This act permitted federal research labs, scientists paid by the federal government, and grantees of public research funds to collaborate with private industry in order to develop commercial patents. Private companies could gain the exclusive rights to patents, while universities and scientists could receive royalties.

With these changes in public policy, universities had a clear economic incentive to establish university-business partnerships. Whatever qualms Congress had previously had regarding private benefit from the expenditure of public funds were erased by the growing threat of international economic competition and by the perceived decline in research and development capabilities of American industry. Moreover, Congress had cut direct government support for basic research. Universities had a double incentive to work cooperatively with industry. In addition to the carrot of new opportunities for royalty income, the universities were given the stick of funding cuts, which forced them to seek offsetting income elsewhere.

In effect, the federal government was limping toward a sort of industrial policy. Since American industry was failing to invest in sufficient research and development to bring new products to market that could compete internationally, especially with the Japanese, the government provided public funds to universities to help move the fruits of basic research into the marketplace. Whether accidentally or by design the federal government virtually forced universities into the technology transfer business. It was hoped that more university basic research would have a commercial payoff. Hence, the federal government was simultaneously shifting the research interests within universities so that commercial applications became more significant and was subsidizing corporate efforts to become more competitive.

The incentives at the federal level were matched by many state governments. One of the oldest programs is found in New York State. The New York Science and Technology Center was chartered in 1963 for the purpose of supporting the development of new technologies and improved access to technology for New York businesses. Seven Centers for advanced technology at New York universities have been established.

During the 1980s a number of state governments made significant financial investments in university-business partnerships within their states. The decision to embark on such programs was extremely practical—they were to help improve the economy of the state. Indiana committed $150 million for a ten-year period beginning in 1982 to support the Indiana Corporation for Science and Technology, which gives grants that, among other things, promote productivity. The Michigan Industrial Technology Institute was funded jointly by the state and the W. K. Kellogg Foundation to help retain Michigan's manufacturing industry and to support improved competitiveness (Foden et al., 1988). Pennsylvania's program is typical and one of the best known. In 1982 Pennsylvania initiated the Ben Franklin Partnership. Program guidelines indicate that the "mission of the Partnership is to support initiatives which will strengthen the state's economy." Appropriate activities for support are those that lead to job creation and retention, diversification of the economy, creation of new advanced technology enterprises, improvement in the competitive ability of technology-oriented companies, and the development of a technologically skilled work force. University-business partnerships were believed central to this mission. "Investments made by the Partnership are intended to establish new working relationships between Pennsylvania academic institutions and private industry in the Commonwealth."

To make decisions on grants, the state designated four Ben Franklin Technology Centers. The Technology Centers are independent nonprofit corporations governed by boards composed of both university officials and industry executives. As of the 1988–89 reporting year, Pennsylvania had invested $137 million in the program. This expenditure has attracted more than $526 million in corporate, federal, and university support. Each of the four Technology Centers is to develop patent policies and royalty and equity payback agreements.

Utah also has an extensive program. The crown jewel in Utah's program is the Centers for Excellence. Begun with state funding of $2.5 million, the centers have received over $38 million from 123 companies and fourteen federal agencies. The centers were modeled after NSF's Industry-University Cooperative Research Centers Program. Centers are located at Brigham Young, Utah State, and the University of Utah. They include six centers that focus on biomedical technology or biotechnology; three that emphasize manufacturing technology; two engineering technology centers; three natural resource centers that help industry develop more environmentally efficient products and processes; five communication and information centers, most of which are heavily involved in advanced communication technology; and two centers that focus on space engineering.

What can we conclude from this description of federal and state legislation? University-business partnerships have broad bipartisan support. They are believed important for improving a given state's competitive economic position and for improving America's competitive position internationally. The fact that such collaborative arrangements exist in Japan and Western Europe adds to their attractiveness. Given Japan and Germany's economic success, it is not surprising that features of their economic system would be imitated. Despite the doubts expressed before some congressional committees and despite the reservations of some congressmen like then Senator Albert Gore, neither the federal government nor state governments show any wavering of support of university-business partnerships. As a matter of public policy, university-business partnerships are remarkably uncontroversial both in the public arena and in the legislative halls.

To what extent have these NSF-supported and state-supported centers been plagued by problems that afflicted WARF and MIT in the beginning of the century? It is significant to note that the NSF program guidelines stipulate that the "prompt publication of research results is expected." "Appropriate" (six months to a year) delays to safeguard patentability or proprietary information are acceptable, however. At least one review study of the Centers program (Gray et al., 1986) indicates that industry participants in the centers program concurred with university participants that "expansion of knowledge" was *the* most important goal in a list of seven presented by the researchers. The development of patentable projects was ranked seventh. These rankings were reversed for industry participants in the Industry-University Cooperative Research Projects Program. This study provides some support for the view that the Centers really are more oriented toward academic values. (An edited version of the most recent program announcement is included in the document section.)

The author is unaware of any patent disputes or other legal problems at any of the government-sponsored centers. On the surface, at least, it seems that some of the earlier difficulties of the early centers have been avoided. However, the reader must keep in mind that the centers discussed here are monitored by government agencies since government funds are involved. Neither WARF nor the MIT centers discussed earlier were part of a government program. As we shall see, a number of disconcerting issues have arisen at several centers that are primarily partnerships between a university and a business or businesses.

The Role of Private Business in the Development of University-Business Partnerships

Although changes in patent law and other inducements provided by government may have been necessary for the growth of university-business partnerships in the 1980s, these inducements were hardly sufficient. What was needed were some corporations ready to take the plunge. What provided the catalyst was the revolution in genetics that occurred primarily in the laboratories of American universities. Gene splicing was achieved by academics, and the key patents for the products of recombinant DNA technology were held by universities. Moreover, the commercial applicability of gene splicing was obvious from the start.

The decade of the 1980s began with a major $70 million cooperative venture in molecular biology. The partners to the agreement were Massachusetts General Hospital affiliated with the Harvard Medical School and Hoechst G.A., a West German chemical company. The person responsible for bringing this idea to fruition was biochemist Howard M. Goodman, who was the first (with collaborator William Rutter) to clone insulin genes. His other successes included cloning experiments with growth hormones and a protein on the hepatitis B virus. Under the terms of the contract, four Hoechst scientists would work with Goodman on projects Goodman chose. Massachusetts General Hospital would hold any patents arising out of the research while Hoechst would be granted a license for any commercial development. In return Massachusetts General would receive royalties on any commercial products successfully developed. Early drafts of research results were to be submitted to Hoechst not less than thirty days prior

23

to submission for publication so that Hoechst could determine if there would be any patentable results.

The announcement of the Mass General–Hoechst Agreement immediately raised a number of concerns. Originally Goodman intended to establish the new Department of Molecular Biology at the University of California at San Francisco where Goodman had done his research. Goodman perceived that the University of California bureaucracy would present an unacceptable delay in reaching an agreement. No such bureaucracy stood in the way at Mass General. Although the hospital was affiliated with the Harvard Medical School, Mass General was not governed by Harvard's rules nor was it in any way financially obligated to Harvard. In response to a request to comment on the agreement by *Science*, Harvard President Derek Bok replied, "I prefer not to comment on it. It was signed without our participation" (Culliton, 1982). The only people at Mass General that Goodman had to deal with were the hospital trustees and the head of Mass General.

There had been no intention to make public the terms of the contract. This action followed a Harvard tradition that dates back to 1974, when Harvard changed its patent policy to allow Harvard to assign patents to industry. Indeed, shortly thereafter Harvard and Monsanto entered into a twelve-year agreement. The Harvard Medical School received $23 million in research and endowment funds. Monsanto was given patent rights to the research. This agreement was kept quiet until 1985 and even after its existence was made public by a Boston newspaper, neither side would comment on it except in a general way. In early 1977, Monsanto announced the formation of a five-person committee to see that both sides honor their duties to protect academic freedom, especially the right to publish, and to "develop any products that may emerge in a manner consistent with the public good" (Culliton, 1977). People speculated as to the motivation for setting up the committee. The conditions for great concern with the Massachusetts General–Hoechst partnership were in place in the 1970s after the secretive Harvard Medical School–Monsanto partnership.

But the early eighties were unlike the mid-seventies. There was extreme pressure from three sources to make the terms of the Mass General–Hoechst agreement public. The Harvard faculty wanted to see if academic freedom had been protected. Goodman had been granted an appointment in Harvard's Department of Genetics, as had all the academic personnel at Mass General. Other universities wanted the terms made public to assist them in their negotiations with industry. Most interestingly, the chairman of the Subcommittee on Investigation and Oversight of the House Committee on Science and Technology, Albert Gore Jr. (D-Tenn.), wanted the terms made public. As noted, Gore was one of the few politicians who had taken a special interest in industry-university relations and some of the conflicts of interest that can result. Gore was especially concerned about this agreement because it involved a large foreign company. After all, the chief justification for these partnerships was that they were a device to increase America's competitive ability in the international marketplace. Yet the business partner in the first modern major university-business partnership was a German company. This fact raised a number of important public policy questions that will be discussed later. Gore prevailed and received a copy of the agreement, which was later made public.

The agreement did contain items that were unsettling. Mass General agreed that Hoechst would be the sole funding agent for the Department of Molecular Biology. No third party, including the U.S. government, was to acquire any rights or equity in any work done solely in the department. This decision generally precluded Mass General personnel from seeking National Institute of Health (NIH) funding. It also took them out of the review process, a situation that Goodman attempted to fix by creating his own review process (Culliton, 1982b). Although the agreement allowed Mass General to collaborate with faculty at other universities who were funded from other sources, many were skeptical. The agreement stated that with collaborative work Hoechst was guaranteed at least a nonexclusive license (Culliton, 1982b). The agreement also provided Hoechst with the option of five-year renewals beginning in 1990. What would happen if at any point the grant were not renewed? This first major agreement in the 1980s alerted both academics and industrialists of the myriad of issues that would have to be resolved if large numbers of these agreements were to be signed.

Another of the often-discussed early agreements was between Washington University and the Monsanto Company. In May 1982 a $23.5 million agreement between the Washington University Medical School and the Monsanto Company was announced. The research area was biotechnology. According to a Monsanto company spokesperson, discussions culminating in the agreement went on for two years. Royalties from the research were to be distributed equally between Washington University, the Washington University Medical School, and the principal investigator's laboratory (Maurer et al., 1984). None would go to the individual investigator himself or herself (Guze, 1983). The principal reason for this decision was to prevent a morale problem from developing: "The morale problem I mentioned earlier would be a real issue . . . if individual Monsanto scientists were expected to collaborate on work which might make their associates rich, but would be business as usual for them" (Maurer et al.). In industry, an individual typically gains nothing from one's patentable discoveries. Moreover, faculty not involved in cooperative partnerships like Monsanto's would have no opportunity to gain extra income from patentable research. Hence the decision to provide no economic reward for the Washington University faculty was made. Significantly the Monsanto–Washington University agreement did not establish a precedent. Under most agreements university faculty routinely receive a portion of the royalties from their patentable research. Since the morale argument is as valid today as it was in 1982, it is interesting to speculate as to the causes of the shift.

The Monsanto–Washington University Partnership has an oversight committee consisting of four university representatives and four Monsanto representatives. Each group has veto power with respect to whether or not an individual research project is funded. "By agreement, a specific research project will not go forward unless both Monsanto and the University endorse it" (Maurer et al., 1982). This provision of the agreement has been criticized as giving Monsanto too much control. In response, Samuel B. Guze, vice chancellor for medical affairs at Washington University, has said:

> It is certainly true that any research proposal rejected by all of the Monsanto scientists—or all of the university scientists—could not be funded from this source. This is no different, however, from the situation with any other funding agency. If the majority of an NIH study section does not support a particular proposal, the proposal does not receive funding from that source. In some sense, this is a veto but there is nothing to prevent a scientist from seeking support elsewhere. (Guze, 1983, 55)

Other provisions of the Monsanto–Washington University agreement include an antisecrecy provision, the right of Monsanto to early review of any paper for patent possibilities, and a right of first refusal to Monsanto to develop a product.

Given the $23.5-million price tag, Vice Chancellor Guze provided some perspective on the percentage that amount represents of Washington University research funding. The total amount is spread out over five years. On average the Monsanto contribution will be 5 to 6 percent of the university's total funding for biomedical research in any of the five years (Guze, 1983). Guze argued that this percentage is sufficiently small so that the overall biomedical research program will not be distorted by the Monsanto gift.

The third early joint partnership that is often discussed was between a foreign company, FIDIA S.p.A., an Italian drug company, and Georgetown University. The funding would establish an institute to be called the FIDIA–Georgetown Institute for the Neurosciences. The Institute would receive $3 million a year (adjusted for inflation) for twenty years. A number of issues that had concerned faculty and others with the Mass General–Hoechst and the Monsanto–Washington University joint partnerships were discussed and settled in the Georgetown-FIDIA agreement. Georgetown Vice Chancellor of the Medical Center, John Rose, said in a press conference, "This would be an institute devoted to basic research, to the discovery of fundamental mechanisms in the brain, without commercial objectives, and that the work would be published freely in the scientific literature, and that the ethical and scientific guidelines of the university would be observed. . ." (Barnes, 1985, 1255).

The fact that the Institute would be devoted to research without commercial objectives is unusual. It may have been influenced in part by negotiations with the District of Columbia zoning authorities. To receive approval, Georgetown had to convince the zoning council that the research would be "in keeping with the traditional academic roles of the university" (Barnes, 1985). Given the noncommercial nature of the research, what could FIDIA expect for its $60 + million? Among the perceived advantages were increased visibility, improved scientific credibility, and future communication with U.S. scientists. Even more important, scientists from FIDIA's research labs will be working with U.S. scientists at the Institute. Should patentable research occur, FIDIA–Georgetown Institute will have the right of first refusal. After that the right reverts to Georgetown University. Only after Georgetown's refusal would FIDIA have a right to acquire the patent for a fair price. Sixty percent of any patent royalties would go to the Institute and 40 percent to Georgetown (Barnes, 1985).

As this book goes to press, it appears that the Georgetown–Fidia partnership may be the first of these early paradigmatic partnerships to unravel. In July 1993, FIDIA S.p.A. filed for "controlled administration"—the Italian equivalent of bankruptcy. Because of its financial difficulties FIDIA has reneged on one important agreement with Georgetown and has reduced the amount of financial support for the partnership. FIDIA has failed to provide the promised support for a new neurosciences research building that now stands half-completed on the Georgetown campus. Georgetown has sued for the promised financial support. In the meantime contributions for established cooperative programs fell from $3.8 million in 1992 to approximately $3 million in 1993. The prospective budget for 1994 is less than $2 million. Meanwhile the FIDIA Research Foundation currently employs one person compared to the nineteen it employed formerly (Nicklin, 1993).

FIDIA's current financial difficulties and the resultant decline in support are not the only difficulties. Although the agreement between Georgetown and FIDIA tried to allay faculty concern about such issues as freedom to publish and patent rights, it highlights the public policy issue Senator Gore raised with the Mass General–Hoechst partnership. Congress had changed the patent law so that universities and business could receive commercial benefit from projects where public funds were involved. The justification for using tax dollars to support commercial enterprises was that America's competitive position in the world would be enhanced to the benefit of society as a whole. Yet two of the three early and largest university-business partnerships involved foreign business firms and that is not the end of the story. An increasing number of foreign companies are financing university-business partnerships in the United States. Akzo, a Netherlands global chemical and health care company, had $4 million worth of contract research in the United States in 1991 (Vleggaar, 1991, 19). Research through the partnership costs half what it would if Akzo did it by itself.

Japan is extremely active. Over 100 Japanese organizations are engaged in research and development in the United States. One-third of the fifty-five corporately endowed chairs at MIT are endowed by Japanese companies. Of the 300 member organizations in the MIT Industrial Liaison Program, approximately half the foreign memberships are held by Japanese firms. Japanese corporate sponsors include NEC, Hitachi, Nippon Telegraph and Telephone, Fujitsu, and Matsushita. Matsushita also participates in the industry affiliates programs at Stanford and the University of California at Berkeley (Herbert, 1989, 13).

As we have seen, American political support of the partnerships is premised on the idea that they will promote American economic growth and enhance our competitive position against foreign rivals. But our foreign rivals are forming their own partnerships with American universities. This creates a difficult dilemma that will be discussed in more detail in the section that evaluates university-business partnerships. If we do not limit participation in these partnerships to American firms, then one of the chief arguments on behalf of them is lost. On the other hand, if we do limit foreign participation, we limit access to new knowledge and thus violate the value of open access that is such a fundamental value in American universities.

Although the vast majority of university business partnerships are in the biological and natural sciences, there are examples from other disciplines. The development of mathematical models of the economy led to the development of sophisticated economic forecasting techniques that were extremely valuable to major corporations. One of the pioneers of economic forecasting, Lawrence Klein of the University of Pennsylvania, created a private not-for-profit corporation, Wharton Econometric Forecasting Association (WEFA), that provided economic forecasting services. The University of Pennsylvania provided a quarter-million-dollar line of credit, 40 percent of which was equity and 60 percent of which was counted as debt for the data, software, and use of the Wharton name. WEFA was to donate the subscriber fees to Penn, and by the mid-1970s the annual payment to the university was $150,000. In 1980, the university sold 80 percent of its equity for an estimated $7 million (Omenn, 1983, 26). One of the benefits of the sale was the establishment of an Economic Research Institute endowed by proceeds from the sale. The university also retained a 20 percent equity position in WEFA and negotiated a five-year agreement that allowed university faculty and students access to WEFA's models and database. Although knowledgeable observers felt the arrangement was extremely beneficial for Penn, there was much criticism of the deal on campus. As with other university-business partnership arrangements, the secrecy regarding the terms of the agreement was found objectionable (Omenn, 1983).

Yet another example of a university-business partnership in business is the Institute for the Study of Business Materials at Penn State. This institute was founded in 1983 and by 1990 had forty sponsoring corporations, two affiliated research centers at other universities, and total revenue of over a half-million dollars a year (Lilien, 1990, 94). This institute differs from most university-business partnerships in that its mission is to conduct publishable academic research, albeit both basic and applied. The research areas include 1) new product research, 2) market structure and operation studies research, 3) buying strategies and operations, 4) public policy studies, 5) looking at how buyers value products, 6) studying the way buyers, sellers, and channel members interact, 7) negotiations studies, and 8) communications research. The Institute offers executive education, which is only available to sponsor companies (Lilien, 1990, 95). The Institute has tried to maintain its academic integrity by insisting that it is a research rather than a consulting institute. The path to publication is somewhat circuitous. The sponsor receives the results of the project first. The Institute has not been able to get permission to publish first. Only after the sponsor has obtained the results is the academic article written. Proprietary information is disguised. The sponsor reviews the article before publication. Permission to publish has never been denied. On occasion the sponsor has asked that the proprietary information be disguised in a different way (Lilien, 1990, 97).

With a few specific examples in front of us, let us try to sketch a broad picture of university-business partnerships. One study asserts that nearly half the firms conducting or supporting research in biotechnology are involved in university-industry research relationships. The same study indicated that such research relationships provided 16 to 24 percent of all external research funds for biotechnology (Blumenthal et al., 1986b). This percentage is much higher than the 1 to 3 percent figure frequently used as an indicator of private support for university research. But the growth is not limited to biotechnology. In the last five years, membership in the principal national organization of university patent officials has nearly tripled. Four-hundred people representing over 125 universities belong (Fuchsberg, 1989c).

Although it is unusual, some universities seem to have industry-related research as their top priority. A particularly poignant example is provided by the College of Textiles of North Carolina State University. This new college opened in April of 1991 and is the cornerstone of N.C. State's new Centennial Campus. The purpose of the College of Textiles is "to serve the textile industry" (Isaacs, 1991, 57). The Centennial Campus resembles technology cities found in Japan. Eventually, the campus will contain private laboratories, residential housing, retail stores, and a hotel/conference center. In the center of the complex is Lake Raleigh. Corporate donors had given $1.7 million of an expected $2.7 million by March of 1991 (Isaacs, 57). In the College of Textiles building one finds an ultramodern, completely functioning Model Manufacturing Facility. "The Model Manufacturing Facility will function much as medical and veterinary hospitals are currently run on university campuses" (Isaacs, 58). The new dean, Dr. Robert A. Barnhardt, is reported to have said, "We'll have the best possible situation—industry and academia living side by side, parking in the same parking lot, eating lunch together and working on research together. . . . The technology transfer will be fantastic" (Isaacs, 57).

The 1980s provided multi-million-dollar, headline-making partnerships like those discussed in this section. The magnitude of the partnerships was certain to whet the appetites of university development offices throughout the country. The magnitude of these partnerships brought them under public scrutiny in ways that more limited university-business partnerships in the period 1950–1980 did not. As concerns about academic freedom, the freedom to publish, and secrecy were voiced by both academics and nonacademics, a number of conferences and seminars took place designed to address these concerns head on and if possible to formulate some universal standards to which research universities would adhere. Two of the more famous conferences took place at Parajo Dunes, California, and the University of Pennsylvania. The draft test of the Parajo Dunes conference and some selected remarks from the University of Pennsylvania conference are included in the document section. These conferences failed, however, to provide universal standards. Far more effective in providing leadership in the area of universal standards was a cooperative partnership consisting of officials from universities, business, and government. We now provide a brief account of this important alliance.

The Government-University-Industry Roundtable

The development of university-business partnerships was also aided by interest-group alliances. By far the most important was the Government-University-Industry Research Roundtable. The Research Roundtable was founded in 1984 to "provide a forum where scientists, engineers, administrators, and policy makers from government, university and industry can come together on an ongoing basis to explore ways to improve the productivity of the nation's research enterprise." The Roundtable is sponsored by the National Academy of Sciences, the National Academy of Engineering, and the Institute of Medicine. It is governed by a council of twenty-five persons from its three constituencies. To accomplish its tasks, the Roundtable is organized into four working groups that focus respectively on 1) the development, identification, recruitment, and retention of talent for science and engineering research; 2) federal university-sponsored relationships; 3) new alliances among universities, industry, the financial community, and federal and state governments; and 4) major issues underlying the entire research and engineering enterprise. It is the activities of the third working group that are most germane to our task here.

The most successful endeavor of the Roundtable was accomplished in partnership with the Industrial Research Institute. A document entitled *Simplified and Standardized Model Agreements for University-Industry Cooperation* was published (1988). As the title implies, the document was meant to present models for university-business partnership agreements. The document contained a one-page model for a research grant. For university-business partnerships the model research agreement was most useful. (A copy may be found in the document section of this book.) The document also contained an Appendix of Optional and Alternative Clauses. By the end of 1989 over

33

14,000 copies of the document had been distributed. In this case, the Roundtable was willing to set standards on controversial issues. As the 1989 annual report of the Roundtable said, the purpose of "Model Agreements" was "to decrease the time and effort required for such negotiations and provide companies and universities new to research alliances a sense of what is reasonable to consider in establishing a contract." The agreement establishes the right of the researchers to publish subject to a negotiated delay for purpose of the university applying for a United States or foreign patent. Under the agreement all rights and title for intellectual property belong to the university. On its part, the university agrees to file for a patent if requested to do so by the sponsor. The university also agrees to give the sponsor first option for a license that can be either exclusive or nonexclusive depending on the negotiated contract.

In 1990 the Roundtable undertook a survey to assess the usefulness of the model agreements. Perhaps the most important result was that the model was accepted and used—at least to a degree—by survey respondents. The most extensive concern was directed toward the sections on intellectual property rights and licensing arrangements. Survey results showed that many university research administrators were not happy to have a nonexclusive royalty-free option in the agreement. There was a general response that industry should not receive commercialization rights free of charge. Several respondents wanted more in-depth discussion of intellectual property rights and several strategies for dealing with the intellectual property issue, as well as the advantages and disadvantages of each strategy. More variety was also requested for licensing agreements. Some respondents wanted a section on trade secrets to be added to the document.

As might be expected, nearly every section received a critical comment. My own reaction to the report of the survey results is that the chief difficulty with the model research agreement is that the specific needs of both the university and the business firm could not be completely accommodated by a general agreement. The research agreement is not a model but a guide. Although it is widely used, it is not used as boilerplate. When universities and businesses use the model research agreement they do and will modify it to suit the specific needs presented by each contract situation.

In 1987 the Roundtable's council undertook a comprehensive review of U.S. academic research in the sciences and engineering. The report of the working group responsible for the research was published in October of 1989 under the title *Science and Technology in the Aca-*

demic Enterprise; Status, Trends, and Issues. Surprisingly, the report contained almost nothing about university-business partnerships. However, it did point out a dilemma that universities face regarding the development of research capacity. On the one hand universities are under pressure from business and government to develop research capacity; indeed the report indicated that local and state politicians wanted the universities to assist in their efforts at economic development. On the other hand the universities put themselves at risk if they do expand their research capacity. Scientific research is very expensive. Good faculty require laboratories and doctoral students to staff them. The costliness of scientific research increases the financial risk to the institution whenever the university expands in the science area (1-10). This increases the pressure on the university to enter into partnerships with business. As we shall see, these partnerships help lessen the financial risk but they raise problems of their own.

More surprising than the lack of emphasis on university-business partnerships in the *Science and Technology in the American Enterprise* report was a lack of discussion of the concerns that were being raised about university-business partnerships in a report specifically about university-business partnerships issued in 1986. The Government-University-Industry Roundtable, in conjunction with the Academy Industry Program, prepared a significant report, "New Alliances and Partnerships in American Science and Engineering." That report was based on a literature search on the topic; an examination of published materials and interviews about twenty-one partnership programs; a specially prepared paper by two scholars on this topic; and a December 1985 conference attended by 200 representatives from government, universities, and industry.

The purpose of the report was to examine the impact and effectiveness of the major alliances existing at that time. The report indicated that the alliances were proceeding without difficulty. With the exception of a few skeptics, the conference attendees seemed to indicate that all was "sweetness and light." The authors of the report also thought things were going well, but probably not as well as the conferees believed. After all, many of the conference participants were active players who had an interest in the success of these alliances. Unfortunately, Part II of the report, "Discussion of the Issues," was primarily summaries of the positions of various speakers at the conference. The working group did have eleven position statements in italicized boxes scattered through Part II, but these statements tended to be very general and often somewhat tangential to the issues discussed at the conference. For example, the working group did not express any opinion on the issue of freedom of communication and restraints on publication. Its comment on the issue of commercial work distorting faculty loyalties ran as follows:

> The Working Group recognizes a change in faculty loyalties over the past forty years. Prior to World War II little funding was available outside the university, and faculty concerns were directed to their own institutions. With the significant increase in federal support there came incentives for promoting individual disciplines and growth in professional and scientific societies. Faculty loyalties were directed toward their disciplines and their colleagues in the relevant societies. Now the potential for significant increase in academic salaries through alliances with businesses and the financial community may diminish faculty loyalties to their universities and their disciplines. The Working Group sees this as the exception rather than the rule, however; generally faculty loyalties to science and engineering run high in spite of the possibility of individual financial gain.

I think the reader will agree with me that this statement is neither concrete nor clear. However, the Roundtable indicated we should not infer that the ambiguities reflected in the statement result from the unwillingness of the working group to take a position. Rather we should look to the working group's assessment that "most of the arrangements are too new to evaluate that matter." However, given the Roundtable's achievement with the model agreement and given the fact that the concerns about university-business partnerships had a history at this point, the appeal to the novelty of university-business partnerships does not ring true. For whatever reason, the 1986 report did little to advance resolution of some of the controversial questions surrounding university-business alliances.

The Roundtable's most recent sponsored research focuses on the perspective of industry on how successful university-business partnerships have been and can be in promoting technology transfer and increased industrial competitiveness. The research base is seventeen senior research managers from a variety of companies that are involved in university-business partnerships. These managers were asked for their perspective on the nature of the relationships of their firms to universities and the implications for national R&D policy. The results of that research were published in 1991 and were so shocking that hearings were held before a House committee. The analysis was overwhelmingly negative. Few of the advantages of the partnerships had been achieved. The industrial spokespersons were highly critical of universities. Given the importance of the report and its unexpected conclusions, the vast majority of it is included in the document section. A full discussion of the report is found in the section focusing on an evaluation of the economic justification for university-business partnerships (pp. 65–66).

Despite the surprising results of the survey, there is little sign that the Government-University-Industry Research Roundtable has lost any of its enthusiasm for university-business partnerships. A recent issue of *Fortune* praises them highly and urges more of them. Thus the consensus in support of these partnerships remains strong. Before turning to an economic and moral evaluation of university-business partnerships, let us consider the extent to which these partnerships exist in other industrialized countries.

SECTION FIVE

International Comparisons

Since a major justification for university-business partnerships is their ability to allow American industry to compete more effectively against other industrial countries, a word should be said about what our competitors are doing with respect to university-business partnerships. As we consider the public policy implications of foreign partners for American universities, it may be interesting to know whether these foreign firms are simply behaving opportunistically or whether they may be operating from an established tradition of university-business partnerships in their own countries. Moreover, the existence of a tradition of university-business partnerships may provide some indication of the implication of these partnerships on our economic development and their potential effect on the character and values of American universities.

Not surprisingly, Japan has developed one of the most extensive systems of university-business partnerships. What is surprising is how recent they are. There is no tradition of university-business partnerships in Japan. Japanese industry has always had a remarkable competitive edge in transferring basic research to profitable products in the marketplace. The government has played an active role as a partner with industry in technology transfer. As would be expected, Japanese research is very team oriented. More importantly, the Japanese researchers do not seem to make the distinction between basic and applied research that is so important in the American university context (Cutler, 1989, 72). However, Japanese universities are no more experienced with obtaining patents than are American universities. Until recently Japanese educators believed that the university was *primarily* for teaching students; there was little commercialization of research until the early 1980s. Now that commercialization is underway, it is being assisted by the Japan Research Development Corporation (JRDC)—an agency of the central government (Cutler, 73). The task of the JRDC is made easier by the fact that there is an established "old boy" scientific network. The top engineers, company presidents, and university scientists all know one another.

Another government influence comes from the Ministry of International Trade and Industry (MITI). MITI has an effective committee system on technology and industry "ranging from restructuring a weak industrial sector to organizing a national program for advanced robotics or for manned space flight" (Cutler, 75). A national consensus develops on what areas of new technology should be emphasized. The Japanese government orchestrates the coordination but Japanese business pays the costs for R&D research. In Japan 80 percent of R&D is provided by business rather than the government (Cutler, 76). In the United States the government supports a much larger percentage of R&D. In addition, U.S. antitrust laws would prevent the kind of intra-industry cooperation permitted in Japan. Finally, a number of the values characteristic of Japanese industry permeate Japanese cooperative research efforts. Cutler observed a high level of interpersonal communication and group decision making, a high level of trust among members of the research team, and a high degree of stability since the turnover in personnel is small (Cutler, 76).

As with Japan and the United States, the growth of German university-business partnerships came during the 1980s. "Between 1980 and 1985, the financial support of the universities by firms rose from 0.5 percent to 6 percent of all separately budgeted research funds" (Schimank, 1988, 332). These partnerships have taken the form of technology parks in the neighborhoods of universities, transfer bureaus, or jointly directed and financed research institutes. As of 1988, twenty-five of the fifty-six universities had transfer bureaus. These transfer bureaus have functions very similar to Offices of Technology Transfer in the United States. They put university faculty and industry in touch with one another, they assist faculty in securing patents, and they seek out industries that might be interested in the commerical application of university research (Schimank, 330). As in the United States, transfer institutes are supported by one or more companies, and, as in the United States, some of these partnerships involve a lot of money. For example, the Institute für Biotechnologie was founded in 1984 at the Frie Universitat Berlin by the large German pharmaceutical Schering AG. Schering will invest 40 million DM ($80 million) until 1994 (Schimank, 333).

Unlike the situation in the United States, these transfer offices do not have much of a role in protecting patents or other intellectual property. That is because few of the benefits from such arrangements are captured by the universities or university faculty. In that respect, the transfer bureaus are more like agricultural extension programs that are provided as a public service by universities although it is hoped that the goodwill provided by the extension services will not be forgotten by state legislators at appropriation time. In Germany, the inventor, not the university, is the legal owner. On occasion, especially when there is more than one inventor, royalty funds are diverted to the inventors' university labs (Waugaman, 1990).

Technology transfer is actively supported by all levels of the German government. The BMFT (Bundeministerium für Forschung und Technologie) was established in 1984 to stimulate joint research projects that involve state-financed research institutes. Its funding increased dramatically throughout the 1980s. Unlike the NSF program in the United States, the BMFT provides support for large numbers of industrial scientists to do research in government-supported labs (Schimank, 1988, 332). In fact, exchange of university and industry personnel seems to be far more typical than in the United States. As in the United States, laws are being modified to provide incentives for university scientists to participate in projects that lead to technology transfer.

Although the industrial powers of Germany and Japan are of most interest, some brief mention should be made of developments in some other countries. In Great Britain an early attempt to foster university-business partnerships through the National Enterprise Board was a failure. The Board has been renamed the British Technology Group and the British government, with four industrial partners, has created a technology transfer company for health fields called Cell Tech Ltd. Partnerships between individual universities and businesses are evolving in a pattern that is similar to that in the United States.

The Canadian situation is also similar to the situation in the United States. Canadian universities, like their American counterparts, are aggressively seeking partnerships and aiding in the creation of companies that develop commercial products from faculty research. For example, the University of British Columbia in its annual report for 1986 reported 1985 revenues of $87.5 million from the fifty-three spin-off companies it had created (Buchbinder and Newson, 1990, 357). This aggressiveness on the part of Canadian universities was created by the same economic forces that account for the initiatives of American universities—severe cuts in government funding for universities and the underfunding of higher education. As in the United States, university-business partnerships have been encouraged by government agencies and third-party organizations like the Government-University-Industry Research Roundtable. Canadian third-party organizations include the Corporate Higher Education Forum and the Science Council of Canada. The Province of Ontario has provided financial support for Centres of Entrepreneurship just as numerous states have done in the United States. Finally, the development of university-business partnerships in Canada has had solid support from all the affected constituencies—government officials, business executives, and university faculty and administrators. There is a small contingent of critics, however, who raise the same issues that are being raised with respect to American university-business partnerships.

What conclusions can we draw from this brief international study? All industrial countries are concerned with the speed and effectiveness of technology transfer as they compete internationally. Nearly all are developing university-business partnerships as one stragtegy for increasing technology transfer. However, in some countries like Japan, these partnerships are but one piece of a coordinated strategy of technology transfer. Given the dangers of university-business partnerships to be discussed shortly, we can question the United States and Canadian strategies of placing so much emphasis on university-business partnerships. Perhaps government funding of private laboratories would be both more efficient in terms of the technology transfer obtained and present less of a threat to traditional academic values. These questions lead us to the second part of this monograph, which is directed to a systematic evaluation of university-business partnerships.

PART TWO
An Evaluation of University-Business Partnerships

SECTION ONE

Advantages of University-Business Partnerships

That university-business partnerships receive bipartisan political support at the state and national levels speaks highly in their favor. Seldom
does an expenditure of public funds receive such widespread support.
Why do people believe these partnerships are such a good thing?

Perhaps we can better grasp the rationale behind this bipartisan
support if we summarize the causes for the explosion of university-
business partnerships in the 1980s. The causes are accurately listed by
Nelkin et al. (1987, 68).

1. An increase in the cost of university research coupled with a drop
in federal funding.
2. The perception that the United States had lost its technological
superiority.
3. Two areas of cutting-edge technology, computers and biotechnology, were closely linked to academic science.
4. Patent reform and state-initiated programs.

As is readily apparent, both sides had economic reasons to enter
into university-business partnerships. The universities needed to find
funds to offset the decline in federal support. Businesses recognized
the severity of international competition and realized that shortening
the product cycle from invention to marketable product was extremely
important for one's competitive position. Speed in technology transfer
became essential. Fortunately, discoveries and inventions in computers and biotechnology have obvious commercial applications. That
reduces the time it takes to bring commercial products to market. The
discoveries and inventions in these two areas, however, were being
made by academic rather than industrial researchers. Industry needed

45

to tap into the universities. Patent reform and government support (both federal and state) for university-business partnerships followed.

At the national level, probably the dominant perceived value of university-business partnerships is the possibilities they provide for improving America's competitive economic position vis-à-vis other industrialized countries, especially Japan. Herbert I. Fusfeld, head of Rensselaer Polytechnic Institute's Center for Science and Technology Policy, is quoted as saying, "Many corporations are realizing they can no longer be self-sufficient technically" (Main, 1987, 81). As was noted above, research in several areas of commercial interest like gene splicing and artificial intelligence has been primarily located at universities. Competitors in Japan and elsewhere have greatly shortened the time requred for product development. There are intense competitive pressures to transfer basic and theoretical applied research into marketable commercial products. Thus American industry needed access to the new biotechnology. That fact alone explains the vast interest in university-business partnerships in the biotechnology area.

Moreover, business was more than ready to enter into any agreement that would bring new or improved products to market faster. Business believed that partnerships here would increase our competitiveness. The states use a similar rationale to support university-business partnerships; they believe such partnerships will aid them in their efforts at economic development.

Some of the initial hopes for university-business partnerships have been realized. Fusfeld claims that each professional researcher adds about $125,000 a year to the local economy. North Carolina's Research Triangle area employs 9,000 Ph.D.s (Main, 1987, 84).

Another writer describes the gains for partnerships in biomedicine in terms of the 5 P's:

1. To gain *patentable* ideas or entities,
2. To have access to *patients* for clinical trials,
3. To have *publications* of clinical studies, which are valuable as promotion aids,
4. To attract *personnel* to the company as a staff of consultants,
5. To have the *prestige* of association with its implied reliability and quality (Cooper, 1982, 301).

An early 1984 study of biotechnology companies published in *Science* in January 1986 concluded that per dollar invested, university research generated 4.2 times more patent applications than other company research. This same study indicated that 41 percent of the biotechnology firms involved in university-industry research relationships derived at least one trade secret from their association (Blumenthal et al., 1986a). A 1989 study by Adam Jaffe found evidence that "university research causes industry R&D and not vice versa." Jaffe goes on to argue that states that improve their university research systems can attract industrial R&D and increase the productivity of those already in place.

Businesspersons see opportunities here as well. Testifying before the House Committee on Small Business, Motorola Executive Vice President Christopher Galvin proposed a 3 percent tax credit against a company's research and development expenses if that money was spent in conjunction with university research, consortia, or national laboratories (Small Business Hearings, 1989, 65). As examples, Galvin suggested an IBM-MIT partnership to build future generations of memory chips or North Carolina textile companies in partnership with the University of North Carolina to build the world's most advanced loom.

The work of some centers is even directed at solving social problems. The National Environmental Technical Applications Center at the University of Pittsburgh is a partnership whose members in addition to the university include the Environmental Protection Agency and several businesses whose purpose is the development and commercialization of pollution control technology (Small Business Hearings, 1989, 91–92).

Business firms believe the partnerships are good for business because they will enhance revenues (increase profits). As Thomas Kiley, vice president of Genetech, said,

Make no mistake about it: for-profit corporations are, by definition, not in business to give away money. Where they provide money for research, they invariably do so in order to gain competitive advantage. (Kiley, 1983, 63)

There are a number of competitive advantages that industries can gain from these partnerships including:

1. receiving employee training at the university,
2. gaining lead time by getting a first look at research,
3. getting the right of first refusal for an exclusive license,
4. becoming identified as an industry leader,

5. obtaining exclusive access in an area of corporate concern (Kiley, 1983),

6. gaining access to certain technology that may be hard to come by,

7. gaining access to special university facilities that would be too expensive for the corporation,

8. gaining access to nonuniversity personnel who bring skills and abilities not present on the faculty (Cooper, 1982, 301),

9. obtaining inexpensive physical space in university-business research parks for small entrepreneurial companies, and

10. obtaining venture capital for many small entrepreneurial companies that some universities are willing to provide.

Corporate leaders see access to personnel as a major advantage. Partnerships with universities provide opportunities for corporations to discover and hire highly trained personnel. Even if persuading senior professors to give up the advantages of the university is a formidable task, selling graduate students—many of whom have had quite enough of the university—on a position in industry is likely to be successful. Jack Sparks, chairman of the board and chief executive officer at Whirlpool, puts the point succinctly: "We gain access to outstandingly creative people—both faculty and students. And we get to hire some of them, notably top-quality students with experience in one or more areas of technology in which we already have interests" (Sparks, 1985, 19). Furthermore, it is hard to underestimate the value that comes from advance knowledge. As Robert Barker points out, the public literature is "often miles behind the front line of what's happening in the universities" (Barker, 1985, 24).

If business perceived opportunities for economic gain, so did universities. Indeed, universities are the chief initiators of university-business partnerships. In a study of thirty-one state-supported technology transfer programs at universities, 80 percent were founded because of the initiative of universities (Wyckoff and Tornatzky, 1988, 473). Engineering colleges alone accounted for a full 27 percent. The most obvious benefit to universities is increased funding to support their research programs. The Massachusetts Institute of Technology began charging industrial clients a fee for access to the university in 1948. By 1987 MIT had 300 industrial affiliates, including one-third of the *Fortune* 500 companies that do serious research. Depending on their size, MIT affiliates pay MIT $10,000 to $100,000 per year (Main, 1987, 84). The Indiana University Foundation received $3 million in royalty income from Procter and Gamble for using the foundation's patent on stannous fluoride in Crest toothpaste (Omenn, 1982b, 696). Both business-associate fees and royalty payments from products using university-patented products could provide substantial revenue to financially strapped universities.

During the 1970s universities began to produce more students with advanced degrees than they could hire. Universities needed industry to absorb these students. Partnerships with industry served as an excellent vehicle for introducing students to a specific company. These partnerships also gave faculty a sense of what industry wanted in terms of training. In this way a better match could be made between the university's curriculum and the needs of industry.

SECTION TWO

Problems: Publication Delay, Secrecy, and the Withholding of Products

Despite the overwhelming support university-business partnerships have received, there are issues and concerns that are disquieting. As university-business partnerships were developing during the first half of the 1980s, a number of fairly specific questions arose about the ownership of intellectual property, patent policy and the withholding of products, the rights of academics to publish, and concerns about increased secrecy in a university environment traditionally characterized by norms of openness and the prompt disclosure of information.

One of the earliest concerns that appeared in the vast majority of articles on the subject was that publication would either be prevented or unduly delayed on the grounds that proprietary information had to be protected. Corporations have little incentive to invest in university-business partnerships if they cannot be assured that they can profit from any technology transfer that results. In order to have a chance at making a profit, the business partner must protect its proprietary information either by obtaining a patent or a license based on a university patent. To further protect proprietary information, publication of the research must be delayed until a patent application has been filed. But some critics feared that publication delays would threaten the academic value of openness that is reflected in prompt publication.

However, the delay-of-publication fear now seems overblown. In nearly all university research business partnerships freedom to publish is guaranteed subject only, in most agreements, to a delay that would allow a company to file for a patent. The typical delay permitted is around six months. Sometimes a person must wait a bit longer to obtain a patent that will protect the company internationally. Delays of this magnitude do not seem to constitute much of a threat to the freedom to publish. Some writers have also pointed out that secrecy

51

should be much more of an issue with government research—especially research for the Department of Defense (Rosenzweig, 1985). Although a few campuses have rejected defense contracts and many have imposed some rules, defense contracting and some other government-funded research require far greater secrecy than commercial research.

Nonetheless, isolated reports regarding the suppression of publication or excessive publication delays still appear in the most recent literature. Two researchers have charged that one university administration tried to have members of the science faculty agree to a statement that graduate students would be required to sign. The statement required that students who worked for a professor who had set up a private lab would not discuss their research and would delay dissertations until patent protection could be obtained for the company (Buchbinder and Newson, 1990, 372). Since no specific information was given on this incident and we do not know how long ago it occurred, we may be justified in dismissing it as an isolated event.

There are other issues concerning nondisclosure and secrecy besides publication delay that cannot be so easily dispensed with, however. In testimony before a House committee, Thomas Murray pointed out that it may be in a scientist's interest to withhold information. A scientist may want to hold on to information that might result in a commercially viable product until arrangements with a corporate sponsor can be made (House Hearings on the Use of Human Biological Materials in the Development of Biomedical Problems, 1985, 100). The point at issue is that the problem of secrecy is not simply a matter of one party exacting a pledge of secrecy from another. Rather, secrecy can be self-imposed. Proving that secrecy of this type has increased is difficult but writers about university-business partnerships widely believe that it has.

Just as the university scientist may have self-interested reasons to withhold publication, so may a corporation have self-interested reasons to delay the introduction of a product. Companies might fail to market something invented in a university-business partnership. Suppose a partnership with General Motors discovered an alternative to the combustion engine and GM refused to market it. Since the academy is committed to advancing the cause of truth, it seems that any university engaged in these partnerships would want to make sure that the potential product made possible by the research actually gets developed. In our discussion of the Wisconsin Alumni Research Foundation, we noted that the WARF's patent was used to prevent the development of oleomargarine. In the 1970s MIT canceled a project to explore methanol as an alternative to gasoline. It was alleged although never proven that Exxon, which was providing significant funding for the laboratory, forced the cancellation (Biddle, 1981; Yamamoto, 1982). If the allegation was true, the cancellation would seem unacceptable given the university's commitment to openness and the advancement of knowledge. Testifying before the Gore Committee, Dr. Zsolt Harsayni testified that Johnson and Johnson had purchased technology from university scientists but had never developed the product based on the technology. Incidentally, the scientists reportedly sued for $250 million and won (Harsanyi, 1982, 313). Finally, some critics of university-business partnerships have raised the issue that privatizing biotechnology might deprive developing countries of needed information (Lepkowski, 1984b, 8).

It might seem that nonexclusive licenses would be the best way to ensure that the product of the research would be developed. After all, if one company does not develop it, another will. However, early on, E. E. David Jr., president of the Exxon Research and Development Company, made a case for exclusive licenses. He argued that the development of a product is a risky activity. In the absence of an exclusive license, the risks might not be worth taking economically. He stated, "the risks of development may be so great that what is nobody's exclusive license may turn out to be nobody's development" (David, 1982).

As university-business partnerships have developed, David's argument has been persuasive. The granting of an exclusive license is a common occurrence. Perhaps the way to solve the problem of the nondevelopment of a product is for the university to insist that if an exclusive license is granted, it should carry some contractual obligation to develop. Such contractual obligations could then put this problem to rest.

Those concerned with a culture of secrecy that might develop as university-business partnerships increase should consider the fact that cultural influence moves in both directions. There is a possibility that university-business partnerships might bring about less secrecy in business. We cannot ignore the fact that the relative openness of the universities might infect their corporate partners. Michael Davis has made just this point. "One benefit that business may derive from profitable links with a university department is an argument to keep controls on information within the company to a minimum. Since university researchers tend to resist secrecy on principle, businesses learn to allow more open communication or lose valuable university contributions" (Davis, 1991, 34). Davis has a valid point. So much of the focus of the critics is on how these university-business partnerships undermine the values of the university. But if we believe that some of these educational values have a legitimate role to play in business, university-business partnerships provide an opportunity as well as a danger.

In addition the introduction of some business values into the university may have a beneficial effect on the university. One intriguing argument was made in 1984 by Merrill Whitburn. Whitburn argues that in many humanities departments there is a strong cultural bias against university-business cooperation. He cites English departments where persons specializing in English composition and communication are second-class citizens. These subjects are often taught by adjunct professors. Cooperative research and teaching between the university and industry in these areas are discouraged. Often the rationale used to prevent the development of programs in these areas is that they are too vocational and hence are inappropriate to the university's mission. Whitburn assails the situation as a violation of the academic freedom of specialists in these areas (1984, 38).

The violation of academic freedom charge is probably extreme. The paradigm case of a violation of academic freedom occurs when a professor is forbidden or pressured to keep silent about his or her own view on a subject in his or her area of expertise. The protection of academic freedom, however, does not require that the university take positive steps to make sure that every view is heard. For example, a medical school that refuses to offer a course on homeopathic medicine does not thereby violate the academic freedom of those who believe the medical school should offer such a course. However, if a subscriber to homeopathic medicine were forbidden to discuss a homeopathic remedy for colds and flu in a course where the treatment of colds and flu was the subject under consideration, the academic freedom of the subscriber to homeopathic medicine would be violated.

Even if Whitburn is wrong in making the violation of academic freedom charge, his discussion raises an important point. Many academics, particularly many academic humanists, have a strong antibusiness attitude. Humanists with a more probusiness perspective usually have difficulty in developing programs that support their research agendas. Orthodoxies do develop in departments. Financial pressures that encourage academics to take research that is of interest to business seriously may expand discussion and debate on university campuses rather than stifle it. For example, Whitburn argues

> Those humanists interested in participating in cooperative ventures will find themselves working with literary scientists, computer scientists, telecommunication specialists, psychologists, philosophers, and others. This participation will enhance their understanding of the scientific-technical culture and should, in time, allow them some influence in this sphere. (1984, 38)

Thus even as the issues of publication delay and the suppression of discoveries are resolved by the development of norms of good practice, issues of self-imposed secrecy and research priorities have no obvious solution. A scientist who keeps his or her discovery secret until a commercial contract is struck behaves no differently from a scientist who keeps his or her discovery secret until the publication of the results appears. In both cases there is little that can be done except to rely on the conscience of the researcher. University-business partnerships do not create a new problem; rather they augment an old one.

As for the institutional encouragement or discouragement of various research agendas, the issue is in doubt. University-business partnerships could move research away from basic research and away from the traditional research interests of university scientists and engineers. On the other hand, university-business partnerships may also break down the bias against applied research and some of the research orthodoxies in the various departments. If university-business partnerships do have these effects, whether the results are good or bad will depend on one's perspective on the legitimacy of applied and nontraditional research. We will have more to say about this issue later.

SECTION THREE

Economic Risks

As we recall, the chief advantage of university-business partnerships was the perceived potential economic benefits for all parties. All the early articles focused on the potential benefits; there was little discussion of the potential economic risks. Now, however, there is a growing concern that universities are overestimating the opportunities for financial gain and underestimating the financial risks, including the risks of lawsuits to defend patents. Let us examine some sobering statistics. In 1982, industry funded $39 billion of U.S. research and development. Only 1 percent—about $250 to $300 million—was used to fund R&D at universities. That amounted to only 4 percent of the university R&D budget (Fusfeld, 1983, 12). Also, ten companies account for 33 percent of all R&D funded by industry. Two companies account for 20 percent (Fusfeld). It would be a mistake for the average university to think that it could approach the businesses in its community and expect much in the way of university-business partnerships. As many commentators have warned, there is no way to expect business to provide the support that has been provided by the federal government. If a university has its government support slashed 10 to 20 percent, it is unrealistic to expect that the university can recoup its losses through increased support from business.

What about royalties from patents? One writer characterizes the odds as follows. Very few discoveries are patentable. Of those that are patentable only one in ten will even make enough money to recover the costs of filing. One in 100 make between $20,000 and $50,000. Only one in 1,000 will prove a major money maker. These odds are consistent with the figures given for the Wisconsin Alumni Research Foundation cited earlier on p. 6 (Fuchsberg, 1989c). The Forum for College Funding reports that revenues from the licensing of intellectual property almost never exceed more than 1 percent of total revenues

(Anderson, 1990). There are good economic explanations for these results. Figures reported in *The Scientist* indicate that in fiscal 1990 universities received 1,200 patents and $60 million. A U.S. patent costs about $10,000 and an international patent costs about $30,000 to $50,000 (Dickinson, 1991, 6). Since most of that income goes to a handful of universities, most universities are spending more obtaining patents than they are receiving in royalties. A recent study by the University of California indicated that it takes an average of eight years for a university invention to receive royalties, while patent costs for inventions protected by several U.S. patents and protected internationally can cost hundreds of thousands of dollars (Theunte, 1992, 1). The University of Minnesota, which is a big player in the technology transfer sweepstakes, is about breaking even (Theunte).

Others complain that the universities are being so greedy in their requests for licensing fees that partnerships are being discouraged. This point has been made by E. Michael Eagen, director of business development at Repligen Inc., a medium-size biotechnology company, and John F. Thuente, director of patents and licensing at the University of Minnesota (Fuchsberg, 1989c).

Of course some universities have "hits." As early as 1981 *Business Week* reported that MIT had made $19 million from its patent on the core memory of computers and $10 million from its patent on synthetic penicillin. The successes make good news copy but many in the university community do not seem to realize how atypical these successes are.

In order to receive greater financial returns, a university might consider a nontraditional investment strategy. If a university cannot reap a sufficient return profiting from the inventions of its faculty, it might try investing in their inventions. This strategy was actually endorsed in an article in *Forbes*. "They [universities] already invest portions of their endowments in venture capital funds; it's not hard to make the leap to investing in their own research" (Morgenson, 1988, 210). A venture-capital investment strategy is one way for smaller, less-known universities to get more involved in research. As Walter Channing, head of the venture-capital group CW, is quoted as saying, "NIH money goes to Yale, Stanford, Harvard, the usual suspects. NIH doesn't have the guts to give money to unknowns" (Morgenson).

Investing in faculty research is far more risky, yet some universities are doing just that, with mixed results. The MIT Development Trust, created in 1972 to identify commercially promising research and to bring together funds and management, folded after six years. The

University of Utah started a program called Creative Capitalism that has invested in fifty companies since 1978. These companies have provided 4,500 jobs and $20 million in tax revenues. However, only a few are profitable (Morgenson). As we will see, one university, Boston University, may already have suffered serious reversals.

A common means for implementing this investment strategy is the venture-capital fund. These venture-capital funds assume many forms. The least risky are those that encourage faculty inventions but do not contribute any university funds to the venture partnership. Jaron Bourke and Robert Weissman (1990) reported some of the details of some university venture-capital funds. Harvard's Medical Science Partners (MSP) was established in 1988 with $30 million in nonuniversity funds. The fund is administered by a former executive of the American affiliate of the French drug firm Merieux. Washington University entered the game two years earlier in 1986, when it entered into a partnership with the Alafi Capital Company and created the Alafi/ Washington University (A/W) Corporation. Each holds 50 percent of the stock but Washington University put up none of its own money. However, Washington University also relinquished control. Only Alafi controls investment decisions and manages the fund.

The University of Chicago takes more of a hands-on approach. Arch Development Corporation resulted from the partnership between the University of Chicago and the Argonne Federal Research Laboratory. The university appoints Arch Development Corporation's board of directors, the associate dean of the business school serves as the president, and students from the business school volunteer for the company. Critics argue that the school is too intimately involved and that the dangers of conflict of interest and a distortion of values to be discussed later are very real. Not surprisingly the University of Chicago denies the charges.

Princeton has developed venture-capital funds and so has Johns Hopkins University. In 1990, Duke spun off an investment management operation that will oversee the investment of more than $1 billion in university assets, including $560 million in endowment funds and $150 million in pension funds (Chernoff, 1990, 1). A major responsibility of the investment arm is to pursue technology transfers. There are no venture-capital funds involved in the Duke arrangement, however. The assets are invested in other ways. Cornell has used its alumni to put money into a venture fund rather than use university funds to do so (Fuchsberg, 1989b, A 29, 30).

Some have argued that universities should allow persons who have used university facilities and personnel to spin off companies in which the university (and often the inventor) will acquire an equity position. The University of Utah's policy is to both receive a royalty payment and take an equity position in the company. This policy resulted from the fact most of the spin-off companies that did not use university patents, but nonetheless obtained the technology or expertise required for the company from the university, left without providing any compensation to the university in the form of an equity position or royalty payments (Brown, 1985, 22–23). The university seems justified in expecting compensation for the assistance it provided.

Wayne Brown recommends a rather complicated arrangement whereby a corporation, limited partnership, or other appropriate commercial entity be established with the express purpose of assisting in the commercialization of university-developed technology. This corporation would neither manufacture nor market products. Instead it would become a shareholder in various companies that would be established to manufacture and market products. This corporation would recruit the management team and be active in the day-to-day affairs of these newly created companies. Among the advantages claimed for this arrangement is the fact that the university would not be involved in the details of the business of manufacturing and marketing products; neither would its faculty, who would serve only as advisors to the shareholder company (Brown, 24–25).

Whatever form these investments take, life becomes complicated for the university. As one knowledgeable business professor has remarked,

> Taking an equity position in a new venture will entail all the difficulties of dealing with a small firm, plus potential financial, organizational, legal and political issues related to the university's dual status as research institution and commercial shareholder. (Mitchell, 1991, 214)

Even the less risky strategies, including collecting royalties from patents, raise the danger of creating internal conflicts. Consider decisions by the university's patent office as to whether or not the university should seek a patent for a faculty member's invention. Since the costs of obtaining and defending a patent are so high and since the return from both royalties and venture-capital investments is so small, university officials cannot seek a patent for every faculty invention nor can they invest in every start-up firm that supports a faculty invention. Those turned down will be angry and frustrated. "Folks making venture decisions at universities will immediately become embroiled in battles with faculty since they'll be saying no to most researchers most times" (Morgenson, 1988, 210).

Yet another danger arises from the cyclical nature of business support. The situation here is analogous to what happened with government support. Universities expanded greatly in response to government largesse in the 1960s and early 1970s. When government support was sharply curtailed in the later 1970s and 1980s, the universities turned to business. Where will universities go when business support is cut back? The economy is cyclical; and research and development funds, whether wisely invested or not, are under pressure in an economic downturn. With the huge deficit and multiple social problems facing Congress, there is no guarantee, and indeed no reason for optimism, in thinking that the government will offset declines in corporate support. Indeed, the 1990s look like a time when both federal and state government support will be sharply curtailed and business support will be under severe pressure.

To illustrate the seriousness of the danger let us consider the case of Boston University, which may be in serious financial trouble because of its use of university endowment assets as venture capital. Boston University has a tradition of an aggressive investment policy. Up to 10 percent of its endowment has been invested through the Community Technology Foundation in limited partnerships that in turn invest in early stage companies with high growth potential (Morgan, 1990). At first the success of this policy was extraordinary. In the early 1980s returns ran from 30 percent to 40 percent as compared to the 10 percent to 12 percent of the best of the traditional investments. In 1987 Boston University shifted its strategy and put most of its venture-capital eggs in the basket of one of its professors. In 1987 Boston University purchased 71.4 percent of the issued stock of Seragen Diagnostics Inc. and guaranteed a $10 million loan to the company. The cost of the stock purchase was $25 million, so Boston University's investment was $35 million. Why did Seragen Diagnostics Inc. merit such a significant investment?

A bit of history is important here. Seragen was founded in 1980 to develop and sell diagnostic products. In 1982 it acquired the diagnostics division of Dow Chemical. At that point the investors in Seragen included two Boston-based venture-capital firms and Nycomed, A.S., a Norwegian pharmaceutical company. Boston University had invested $1,224,028 of "funds functioning as endowment." In 1985 the diagnostics arm of Seragen was spun off and Boston University acquired a 67 percent interest in the new firm of Seragen Diagnostics. Later Seragen Diagnostics was sold and Boston University received income of between $9 million and $10 million—an exceedingly good return (Morgan). That is the good news.

Meanwhile Boston University's interest in the parent company Seragen continued. In 1987 the Norwegian pharmaceutical Nycomed was taken over by another Norwegian pharmaceutical company that wanted out and offered to sell its share. Boston University then acquired Nycomed's position for the $35 million investment quoted earlier. Boston University President John Silber is quoted as saying that Seragen will become a $5 billion company. If Silber is right, Boston University's $35 million investment would be exceedingly profitable. How well has Seragen been doing? Not very well.

Seragen is suffering operating losses. Boston University has been supporting those losses through cash and loans. As of June 30, 1989, more than $16.3 million has been written off (Morgan). Seragen was not expected to earn a profit until 1993. Unless the situation turns around, Boston University may face an $80 million exposure. The Boston University endowment is around $200 million. If Seragen fails, Boston University will have a most serious financial setback.

As we shall see with some of the criticisms of university-business partnerships, the difficulties do not pertain to the partnerships themselves. Boston University is not at risk because it pooled its money with venture capitalists. It is at risk because it made a large, risky investment—an investment that seems imprudent given the fact that Boston University is an educational institution, where those who contribute to its endowment assume that it will make prudent investments. Boston University would have been equally imprudent to invest heavily in junk-bond financing. If there is a message for us here, it is that the university should not treat its endowment and other assets the way a private firm treats its assets.

There is a difference in purpose between a university and a private firm. A stockholder in a private firm has a different purpose in mind for her investment than a person has when making a contribution to the endowment. Taking risks for a larger return is not an accepted norm of investment behavior for a university. What Boston University is doing is akin to violating an implicit social contract it has with those who have contributed to its endowment. Perhaps the norms for prudent investment should change, although this book will present many reasons why they should not. In the present context Boston University seems to have behaved inappropriately, but it is the riskiness of the investment rather than the fact that they were in a partnership with other financial investors that creates the inappropriateness. In evaluating the various investments that universities make in university-business partnerships, two things must be considered: the source of the investment funds and the riskiness of the investment. It is the obligation of university officials to make sure that these risks are appropriate given the source of funds. Alumni who put up their own money in a venture-capital fund are probably making an appropriate investment. Using endowment funds is not acceptable given the risks that go with venture-capital investment.

Lawsuits are another way university-business partnerships can cost universities money. As of this writing no university has been subject to a product liability suit and perhaps the commonplace requirement that a license is granted on the condition that the licensee carry liability insurance may protect universities from this legal peril. Defending patents is another issue, however. In 1988, Cornell University won two patent-infringement cases, one on a patent that had already earned Cornell $300,000 in licensing fees (Fuchsberg, 1989). The University of California, San Francisco, is currently suing Eli Lilly for patent infringement. Lilly sells insulin products and UCSF claims that the manufacture of insulin requires use of a gene sequence and transformed microorganisms patented by UC to produce it. Lilly doesn't deny it uses the process; their lawyers argue that the UC patent is invalid. The University of California must now defend its patent in court. Moreover, the court fight did not arise because UC serendipidously discovered the alleged infringement. The University of California and Lilly have been trying to negotiate a licensing agreement for six years. Finally UC sued. The good news is that this is the first time UC has sued for infringement of any of its more than 100 biotechnology patents (Thayer, 1990).

The University of Illinois is joined with the two companies with whom they have exclusive licenses, DuPont and Pfister Hybrid Corn Co., in a suit against Pioneer HIBred International defending their patent on oil-rich corn seeds. This court action was taken in January of 1990. The suit claims that Pioneer obtained the seeds improperly by pressuring a university employee who was having health problems (Looker, 1990b). Court depositions indicate:

Alexander, who was in failing health due to heart and prostate complications which resulted in surgery two months later, and who was placed in a stressful situation due to Pioneer's persistent requests for seed from the gene pools and inbred lines, agreed to provide Pioneer with seed without the knowledge of university officials.

What makes the seeds so valuable? High-energy corn would enable livestock to put on weight with less food. Hence a license on the corn was valuable enough to have Du Pont and Pfister pay the University of Illinois $50,000 each plus royalties. Pioneer had also been a bidder for a license but they withdrew after they had obtained the seeds from Alexander.

It looks like Pioneer is obviously in the wrong and the University of Illinois is obviously in the right. So long as the frame of reference is private market transactions, the University of Illinois *is* in the right. A complication arises when the question is asked, "Should discoveries at land-grant public universities belong to the public and hence be unavailable for private purchase?" Until recently the tradition was to make all new genetic lines of corn public. In essence they were free to any one who had a use for them (Looker, 1990). Biotechnology has increased the value of specialty grains. As a result they are now subject to the rules of the market and they no longer belong to the public. Does that matter?

Some experts are concerned. They remind us that the land-grant universities had conducted a comprehensive public breeding program. In the absence of biotechnology, plant breeding was "too costly, too long term, or too uncertain to be attractive to industry breeders" (Buttel et al., 1984). Now, as a result of the fact that there is money to be made by the university, however, public breeding is virtually nonexistent. These experts see a decisive move of personnel to private industry and a decline in university breeding programs. One could respond by saying that university-business partnerships will stem the tide and that commercial university breeding programs will increase. But even if that is correct, university breeding departments will be oriented toward private profit-making firms rather than to the general public. The decision to move something from the realm of the public to the realm of the market is a public policy decision. We will have more to say about this shift from a public interest focus to a private for-profit focus later.

The underlying message here is that university partnerships cannot be counted on to provide economic benefits to universities. They provide no panacea for the declining economic fortunes that have befallen universities in the 1980s and early 1990s. Indeed efforts to gain economic benefits from university-business partnerships may end up costing the university more money rather than providing additional income. And as the University of Illinois lawsuit indicated, the constant search for patentable products may change the very nature of the university and its core values.

A somewhat startling but similar recognition regarding the limited economic return for university-business partnerships has occurred on the side of industry as well. In 1991, the strongly supportive Government-University-Industry Research Roundtable, described in some detail earlier, published interviews with seventeen industrial officials whose companies had been deeply involved with technology transfer partnerships. Their generally negative evaluations were surprising. For example, the Monsanto representative indicated that no products have been developed from either of its two alliances with Harvard and Washington University. The Monsanto official indicated that products would have been expected from a Monsanto in-house research and development effort. The language of a charitable donation was being used to describe Monsanto's alliances with Harvard and Washington University. (Recall that Monsanto's partnership with Washington University was one of the star partnerships of the 1980s and that not one product has resulted. Twenty-three million dollars is a large charitable donation.)

These industrial officials argued that "technical advance occurs most often through small incremental improvements to existing products and processes rather than as large technical breakthroughs" (Government-University-Business Roundtable, 1991, 1). Since most university research is broad theory-based research, universities have little role to play in these small incremental improvements. Moreover while these industrial officials value theoretical university research, they do not want the university to become involved in product development. In the area of biotechnology, industry officials expect to rely less on universities than they do now. Industry wants universities to train and educate scientists. In this respect the industry officials urged the universities to do a better job in providing scientists and technicians with management skills, communication skills, quality assurance, and a team approach to problem solving.

Thus universities have an important role to play in training the next generation of scientists and engineers and in providing theoretical knowledge that may have a future payoff, but their role in product and process development is perceived to be relatively unimportant. This assessment by the officials of industry stands in sharp contrast to the important role university officials think university research can contribute to technology transfer. Indeed some of the interviewee statements of industry officials sound little different from the academic and political criticisms of university-business partnerships.

> Universities should not attempt to orient their research more closely to product discovery; this is not an appropriate role for universities, nor is it a task for which they are generally well suited, said the interviewees. Rather they must try to foster creativity, and to advance the frontiers of knowledge through long-term basic research (Government-University-Industry Research Roundtable, 1991, 10).

This developing difference of perception regarding the importance of university research in technology transfer is certain to create misunderstanding. For example, several of the industry officials indicated they resented the difficulties in negotiating patent and licensing agreements with universities. Given the paucity of the payoffs, the industry officials find this perceived tough bargaining stance to be ironic.

Thus the economic justification for university-business partnerships that provided the basis for their support is eroding. The failure of these partnerships to bring economic benefits either to the university or industry makes some of the other criticisms of these alliances even more serious.

SECTION FOUR
Conflict-of-Interest Problems

One of the most common criticisms of university-business partnerships is that they often create serious conflict-of-interest issues. These issues are so serious that the National Institutes of Health has been drafting guidelines to try to eliminate some of them. Indeed, the NIH issued guidelines in 1989 for discussion. The guidelines created such an outcry from scientists that they were withdrawn. NIH is trying again and many universities are waiting for the publication of these guidelines before they complete or revise their own. Another indication of the seriousness of the problem is the fact that the House of Representatives had hearings on conflicts of interest in university-business partnerships in 1989.

Discussions of conflicts of interest in university-business partnerships are inhibited by the lack of a concise definition of what constitutes a conflict of interest. Despite the frequent use of the term there is no standard definition. *Webster's New Collegiate Dictionary* has a reasonably good definition: "A conflict of interest is a conflict between the private interest and the official responsibilities of a person in a position of trust." After examining the American Bar Association Code of Professional Responsibility, Michael Davis has proposed a definition that applies to a generalized agency relationship. "A person has a conflict of interest if a) he is in a relationship of trust with another requiring him to exercise judgment in that other's service and b) he has an interest tending to interfere with the proper exercise of that judgment" (M. Davis, 1991). A similar definition is provided by Tom Beauchamp. He maintains that a "conflict of interest occurs whenever there exists a conflict between a person's private or institutional gain and that same person's official duties in a position of trust" (Beauchamp, 1992, 9).

What makes the claim of a conflict of interest so emotionally charged is that often the person accused of a conflict of interest does not believe he or she violated their position of trust or was improperly influenced by the possibility of personal gain. Thus a professor who was doing research on possible side effects of a drug manufactured by a company in which she had an equity position could claim that there was no actual conflict of interest because her objectivity was not compromised. This is analogous to a mother having her son in class claiming there was no conflict of interest because she graded her son on the same standards she graded everyone else. The distinction being made here is between a perceived conflict of interest and an actual conflict of interest. What looks like a conflict of interest to the outside observer may not be an actual conflict of interest if the professor's judgment was not compromised. It is relatively easy to spot circumstances where a conflict of interest could occur. It is more difficult to determine if a conflict of interest did occur.

Given the fact that it is often difficult to determine whether a conflict of interest has occurred, some may argue that the operating principle should be that one should avoid even the appearance of a conflict of interest. But that principle would be unduly restrictive. A manager of a corporation is always or almost always in a position to benefit personally at the expense of the corporation. It is impossible to avoid the appearance of a conflict of interest. And although we have become increasingly cynical about claims that people can maintain their objectivity when they are in situations that could be perceived as conflicts of interest, there are occasions when the integrity of the person is sufficiently established that we do trust them to maintain their objectivity in such situations. For example, Richard L. Cook, an executive of the Du Pont corporation, was appointed to a one-year term to Virginia's highest environmental post even though Cook maintained his ties to Du Pont and would return to Du Pont at the end of the term and even though Du Pont and Virginia had recently been and at present were in conflict over environmental matters. Despite the high potential for a conflict of interest, all parties agreed that Cook was the best person for the job.

To accommodate cases like Mr. Cook's, a distinction between a potential conflict of interest and an actual conflict of interest is needed. People have potential conflicts of interest when they are in positions of trust where their objectivity *could be* compromised and they have actual conflicts of interest when their objectivity *is* compromised. This distinction allows for a continuum of situations from a high risk that a potential conflict of interest will become actual to a low risk that a potential conflict of interest will become actual. As Tom Beauchamp has pointed out, "some influences clearly distort judgment, others have some reasonable probability of doing so, and others have some distant possibility of doing so" (Beauchamp, 1992, 10). As we discuss conflict-of-interest situations with university-business partnerships we must be sensitive to the likelihood that a potential conflict of interest will become actual. We also need to think about mechanisms that could be used to allay fears regarding perceived conflicts of interest.

There is a tendency to think of conflicts of interest in financial terms—as situations that provide for unjust enrichment. For example, a university faculty member has a potential financial conflict of interest whenever she has a equity position in a firm that sponsors her research. In order to reap the profits, she might overlook ambiguous test results. Similarly a university has a potential financial conflict of interest when it has an equity interest in the venture-capital firms of one of its faculty. With a financial stake in the firm, how objective can the university be in its appraisal of the faculty member?

But not all examples are financial in nature. Some involve what one writer calls conflicts in commitment (Reams, 1986, 69). In these cases a person's obligation to the partnership may interfere with her other obligations; for example, when a person's industry-sponsored research interferes with her teaching. With conflicts of commitment the conflict lies not between one's obligation to others and one's self-interest, but among one's conflicting obligations to other parties. Some situations are instances of both a conflict of interest and a conflict of commitment. A person who directs a university-business partnership research center and who both neglects his students while directing the center and has the center's business partner sponsor some of his other research is involved in a conflict of interest and a conflict of commitment.

Let us consider examples of unjust enrichment and conflicts in commitment. Our examples will include institutional conflicts of interest (e.g., when the university has a conflict of interest) and individual conflicts of interest (e.g., when an individual faculty member at a university has a conflict of interest). We begin with the previously cited case of a university that takes an equity position in a company where one of its faculty members is either a major stockholder or an officer. Why would that represent at least a potential conflict of interest? In a tenure or promotion case, could the institution be objective if the faculty member is successfully pursuing patentable research that either does or could provide substantial revenue to the university? Publications that would have been judged mediocre might now be seen as acceptable.

As for individual conflicts of interest, a Harvard scientist has pointed out that if a university faculty member has a large equity position or is an officer in a company and for some reason his company is in competition with his university, then he would have divided loyalties. He would have a personal interest that might well interfere with his responsibilities to the university. If the company were publicly held, the conflict would be between his obligations to the stockholders and his obligation to the university (Yamamoto, 1982).

This issue is of more than theoretical interest, as the University of Illinois found out. In 1989 the University of Illinois was involved in an ugly lawsuit with its former professor of computer and electrical engineering, Donald Blitzer. The university had permitted him to start a private company, University Communications Inc. Meanwhile, on campus, Blitzer continued to direct his Computer-Based Educational Research Laboratory. In turn the university received 3 percent of the gross revenues of University Communications Inc. Two of Blitzer's colleagues brought suit, contending that Blitzer used public funds to visit potential investors, required university employees to do company clerical work, and allowed his customers to use university computers at a fraction of the cost of what others paid (Siler, 1989). Since the charges were made by two colleagues, it may be reasonable to conclude that the university was not adequately supervising Blitzer. After all, the university was getting 3 percent of the revenues. As we consider the plight of the University of Illinois, it should be noted that one of the first conferences to discuss concerns about university-business partnerships, the 1983 Pajaro Dunes Conference, had recommended against a university taking an equity position in the firm of a faculty member.

One of the most hotly debated financial conflict-of-interest issues is whether a faculty member should be permitted to do research for companies in which he owns stock. The danger, of course, is that the financial interest in the success of the project will undermine the objectivity of the research. The issue has been particularly touchy at Harvard. Professor Scheffer Tseng was a researcher conducting clinical tests for a potential dry-eye treatment. Professor Tseng owned a large share of stock in the company formed to market the treatment, and Tseng's family apparently made a million dollars from the new company. An independent two-year study showed "indifferent results" and cast doubt on the claimed effectiveness of the treatment. It is also alleged that Tseng tested the treatment on patients not authorized to receive it; Tseng's financial interest in the company might have been the cause of the unauthorized treatment (Bourke and Weissman, 1990: Stipp 1990).

Another case that has been the subject of congressional hearings and discussed in the periodicals involves the University of Florida. Pharmatec was a for-profit company founded by University of Florida faculty member Nicholas Bodor. The company was founded to exploit a system for delivering drugs directly to the brain. Stockholders in the company included two deans in the college of pharmacy and three department chairs. The deans had responsibility for overseeing the university's conflict-of-interest policy. When a question arose as to whether the process might cause delayed Parkinson-like symptoms, the objectivity of Bodor and the University of Florida's response to the question of possible toxicity was bound to be questioned and it was. The financial interests in the firm undercut any attempt at objective analysis. The University of Florida now has a policy forbidding administrators to have an equity position in companies with which the university has a sponsored-research agreement (Marshall, 1990).

Despite these cases, some officers of biotechnology firms opposed a proposed Harvard rule that would bar faculty from doing research for companies in which they hold stock. James Vincent, chief executive of Biogen, claimed the proposed regulations could "really hurt companies that don't have cash [to pay academic researchers] and have to use equity" (Stipp, 1990).

Another argument against prohibiting a faculty member from having an equity position in a firm which sponsors the professor's research is that if the rule is enforced too strictly, professors might have to sell insignificant shares. One Johns Hopkins University professor was forced to sell 200 shares of IBM stock (Stipp, 1990). The point of this argument is that owning a few shares of stock is not sufficient to compromise the objectivity of a professional and thus no real conflict of interest exists or is likely to exist.

Rules forbidding faculty from having a large equity share in an outside firm, or forbidding faculty to accept research grants in firms in which they have an equity stake, have largely been rejected by faculty. Although Johns Hopkins has banned faculty from conducting research of that type, the norm that seems to have developed is disclosure rather than prohibition. Nearly all research universities have a policy requiring disclosure of potential conflicts of interest. (A number of university conflict-of-interest policies are included in the documents section of this book.)

Disclosure seems a sufficient response to a number of conflict-of-interest questions raised in the literature. Some questions currently being asked include:

> Should university scientists let companies pay for their trips to scientific meetings and pay them to talk at those meetings about topics related to the company's products?
>
> Should scientists review other scientists' work for federal research agencies or for scientific journals when the reviewer has a financial stake in whether or not the research they are reviewing receives a grant or is published? (Wheeler, 1989)

An example of a conflict of interest of the first type was discussed in a *Newsday* editorial. A Harvard scientist at an international conference had praised a new method for controlling the disease-bearing ticks that cause Lyme disease, but the scientist had neglected to inform the audience that he was the founder and an officer in the only company that markets the method. Could not a policy of disclosure help here? If the conferees had known that the speaker had a financial interest in the company whose method was being discussed, then they could have been on guard regarding the objectivity of the speaker's remarks.

Similarly the administrator or journal editor in conjunction with the applicant or author can decide whether the proposed reviewer could maintain her objectivity. Of course, that person's review would no longer be totally blind, and in many cases the proposed reviewer would not be acceptable. But some persons with a good reputation for objectivity and impartiality might well be acceptable. On the philosophical side of business ethics, there are relatively few senior scholars in the field and nearly all of them have competing textbooks. However, these scholars often review text proposals of competitors when the publisher and the author are fully aware that the reviewer is a competitor. A relationship of trust exists among these scholars so that the conflict of interest is only apparent.

On the other hand, is mere disclosure always sufficient to resolve an apparent conflict-of-interest situation? Disclosure warns all the relevant parties to take note, but it does not eliminate any potential conflict of interest. Whether disclosure is sufficient to resolve conflicts of interest may depend on the product involved. Perhaps products like medical drugs require stricter rules. David Korn, dean of the Stanford University School of Medicine, is reported to have said,

There is a special sensitivity to commercializing medicine that doesn't apply to other kinds of research. People don't look at developing a better silicon chip or gasoline additive the same way they do at developing a new drug or ointment. (Stiff, 1990)

Historically there is evidence that people have a special sensitivity to medical products and public health. In 1934 Harvard adopted a patent policy entitled "Statement of Policy in Regard to Patents on Discoveries or Inventions Bearing on Health and Therapeutics." It said:

No patents primarily concerned with therapeutics or public health may be taken out by any member of the university, except with the consent of the President and Fellows; nor will such patents be taken out by the university itself except for dedication to the public. (Quoted in Culliton, 1981, 1198)

The public's special sensitivity to medical products had caused immense problems for the University of Minnesota. In 1992, the Minneapolis *Star Tribune* ran three major stories regarding three different conflict-of-interest situations in the University of Minnesota Medical School.

In one case, Dr. David Knighton, an associate professor of surgery, had spent years developing the drug Procuren, which is supposed to help heal chronic wounds, and had created his own company, Curative Technologies Inc., which sold the drug. Curative Technologies entered into a relationship with the University of Minnesota. The university allowed the drug to be sold to its patients in the University of Minnesota Hospital. In return the university received over $2 million in research grants, royalties, and stock in the company.

The most explicit conflict of interest arose from the fact that Knighton conducted effectiveness tests of Procuren in university labs, even though Procuren was Knighton's own drug. This situation developed because the U.S. Food and Drug Administration (FDA) said the drug had not proven effective and had been falsely promoted in violation of federal law. Curative had sold $37 million of the drug in four years. Knighton made an arrangement with the university that allowed Knighton to use university facilities to test the drug and provided him a legal way to sell the drug without federal government approval. Knighton's first tests showed the drug worked; tests by other scientists showed it did not. In a more recent test, Curative excluded a number of patients who did not heal. The *Star Tribune* charged the university with allowing Knighton to turn his lab into "an outpost of the company." The university medical school ignored warnings from their own watchdog committee regarding Knighton's involvement with Curative. Finally, when Curative went public in 1991, it failed to inform investors about its research difficulties (Lerner and Rigert, 1992).

Another conflict-of-interest case arose with the drug ALG, which is widely used in transplant operations to reduce the likelihood of transplant rejection. A *Star Tribune* report characterized the situation as one where the university was operating its own drug business, and charged that it built a new facility for the operation at a cost of $12 million that was to be paid for by sales of ALG. Of the five most commonly used antirejection drugs, AGL is the only one that does not have FDA approval for sale. However, until 1988, the university was selling the drug at a profit. After the FDA forbade sales for profit, sales declined from $10 million a year in 1988 to $1.7 million a year in 1990. An inspection in June 1992 by the FDA uncovered many violations including "unauthorized exports of the drug, improper promotional claims of safety and effectiveness and numerous gaps in the testing records" (Lerner and Rigert, 1992, 6A). Meanwhile, the director of the program, Professor Richard Condie admitted to receiving $12,000 a year as scientific consultant to Hemosol Inc., which was buying blood by-products from the ALG program. Condie was involved in negotiations between Hemosol and the University of Minnesota regarding a university-business partnership while on the payroll of both sides. Condie claims that he disclosed his dual relationship. The implication of the news report is that in this case full disclosure was not enough. Perhaps that feeling was based on a perception that the public interest was not being protected.

Should full disclosure be supplemented by state oversight? California law requires faculty at state-supported universities to disclose their financial interests in the private sponsors of their research. This disclosure is to take place when a faculty member applies for initial project approval or for renewal approval (Leskovac, 1984). When seeking approval, there is a fairly elaborate and uniform procedure mandated by the law. Each campus has a review committee that considers whether the project is one appropriate for a university, whether the project is proprietary in nature, and whether the principal investigator is the only one qualified on campus to undertake the research. All decisions of the campus committee are reviewed by the campus chancellor, who has broad powers to accept, reject, or amend the recommendation. The chancellor's decision is filed with the California enforcement agency responsible for oversight, the FPPC (Lescovac, 1984).

As this discussion indicates, perceived conflict-of-interest situations are difficult to avoid. A necessary condition for keeping a perceived conflict of interest from being actual is full disclosure. This puts the affected parties on guard and enables them to terminate or modify a relationship to protect their interests. In some cases the perceived conflict of interest is deemed so serious that rules are formulated that require that the person in the conflict-of-interest situation surrender one of the interests that creates the conflict. Indeed the rules may stipulate which interest is to be surrendered. These rules may be initiated by the university or by public authorities. What is so striking is the relative lack of specific university rules on conflict of interest. Beyond disclosure, most university policy documents we examined had little specific to say about the subject. The issue will remain in the forefront of public discussions of conflict of interest until most research universities write detailed rules forbidding the more serious instances.

Let us now turn to conflicts of commitment, of which there are many examples in the early literature. In remarks for the 1982 University of Pennsylvania conference, the late Bartlett Giamatti commented, "I doubt that a faculty member can ordinarily devote the time and energy the university requires and also pursue a substantial involvement in any such outside company" (Giamatti, 1983). Conflicts of commitment are hardly new in academe. Allowing faculty members to be affiliated with biotech firms presents the same kind of difficulty as allowing members of the business school faculty to sit on corporate boards. The danger that the faculty member will neglect his or her duties is the same for both. With respect to private consulting, most universities already have policies in place that limit consulting to one day a week per six-day week. Certainly that will help in situations where faculty have responsibilities in private companies. Some faculty and even some universities might find such a rule too restrictive, however. A university might want to keep a faculty member even if he or she wanted to spend more than one day a week away from the university.

Another way conflict of commitment gets activated is in the entrepreneurial professor's relations with students. Most of these professors have a number of graduate students or other university staff working for them. When these people work for the professor, are they working for the professor or the professor's company? Will a graduate student be encouraged to work on a project that is of interest to the professor's company or will the graduate student be encouraged to work on projects he or she is intellectually committed to irrespective of the relevance of the proposed project to the professor's company?

These concerns were highlighted in a 1983 American Association of University Professors report, "Corporate Funding of Academic Research." In response to difficulties of this type, Varrin and Kukich (1985) recommended that professors not hire graduate students to work in their companies. But that recommendation would not go far enough to eliminate the problem. The graduate student would have to be prohibited from working on any project of benefit to the professor's company whether the student was employed by the company, the university, or some third party. But a recommendation of that severity is not practical. The federal laws were changed so that university employees could work on projects that had a commercial application. Presumably these projects cannot be handled by the professors alone.

The danger of a conflict of commitment is inevitable, but it is hardly unique to university-business partnerships. There is always a danger that graduate students will be encouraged to do work that matches the research interest of the faculty member rather than the intellectual interest of the student. The important question is whether the existence of university-business partnerships makes the traditional problem substantially worse. Unfortunately, there is at present no way to answer this question. However, if university-business partnerships were to change the culture of the university so that those faculty involved in the partnerships gained power and prestige and if the number of faculty involved in such partnerships increased substantially, then conflicts of commitment might become a far more serious problem than they have been in the university setting. Let us then turn to a discussion of the impact of business values on the values of the university.

SECTION FIVE

The Clash Between Academic Values and Business Values

Much has been said about the differences in values between academe and business. This issue was expressed nicely by Joseph C. Burke, provost of the State University of New York:

> Academia and business have different purposes and priorities and are peopled by professionals with diverse personalities. The aim of Academia is the search for "truth" through the discovery and dissemination of general principles. The bottom line for business is the search for profit through the development and delivery of salable products. Academic organizations seek an ageless commodity—timeless truth. Business organizations seek a perishable product—something that sells. The different aims of each organization naturally attract professionals with contrasting attitudes and aspirations. . . . A case in point is the business demand, and the academic disdain, for technology and technicians. Many businesses see technology transfer and trained technicians as the secret to their success. Many academics view the demand for technology and technicians as subverting their fundamental mission in basic research and liberal education. (1985; See also Giamatti, 1983, 6)

And more recently Jules B. Lapidus, president of the Council of Graduate Schools, has said:

> The pressure on universities to be research and development labs for industry is destroying research universities. It's distorting the values. I think it's a bad idea. . . . It's been much too easy for universities to shape their values to meet sponsors' needs. (Quoted in Cordes, 1992, A 26)

Of course if the actual divisions were as deep as characterized here, university-business partnerships would never get off the ground. More-

77

over, there is a tradition of university business cooperation. Nelkin and Nelson are correct in arguing

> . . . Propositions about a natural chasm between academic science and industry science have often been drawn too sharply and too globally. . . . These cultures have been living together for a long time. Indeed, academic science and industrial science in the United States grew up together. (Nelkin et al., 1987, 67)

Industrial chemistry and academic chemistry arose at the same point in historical time. Since the chemical industry needed trained chemists, the link between the academic and industrial chemists were both early and natural. At present there are natural alliances among physics, engineering, computer science, and biology departments and industrial research and development. Colleges of agriculture have a long history of a close working relationship with farmers and the agriculture industries.

The success of university-business partnerships indicates that to some extent the divisions have been overcome. But how and at what cost? Many critics argue that the divisions have been overcome because the universities and faculty involved in such partnerships have adopted the attitudes and values of business at the expense of the attitudes and values of the academy. To what extent is that charge true?

In the early 1980s, Leonard Minsky, the head of Ralph Nader's Center for Universities in the Public Interest, said,

> When university researchers are en bloc consultants, when funds are specifically tied to the generation of commercially useful products, and when corporate scientists effectively choose the topics of research for university scientists, we have reached an entirely new level of corporate control. (Quoted in Lepkowski, 1984b, 8)

Although Minsky may be characterized as something of a radical, Harvard's Derek Bok cannot. Recently Bok listed the three greatest dangers facing American universities (Bok, 1991). One of the three was the commercialization of the university. Bok admitted that Harvard has in recent years moved aggressively to capitalize on commercial opportunities. But,

> Like other new activities, entrepreneurial ventures can burden the administration and divert the faculty. Graduate students may be drawn into

projects in ways that sacrifice their education for commercial gain. Research performed with an eye toward profit may lure investigators into conflicts of interest or cause them to practice forms of secrecy that hamper scientific progress. Ultimately corporate ties may undermine the university's reputation for objectivity and, if foreign firms are involved, antagonize the Congress by seeming to favor America's commercial rivals. (Bok, 1991, 15)

What is significant about Bok's statement is that it represents a change in his thinking. In 1980 Bok was a champion of university-business partnerships. In that year Bok tried to get the Harvard faculty to approve Harvard's taking a 10 percent equity holding in the biotech firm of Genetics Institute Inc., which had been founded by two Harvard faculty members. He was rebuffed.

Bok's 1991 statement reminds us that there are limits to the commercialization of academic life. It is obviously unseemly to auction off the last fifty places in Harvard's freshman class even if all those participating in the auction are qualified for admittance. Bok is concerned about how the university is perceived. If it is perceived as a commercial enteprise, then its stakeholders may change the nature of their relationship to the university to the university's detriment.

One of the reasons that society accepts the policies of tenure and academic freedom is because it has been persuaded that the public will benefit in the long run if professors are insulated from pressures that could compromise their impartial search for knowledge. If universities themselves create pressures that threaten academic standards in order to obtain extra income, can they be as sure that the government will continue to have confidence in their work and maintain the conditions of freedom essential to progress. . . . It is still not clear what effect these new commercial ventures will have on the feelings of constituencies whose loyalty are vital to the university: on faculty members who must often do much more than their job description requires if the institution is to flourish; on the alumni who must give generously of their time and money if the university is to progress; on the public, which gives various privileges to institutions of learning in the belief that they are not commercial ventures but organizations that subordinate money to other aims and values of distinct value to society. (Bok, 1991, 17)

Bok points out that in the last two or three generations universities have generally lost their immunity to lawsuits, have been more heavily regulated, and have had their tax-exempt status challenged by local governmental authorities. Certainly some of these phenomena are partly explained by causes other than the commercial ventures of universities. Local communities are in such serious financial shape that the tax-exempt status of universities would be a tempting target even if the university were pure. As for lawsuits, the court rulings that permitted suing nonprofits and government agencies have more to do with the rise of lawsuits against universities than with resentment of university commercial enterprises. Indeed, for the land-grant university, alternative sources of revenue that might relieve hard-pressed states of some financial support are likely to be well received. What are not well received are university commercial activities that compete with the private sector (e.g., showing first-run films or selling clothing) or activities where university faculty become wealthy from inventions that were produced by faculty using university (and hence often public) resources and facilities. A recent case (discussed previously in the conflict-of-interest section) illustrating this point involved Professor David Knighton, a member of the medical faculty at the University of Minnesota who made millions of dollars from the drug Procuren and was roundly criticized in the local press.

It must be pointed out that concerns about the commercialization of universities did not begin with university-business partnerships in the 1980s. In 1971 Robert Nisbet wrote *The Degradation Of The Academic Dogma,* in which he voiced his opposition to the corruption of university values which he believed was taking place because of increases in government sponsored research. The degradation resulted from ''conversion of scholarship into organized factory like research—for the transformation of literally thousands of professors from teachers and scholars into entrepreneurs'' (81).

Moreover, the right to profit from one's inventions that is taken as obvious, even in cautionary discussions of university-business partnerships, was certainly not considered a right in the early part of the twentieth century. Rather, profiting from one's invention was viewed as morally suspect. Consider the controversy surrounding the patenting of the antitoxin for scarlet fever in the mid-1920s. George and Gladys Dicks had found a way to mass-produce the antitoxin by immunizing horses. They published their results and soon a number of manufacturers were producing the antitoxin based on published writings of the Dicks. The Dicks were concerned that some of the manufacturers were producing antitoxin that was inferior and perhaps even dangerous. They offered patents on their process to the American Medical Association in 1924. The AMA turned them down since the AMA membership was seriously split on the wisdom of medical patenting. The Dicks then followed the advice of the AMA to establish a nonprofit committee to patent the process. The committee was established early in 1925. The members of the committee received no income and the patent royalties were used for a program of quality control.

Despite these terms, it is generally believed that the Nobel Prize Committee's decision not to award a prize in medicine and physiology in 1925 was caused by an unwillingness to award the prize to the Dicks. By 1926 there were numerous editorials in major medical and public health journals criticizing the Dicks' decision to patent. The criticism intensified when the Dicks defended their patent rights in court in the late 1920s. (This account of the patenting of the scarlet fever antitoxin is based on Weiner, 1987.)

Even after public attitudes changed and profiting from inventions became morally acceptable, some people still thought the financial advantages given to patent holders had unfortunate consequences. For example, in 1956 Columbia University professor of engineering Seymour Melman was commissioned by the U.S. Senate Subcommittee on Patents, Trademarks, and Copyrights to review the patent system. Melman undertook an extensive survey of private companies and universities. As a result of his survey, he discovered a number of issues which then-current patent policy was unable to successfully address. For example, the system was modeled on the notion of a single inventor. Modern science was primarily a group-centered activity in which it would be difficult to determine who should receive the credit for an invention. Melman also discovered that many believed that the struggle over property rights impeded rather than encouraged invention. For example, people believed that the struggle for property rights encouraged secrecy rather than prompt publication. Ultimately Melman recommended that the patent system in place at that time be replaced by one that focused on nonmonetary awards. Patent lawyers were not amused and the report was not acted on (Weiner, 1987).

Melman's concerns are not totally without foundation as we consider changes in university policies as a result of commercialization. The shift from a public-interest to a for-profit perspective can be seen at the University of Minnesota. Two University of Minnesota faculty patented the honeycrisp apple tree in 1990 and another faculty member patented the autumn spire red maple tree in 1992. Until 1948 the university's horticulture department *gave* new varieties of orchard and garden plants to the Minnesota Horticultural Society and they still release most plants without patents. Before patenting the honeycrisp apple tree, the university had given eighteen varieties of apple trees to the public without a patent. Since the Plant Patent Act of 1930 permitted plants to be patented, the university makes a decision on whether or not to seek a patent on the basis of market considerations. Honeycrisp apple trees are characterized by crisp fruit, late harvest, and winter hardiness—characteristics that give them excellent potential marketability. Some see the honeycrisp as a competitor to the red delicious. As for the ethical issue of patenting and then licensing the honeycrisp, James Luby, patentholder and director of the fruit-breeding program in the University of Minnesota's Department of Horticulture, says:

> In the past the feeling was that agricultural experiment stations got most of their funding from tax dollars, therefore it wasn't ethical to try and collect royalties on something we developed. . . . But let's face it. A lot of research money doesn't come from the public anymore. . . . For virtually all the plant breeding funds, except for salaries, we rely on gifts from indutry and royalties from previously released varieties. (Norcross, 1992, 11)

But can Luby's position be accepted without reservation? Two researchers report that a California-based company had discovered a process for rapidly duplicating strands of DNA *in vitro*. The technique had many useful applications, including the early detection of cancer and AIDS. But the company had a patent on the process that the company insists must be protected. Thus they were not willing to allow the technique to be used for the early detection of cancer and AIDS unless a royalty was to be paid. Suppose that company had been a university. Would it be wrong for the university to delay granting a license for these beneficial uses and charge royalty fees? So long as universities are not viewed as commercial organizations, it is clear that such activity on the part of a university would be wrong. However, it does not seem wrong, or as wrong, when royalties are demanded by a for-profit business. Whether the actions of a university are right or wrong depend in part on the kind of institution it is.

In this particular case as reported in *The Scientist,* April 17, 1989, some universities had consulted lawyers in an attempt to break the patent. They wanted to use the technique for early detection of cancer and AIDS. However, the article reports, the universities were not considering doing this to serve the public good but to obtain revenues for their own labs. In essence these universities were thinking like commercial enterprises in deciding whether it was worth challenging a patent in order to make money for themselves (Buchbinder and Newson, 1990, 372–73).

There is yet another twist. A few scientists believe that the HIV virus is not the cause of AIDS. Suppose one of these scientists was the member of a department or even a university that had a successful university-business partnership that was doing research on the assumption that the HIV virus is indeed the cause of AIDS. Could such a department or university fairly evaluate the dissenting scientist for tenure? How likely is it that the university or department would support the research efforts of the dissenting scientist (Buchbinder and Newson, 1990, 373–74)?

Another argument against an atmosphere of commercialization at the university is that such an atmosphere undermines the university's commitment to basic research and that applied research would come to dominate. Recall this is just the issue that created problems at MIT early in the century. It is one of the major points of David Noble's critique of university research in the first quarter of the twentieth century. Noble said:

Industrial sponsorship and direction of university-based scientific research . . . redefined the form and content of scientific research itself. This involved more than the general shift away from the search for truth toward utility which had already been well underway by the turn of the century. Now the shift toward utility assumed particular forms, molded by the specific, historical needs of private industry, by particular firms intent upon increasing their profit margins and their power. This reorientation affected not only what kinds of questions would be asked but also what particular questions would be asked, which problems would be investigated, what sorts of solutions would be sought, what conclusions would be drawn. Science had, indeed, been pressed into the service of capital. (Noble, 1977, 147)

To what extent are Noble's criticisms made more poignant by the development of university-business partnerships? Concerns in this area have arisen frequently. Those concerned argue that a decline in basic research not only would hurt the university but society would suffer as well since ultimately the success of applied research rests on a strong basic research base (Omenn, 1982; Robbins, 1982; Ross, 1986; Leskovac, 1984; Hill, 1983).

On the other hand, the supporters of university-business partnerships have been able to show that many of the industry partners are supporting basic research and that there is great sensitivity to the issue. Indeed, in the most recent Government-University-Industry Roundtable Research report discussed earlier, even industry officials whose firms were involved in university-business partnerships argued that the primary research responsibility of universities is basic research.

However, in 1981 House hearings MIT Professor of Microbiology, Dr. Jonathan King, distinguished the commercial application of research from the beneficial application of research. Even if university-business partnerships do not interfere with basic research, they may not bring forth beneficial applications. King pointed out that many vaccines were developed and produced by the government because private companies did not think they could get a return on their investment if they tried to develop and produce them themselves. In addition, some of our diseases are caused either by commercial products or by industrial processes. King cited diseases caused by pesticides and the fear that the processes for making synfuels endangers the health of the workers (Hearing on "Commercialization of Academic Biomedical Research," 1981, 67).

King's contention links the concern about the impact of commercialization on basic research to the earlier concern regarding the public service function of a university. King seems to be arguing that even if commercialization does not reduce the amount of basic research, it may nonetheless skew the direction of basic research. Some research is in the public interest even if the products of that research are not commercially viable. Increased commercialization will decrease that type of research. In addition, as the commercialization of the university increases, who will be able to provide objective research on the possible negative impact of commercial products on the workers who manufacture them and the buyers who consume them? Traditionally the university has performed that function but as commercialization increases, the university will likely find itself in a situation where it is supported by an industry and is asked to evaluate objectively the safety of a product of that industry. That situation would present an apparent conflict of interest and, moreover, an apparent conflict of interest that the public may not be willing to resolve simply by complete disclosure.

Perhaps one of the more sophisticated arguments concerning the corruption of academic science by commercialization is made by Nicholas Wade in a background paper for a study of university-business partnerships by a task force for the Twentieth Century Fund (Wade, 1984). Wade contrasts the validation of university research with the validation of industry research. In the university, validation is usually a three-step process. First, applications for funding are examined by a committee of peers. Second, the research results of the funded project are examined by journal referees. Third, the published results are subjected to replication. In industry, validation is performed in the marketplace. With industry-sponsored research there is usually no peer review. Wade is willing to admit that each method of validation is appropriate in its own sphere.

But which method is better? The academic or the industrial? Consider the following two alternative ways of answering the which-is-better question. It might mean: Which method is more efficient in terms of producing commercial applications that people can use? It also might mean: Which method provides the more accurate research? Wade cites many incidents that give us good reason to answer the second question in favor of the academic method and to be agnostic with respect to the first. The search to find a way to make bacteria synthesize insulin was a hotly competitive one involving an alliance of Harvard researchers and Genentech employees versus a research team from the Department of Biochemistry and Biophysics at the University of California at San Francisco. In May 1977, the UCSF team held a press conference to announce their success. Normally, the second step in the academic validation process requires that research results be made public through publication in professional journals. The news conference method of publication is a radical departure from the academic norm even if it is not a departure from the norms of the commercial marketplace. But can't the quality of the science be just as good whether the means of publication is a professional journal or a news release? No, according to Wade. In their hurry to beat the Harvard/Genentech team, the UCSF team allegedly violated government safety rules and then made misleading entries in the laboratory log book to conceal the fact. The pressures of commercialization undermine accurate validation.

But Wade's critique doesn't end there. The UCSF violation threatened attempts by academic scientists to dissuade Congress from passing legislation enforcing the NIH safety standards. Scientists were opposed to the regulations, which they considered too stringent. During congressional testimony on the proposed legislation, the norm was breached again. Philip Handler, then president of the National Academy of Sciences, announced "a scientific triumph of the first order," namely the cloning of the gene for the hormone somatostatin. Again a discovery was announced publicly before being published in an academic professional journal. Moreover, the discovery was a

relatively minor extension of a gene-splicing technique. Its announcement was used politically, but it served no genuine scientific purpose.
Moreover, the research had not been reviewed by peers as it would
have been had it been sent to a journal to be reviewed before publication. Again, accuracy in the validation process had been sacrificed.

Since the journal publication norm was breached by a leader of the
stature of the president of the National Academy of Sciences, the norm
was in danger of being undermined. Wade documents further instances
in which research results have been announced in press conferences,
including some where the information was shown to be scientifically
inaccurate (Wade, pp. 33–34). For example, two prominent scientists,
Nobel prize winner Walter Gilbert and Charles Weissman, officers of
Biogen, announced with much fanfare the cloning of interferon. What
the public was not told was that a Japanese team had already published
a paper that described their accomplishment of the same feat. The
public bid up the stock of Biogen's parent company, Schering Plough,
by sixteen points and doubled the paper value of Biogen. The announcement was designed to serve commercial purposes rather than
scientific ones. The Japanese had published in accord with the traditional norm; the Americans had not. The general question to be asked
is whether the increase in the commercialization of science will undermine the basic norms or values of academic science.

Historically the values of science have been different from and
perhaps antithetical to the values of business. In an early article
criticizing university-business partnerships, Barbara Culliton cited
Robert Merton's 1942 essay, "The Normative Structure of Science,"
to provide traditional norms for the practice of science. In that essay
Merton identified four norms that are characteristic of the practice of
science: universalism, communism (the collective ownership of goods),
disinterestedness in the foregoing of personal gain, and organized
skepticism (Culliton, 1981, 1198). Earlier we discussed whether university-business partnerships required secrecy and hence violated the
openness of science. Secrecy violates Merton's norm of universalism.

Obviously communism in this sense of collective ownership is incon-
sistent with commercialization. The notion of scientific knowledge as
collective property precludes it from being private property. To show
just how far we have moved away from the value of collective property
in a short period of time, Wade discussed two of the central events in
the biotech revolution. The technique for splicing genes was discovered
in 1973 by Stanley Cohen of Stanford and Herbert Boyer of the
University of California at San Francisco. Neither thought of patenting

it and Cohen initially resisted a request by the Stanford patent officer that Stanford do so. Cohen based his case on reasons that appealed to the traditional understanding of the transmission of scientific knowledge. The gene-splicing technique rested on the discoveries of other scientists that had been freely given. To patent the technique would involve owning a portion of the work that had been freely given by others (Wade, 1982, 31). Cohen finally relented to the argument that a patent would provide great benefit to Stanford. However, Cohen took no money for himself. Neither did Boyer.

The other great discovery of the 1970s was the hybridoma technique that enabled the production of pure antibody molecules that could be targeted against the antigen of one's choice. The technique was discovered by two British scientists, Georges Kohler and Cesar Milstein. The technique was not patented. It was the policy of Milstein's sponsor, the Medical Research Council, to make its new methods freely available (Wade, 1982, 31). That this position seems quaint in 1991 shows how far we have come in less than fifteen years.

As for value three (disinterest in personal gain), there has been an informal agreement among scientists working in biotechnology that they share materials such as cells, bacteria, and antibodies that no single lab can supply itself. There was also an implicit agreement that shared material would neither be given to others nor used for financial gain without permission. But this openness would soon change. In 1977 two research hematologists at UCLA, Phillip Koeffler and David Golde, succeeded in making the cells of a dying cancer patient grow and divide. The scientists called the cells KG-1, naming them after themselves. Glode later sent a sample of the cells to Robert Gallo, a colleague at the National Cancer Institute. Gallo passed them on to Sidney Pestka, a friend. Whether or not Gallo had permission to pass them on is in dispute. Pestka discovered the cells were superproducers of interferon. Pestka worked at the Roche Institute of Molecular Biology, which was wholly funded by Hoffmann-La Roche. Dead KG-1 cells showed up at Genentech, with whom Hoffman-La Roche had a secret contract to develop interferon. When Genentech made its announcement, several people became millionaires. Gallo was not one of them. Gallo, who had a reputation of always sharing biological material, has changed his policy. He no longer shares unless he owns the material or has written permission from everyone involved (Wade, 1982, 36).

The moral that Wade draws from this story is that the norm of sharing will be undermined because intellectual property is no longer considered common but rather is considered as something that can be owned. Thus people in the same department will not share information with other members of the department who have commercial contacts because they feel their ideas will be stolen to make money for someone else.

To assess the seriousness of the decline of communitarianism, we first need to consider how realistic the communitarian value was before the biotech revolution. The old rule was that an idea belongs to the person who publishes it first. Thus there was always an incentive to keep an idea to oneself until you could establish in print that it was yours. Nonetheless, although Wade admits that secrecy was a problem in the past, the commercial value of ideas made the secrecy problem much worse.

But two questions need to be asked here. Is the desire for money that much more corrupting than the desire for fame and prestige? Apparently Wade thinks it is and regrettably I agree with him. I think this says more about the values of society, however, than it does about commercial research.

But since society's values on this matter are not likely to change, perhaps we should ask how we can control the abuses of commercialization. To do that we might ask what prevented the incentive for fame and prestige from operating to prevent open communication? Wasn't it a norm that said that you should acknowledge the ideas of others? Papers are jointly authored when the ideas are truly shared. Even intellectual debts are acknowledged in footnotes. Couldn't a new norm develop that dollars be shared? If academics are willing to share credit, why can't they share money?

I doubt that Wade would accept this suggestion of a new norm of sharing. His critique is more radical than showing how commercialization leads to secrecy and a lack of sharing. Rather, commercialization leads to the undermining of the basic values of science: If the university focuses on the commercial gain of its scientific research, the university research enterprise will be different. Commercial research is for profit; it thus crowds out research in the public interest. A high level of commercial research increasingly prevents the university from being an objective evaluator of commercial products. Commercial research encourages the premature release of research results and provides incentives for exaggerating the success of research. And to protect one's personal or one's university financial interests, one is inclined toward less sharing and more secrecy.

Thus the clash of academic and commercial values is not limited to something as superficial as differences in lifestyle nor is it simply a matter of most academics being more theoretical and less practical. Rather, the values of the marketplace are fundamentally at odds with the values of the academic research scientist. In the absence of clear-cut economic gains to either party in university-business partnerships, this fundamental clash of values provides a good reason to move cautiously in developing still more university-business partnerships.

However, some may argue that many of the alleged problems of university-business partnerships are analogous to problems that have been with the universities for a long time (e.g., conflicts of commitment). If that is true, should we be so concerned about the dangers of university-business partnerships? One reason for giving an affirmative answer to that question is that we must also be aware of the dangers that come from the accumulation of small effects. In my initial study of university-business partnerships, I was struck by the fact that the criticisms leveled against university-business partnerships were identical to those being leveled at other aspects of the commercialization of the university. However, as this current study progressed, I became concerned that we are approaching a threshold where further commercialization of the university would transform the university into an institution very different in terms of its values and purpose than it has traditionally been. I concur with the following observation of Nelkin et al.:

> Because each new arrangement is relatively small, each can be regarded as not significantly changing the basic structure of academic science. A new program at one university serves as a precedent, and even a goad, for other programs. And the total effect of many incremental changes is not necessarily small. The threat . . . is that the cumulative effect may be a transformation of large areas of academic science. (1987, 73)

SECTION SIX

Issues of Distributive Justice

The development of university-business partnerships also raises many issues of justice. Critics point out that under these programs, the rich get richer and the poor get poorer. Who are the winners and the losers? I contend that the winners are the large research universities while the losers are the liberal arts colleges and the non-research-based universities. Within the large research universities the winners are the biological sciences, engineering, the medical school, and to a lesser extent information sciences. The losers are basic research science, the humanities, social sciences, and the arts.

With respect to the first point, we are in danger of creating a stratified class system among institutions of higher education. At the apex of the hierarchy are the major research universities that own the latest in expensive high-tech equipment. At all other institutions of higher education, science education, at least, will be much impoverished, especially in terms of state-of-the-art equipment and other scientific resources. This problem was recognized as early as 1982. At that time Charles Lowe noted,

> Industry will seek the best laboratories and the best scientists in the best schools. The rich will get richer and the poor will get no assistance. This is a real cause for concern, since it exacerbates an existing imbalance. For example, the top twenty research centers in this country, 1 percent of the total number, received 44 percent of the NIH budget. To the other 1180 institutions with NIH grants and contracts went the remaining 66 percent [*sic*]. (Lowe, 1982, 244)

Similarly, Herbert Fusfeld reported, "In 1982 the 100 largest research institutions accounted for 83 percent of all academic research and 84 percent of federal funding of this research" (1986, 19). But there has always been a pecking order in higher education, one might

91

reply. Perhaps so but there has been a wide continuum from the strongest research universities to the weaker ones. Fusfeld indicates that there are 500 institutions of higher learning engaged in research, although only 200 really focus on research. Fusfeld then raises the following question:

> Suppose 10 major universities become completely up to date with the most advanced facilities for microelectronics research while another 190 research universities do not. Is the American university research system overall inadequately equipped for such research? (1986, 27)

Fusfeld's point is that successful university-business partnerships may decrease the number of excellent research universities and increase the gap between the excellent ones and all the rest.

Let us consider the fate of liberal arts colleges, which are primarily undergraduate institutions. In the past many liberal arts colleges have competed well with good research universities—even in the natural sciences. But given the expense of programs in the natural sciences, the flow of money to the research universities will lessen the ability of liberal arts colleges to compete. This problem was of deep concern to Oberlin President Frederick Starr in 1984. He noted a 17 percent drop in corporate funding for research in science at the undergraduate level. Oberlin produces a higher than average number of science students. Starr was afraid that science students at Oberlin and colleges like Oberlin would be shortchanged (Lepkowski, 1984b, 11).

The problem is exacerbated by the fact that the burden of trying to compete in science will eat away at the other programs at the liberal arts colleges. Ultimately there is the possibility that a wide quality gulf will exist between the research universities on the one hand and liberal arts undergraduate colleges on the other. Even the best liberal arts colleges may appear weak in comparison with the most favored research universities. This would be unfortunate because many liberal arts colleges have characteristics that enable them to provide undergraduate education that is in some respects superior to that offered by major research universities. Loss of funds to support expensive science education could overwhelm this current competitive advantage to the detriment of undergraduate education in general.

Within the research university, gulfs will open up among departments and among colleges. As a number of critics have noted, there is a danger that university departments will be evaluated on a business model as profit centers. The departments that thrive will be those that generate funds. The implications of this kind of thinking would strengthen some science departments and many professional schools at the expense of the humanities, most social sciences, and the fine arts. University-business partnerships in the humanities are conspicuously absent from the myriad examples presented in this book. They are also absent in the arts and, for the most part, in the social sciences. Moreover, many federal programs in both the United States and Canada require matching funds. However, corporate funds for matching fund support of programs in the social sciences and the humanities, where there is little chance of a commercial payoff, is scarce.

Of course, institutions could take a path similar to the Wisconsin Alumni Research Foundation and share some of the financial returns with colleges and departments unable to generate more than a token number of university-business partnerships. But even if the funds from the partnerships were shared with these disciplines, there is no evidence that the distribution would be even approximately equal. The fine arts, humanities, and social sciences might be better off, but the gap between them and the sciences, engineering, and information systems would continue to increase. This inequality might be defended on the grounds that colleges and departments that bring in revenue from university-business partnerships deserve more since they are contributing more to our economic competitiveness. One does not have to determine the correctness of that argument to point out that, whatever its merits, politically it is very divisive.

Moreover, other institutional squabbles would remain even if the distributive problem between the haves and the have-nots could be resolved. As one commentator has noted,

> What, for example happens when funds from the core budget that might otherwise go to instruction-related facilities or practices are earmarked instead for technology? Or when faculty who spend their time on technology transfer get the salary increases? Or when technicians are hired to do the work traditionally done by graduate students?" (Fairweather, 1990, 34)

There is also the question of how an emphasis on industrial research meshes with the primary function of teaching. Fusfeld argues that the organization of a university should look different depending on which of these missions is emphasized.

> If we set forth an organizational structure that would most effectively initiate and conduct a large-scale research and development activity,

serving multiple interests, involving responsibilities for linkages and transfers, we would almost certainly develop a structure quite different from one that is among the disciplines and under the authority of university departments. The optimal organization of university research that serves many missions and objectives, even though the activity is largely basic research, is not the optimal organization of university research that exists primarily to strengthen education. (1986, 28–29)

University-business partnerships raise a number of governance issues as well. There are at least three major areas of concern. First, the creation of centers will undercut the power of the departments and fragment governance; second, those faculty who engage in patentable research may obtain positions of power and undue influence; and third, the traditional peer review system could be weakened or undermined. How are these areas of concern related?

One of the central features of university-business partnerships is that the work of the partnership takes place primarily in research centers especially created for the purpose of the partnership. Partnership work in traditional departments is rare. One of the major functions of a university-business partnership is to produce income while a traditional department has many functions, including many that are traditionally viewed as more important than producing income. Two such functions are teaching and nondirected basic research. (Nondirected is distinguished from directed basic research in that the former is conducted due to the intellectual curiosity of the researcher while the latter is conducted because it will contribute to a broader, mission-oriented objective [Fusfeld, 1986, 22].)

However, as the university finds itself constrained financially, these income-producing centers become more important to it. Faculty whose chief contribution to the university is to engage in research that produces patentable products gain power and prestige. This means that directors of research centers can bypass the faculty governance structure and work out deals directly with university officials. In addition, when tenure, promotion, and salary decisions are to be made, the faculty entrepreneurs will not be judged by members of an academic discipline in a traditional department but will instead be judged by fellow entrepreneurs from a variety of disciplines. In this way the traditional peer review system is undermined and weakened. For example, as early as 1983 the American Association of University Professors expressed concern that faculty who submitted research proposals to a combined faculty-industry review committee might not receive tenure if their research proposals were turned down (Thomson et.al., 1983).

But there are already many extraneous factors that can contribute to a negative tenure decision. Certain areas of research receive more resources and that makes research in these areas easier. Some research methodologies are more acceptable than others. For example, non-quantitative research in business schools is suspect. Analytic philosophers seldom appreciate the method and style of philosophers working in the continental tradition. University faculty are sharply divided as to whether deconstruction is an acceptable research methodology. The fact that it is more difficult to receive tenure if one is using a nonstandard methodology or is researching an unpopular issue or, more commonly, if one's colleagues do not find a person's research interesting, has not seriously endangered the tenure system. How much of an additional strain would university-business partnerships add?

There is also the issue of whether university-business partnership centers should have tenured faculty. Some have argued that faculty in university-business research centers should not be eligible for tenure. After all, their work will usually take a form that is different from traditional faculty in that neither teaching nor university service is required. There is also the perception, and sometimes the reality, that faculty working in university-business research centers are working on projects where the research is so applied that typical research faculty would not grant tenure.

Fusfeld argues, however, that tenured positions should be offered for reasons of stability and growth. Too often current personnel are "postdocs" waiting for an opportunity to move into a standard academic appointment (1986, 32–35). This creates an unacceptable rate of turnover. Moreover, within the university context, faculty not on tenure-track lines are perceived, and often treated, as second-class citizens. This creates morale problems. If university-business partnerships are essential to the university and play a valuable role in the institution's success, then faculty employed in those partnerships should be treated on a par with typical departmental faculty and given tenure.

One obvious objection to Fusfeld's argument is that university-business partnerships are funded on soft money. Should the funding disappear, the university would be stuck with many personnel that it neither needs nor can afford. Fusfeld counters that argument, saying that universities that have $20 to $30 million in research money can safely commit $1 to $2 million a year for tenured research faculty. On the other hand, those who emphasize the economic instability of industry research contracts and are concerned about centers of power and influence outside traditional departments will be less sanguine than Fusfeld. Whether the university would ultimately be harmed by such an arrangement is still very much an open question.

The debate under discussion here did not originate with the growth of university-business partnerships in the 1980s. Robert Nisbet made the argument in 1971 when he criticized the increase in government spending on research:

> Why should a chemist or biologist or—in due time—a sociologist or economist defer to a faculty committee or dean, much less department chairman, when on his individual prestige alone hundreds of thousands of dollars, even millions could be brought for use by retinues of technicians, graduate students, secretaries, and junior faculty members that would often rival established departments in size. (75)

The scenario outlined above might come to pass. Some would argue that it is already coming to pass. One of the more controversial university-business partnerships in this regard is the Whitehead Institute at MIT. The partnership agreement permitted the Whitehead Institute to appoint full members of the biology department. Such an arrangement is a radical departure from common practice in the academy, where departments normally guard their right to appoint colleagues with a remarkable tenacity.

What is more controversial is whether or not it would be a good thing if the scenario came to pass. There are many champions of interdisciplinary research in the university who argue that the view of knowledge reflected by the current department structure of the university is anachronistic and an inhibitor to good research. A decline in the power and prestige of departments would be a good thing rather than a bad one. And furthermore, center faculty will be judged by their peers; their peers will represent a number of disciplines rather than a single discipline. It can even be argued that a researcher who can gain respect from practitioners of a number of disciplines is a better researcher than one who can gain the respect of practitioners of a single discipline.

Perhaps the crux of the argument focuses on the nature of the research. Many would argue that it is more appropriate that faculty pursue nondirected research based on intellectual curiosity rather than pursue directed research set by the agenda of another. But why is it more appropriate? The other side can argue that the problem with American university research is that the research agenda is set by the idiosyncratic visions of individual faculty. Given the public funds expended on university research and given the fact that land-grant universities serve a public mission, why shouldn't society rather than individual faculty set the research agenda? America needs more jobs and it needs to be more successful in international competition. The public pays a good part of the cost of university research; therefore it has the right to expect that the research result in a payoff to the public. Research conducted on behalf of university-business partnerships has a greater likelihood for such a payoff than research conducted because it meets the intellectual curiosity of the faculty. The price for supporting intellectual curiosity has become too high.

Such a response would not be popular in the academy. Nonetheless I take such an argument seriously. Moreover this argument has been made explicitly by certain members of the Minnesota legislature, and I can only assume that legislators hard strapped for funds in other states have made a similar argument. What can be said against the argument?

One reply is based on the fact that were such an argument successful, society, and especially business, would set a large part of the university's research agenda. The first move in the argument contends that having society set the research agenda will result in a dramatic shift away from nondirected basic research to directed basic research and then to applied research. Many have made the argument that applied research is dependent on basic research and hence if too many resources are spent on applied research now, there will be inadequate applied research in the future. The Canadian Natural Sciences and Engineering Research Council did a study asking holders of their grants to characterize the main thrust of their work as either basic or applied. In 1978–79 the ratio was 33.6 percent "Applied" and 66.4 percent "Toward the Advancement of Knowledge" (Basic). By 1987–88 the ratio was 54.8 percent "Applied" and 45.2 percent "Toward the Advancement of Knowledge" (Basic). (Buchbinder and Newson, 1990, 375.)

But our experience with university-business partnerships indicates that an excess of applied research is not the issue. Note that the Canadian study had a limited selection of responses: "Applied" and "Toward the Advancement of Knowledge," which I have characterized as basic. Our earlier discussion of the criticism that university-business partnerships would undermine basic research uses the more sophisticated "applied," "directed basic," and "nondirected basic" distinction. Most university-business partnership research is basic (albeit directed basic) rather than applied. For the above line of argument to work, one would have to argue that the shift from nondirected basic research to directed basic research would have long-run, untoward consequences for directed basic and applied research. That argument is more difficult to make and much harder to prove.

I can imagine the lines that such an argument would take, however. The fundamental premise is that the exercise of intellectual curiosity by many individuals is more productive in terms of research than having government or business decide the direction that basic research should take. In making this argument I do not have an image of business executives issuing orders to professors much as a manager orders employees. Rather, since business executives are disciplined by market forces, market incentives would drive research for both members of university-business partnerships. Business and perhaps legislatures would only fund research that meets their needs. Thus, the real question is whether research directed by the discipline of the market will provide more productive research in the long run than research based on the intellectual curiosity of a group of individual faculty researchers. A number of people would bet on the market. I predict that one of the most controversial ideas of the 1990s will be attempts by legislatures and, to a lesser extent, businesses to exert more influence on the research agendas in universities. What some are arguing here is that the research agenda of university faculty should be settled as a matter of public policy.

Concluding Thoughts on University-Business Partnerships

Are university-business partnerships in the public interest? This question does not have a definitive answer. These partnerships do have legitimacy. The federal government made changes in patent and tax law to promote them; many state and some local municipalities have provided financial support as, of course, has the federal government. The 1980s represented a period of remarkable consensus. The 1990s will probably be different. Recently, as we have seen, there has been some criticism by industry participants in university-business partnerships and recognition that for most universities these partnerships are risky long-term ventures rather than short-term money-generating machines. Some prominent educators, like Derek Bok, seem to have changed their mind and become more cautious. Caution will likely be the hallmark of the 1990s.

These recent doubts regarding university-business partnerships should give us pause. The underlying assumption of these partnerships was that they would provide a means of providing commercially viable research and development that would improve the ability of American corporations to be internationally competitive and hence would contribute to our economic welfare. In effect these partnerships were to serve as an ersatz industrial policy—a way for the American system to compete against Japan's Ministry of International Trade and Industry (MITI) and Japanese keiretsu organizations. For example, Carnegie-Mellon President Richard M. Cyert believes that university-business partnerships could be an informal answer to MITI (Main, 1987, 86). American firms have become more competitive but there is no evidence that university-business partnerships have been much of a causal factor. And neither university-business partnerships nor increased

American corporate competitiveness has been able to counteract those forces contributing to a stagnant economy. Admittedly, given the multiple factors that cause recessions, we cannot indicate that university-business partnerships have failed to help economic growth, but for the same reason we cannot claim too much for them. However, since an industrial policy is supposed to make a country more competitive and stimulate growth, university-business partnerships have failed as an ersatz industrial policy if they were ever intended to be one. To expect these partnerships to serve as a full-blown industrial policy is to expect too much.

Moreover, some commentators have argued that an emphasis on university-business partnerships leads society to ignore other issues that are even more important to economic success. What America needs most is a well-trained workforce. Technology transfer is important, but a well-educated, well-trained, well-motivated workforce is even more important. Business might get even greater returns if more of its dollars were invested in training (Fairweather, 1990, 40).

Also, I argued earlier that a more effective strategy for business would be for it to increase its research and development expenditure for in-house research and development work. Japanese firms spend a much greater percent of their income on in-house research and development than does the United States. Much less commercial research and development is conducted at Japanese universities than at U.S. universities. This recommendation receives indirect support from the industrial critics of university-business partnerships that appeared in the most recent report of the Government-University-Industry Research Roundtable. Rather than change its underlying philosophy, both the government and business seem to want the universities to provide technology transfer inexpensively. By using the university, business is unlikely to pay the full costs of the research and development it will use. Remember that the taxpayers are paying for some of this research. In effect, university-business partnerships are a subsidy for business. This is probably a shortsighted decision that will not solve our tendency to underinvest in research and development.

If university business partnerships have not as yet done much good, perhaps the very real dangers of such partnerships should be taken more seriously. This may even be the time to consider some unorthodox criticisms of technology itself.

After all, the development of a new product usually makes another obsolete. Thus the gain of some is obtained at the expense of a loss by others. In 1984, the California Rural Legal Assistance Agency sued the University of California, Davis, because the university supported research on automatic harvesters that eliminated the jobs of manual pickers (Lepkowski, 1984, 10). By eliminating jobs, the public university allegedly was not serving the best interests of the public in California. Was the university's research socially optimal? That question is seldom asked about the products being developed in university-business partnerships, although recently, as we have seen, some legislatures *are* beginning to ask that question. What is the answer?

Another way of putting this question is to point out, as Thomas Murray did, that "a company may find that it can make much more money by developing a face cream that it can with a new vaccine for some disease such as malaria" (Hearings on "The Use of Human Biological Materials in the Development of Biomedical Products," 1985, 102). Murray's point is of more than theoretical interest. Merck scientists discovered the cure for river blindness—a disease that afflicted the poor rural tribes of Central Africa. However, there was no other market for the cure and the poor tribesmen in Africa could not afford it. To Merck's credit, it developed the drug, gave it away, and even paid the costs of shipping it to Africa, despite the fact that no international charitable foundations would help. But how many companies would behave as Merck did? How can we be sure that human need is given due consideration with the pursuit of profit?

The issue of human need also rises at the university level. As the university builds partnerships with industry, what about research that benefits the public in general? As we have seen, some critics believe that some universities are already sacrificing research in the public interest for research that benefits corporate sponsors (Cordes, 1992, A26). Additional examples of research in the public interest include research in environmental protection, health care, mass transportation, sustainable agriculture, and the development of an educated and productive work force. The United States is faced with a large number of social problems, and universities, supported by public tax money, should be directing their research skills toward resolving these social problems. Some leaders like Jane L. Delgado, president of the National Coalition of Hispanic Health and Human Services Organizations, and Rand Wilson, coordinator for the Campaign for Responsible Technology, are urging universities to broaden their reliance on representatives from industry and academia to include persons from other walks in life. Broader representation on both government and university advisory boards is needed. Representatives from labor and community action groups are obvious candidates (Cordes, 1992, A26). Public universities are supposed to serve the entire community and they have been traditionally designated as the appropriate institution to conduct research in the public interest—research that business will not undertake. Will the commercialization of the university undermine that traditional mission?

Another troubling issue arises when we consider the justification of university-business partnerships and what might be required to make practice consistent with the national interest. Throughout this book I have argued that federal, state, and local government has supported the development of these partnerships on the grounds that these partnerships are in the interest of the U.S. economy. However, if institutions of higher education are faithful to the values of openness, these partnerships are open to foreign corporations and foreign businesspersons as well. Since U.S. universities have a long research tradition that Japan does not have, it should come as no surprise that Japanese industrial researchers would take advantage of opportunities to become acquainted with the research taking place in American universities. In 1984, then Cornell Provost Robert Barker had an interesting story to tell. Barker had been working at developing a university-industry-government partnership at Cornell. When he inquired if there were representatives from industry already working in Cornell's research activities, he was told there were five. They were all Japanese who had been sent to Cornell by Japanese corporations. Two of them held very responsible positions in their respective companies and were at Cornell to discover what was going on in genetic engineering (Barker, 1985). In testimony before Congress, David Noble testified that at MIT's highly touted industrial liaison program where member firms are charged a fee to gain access to MIT's largely government-funded research, half the members are foreign firms, fifty-seven are Japanese competitors, and that virtually all are multinationals with no special allegiance to U.S. economic interests. Indeed the industrial liaison program has a sales office in Tokyo (Hearings, "Is Science for Sale? Conflicts of Interest vs. The Public Interest," 1989, 24). If the justification for these partnerships is benefit to the U.S. economy, how can the privilege of membership in programs like MIT's industrial liaison program be granted to foreign competitors? On the other hand, to forbid membership would be contrary to the central academic value of open communication. This fundamental dilemma has not been addressed—in all probability because government officials are unaware of the heavy foreign participation.

The earlier problems regarding such things as barriers to publication and the determination of whether universities should grant exclusive or nonexclusive licenses are viewed largely as unimportant. Larger issues have surfaced. The economic benefits to both universities and business are in doubt. In the open university, foreign competitors may benefit as much as U.S. firms. In the meantime research for the public good, as opposed to the good of business, that has traditionally been conducted by universities is in danger of being neglected. I reluctantly conclude that we can no longer treat university-business partnerships as an automatic win-win situation. We are entering an era where new and more penetrating questions must be asked of university-business partnerships. Suddenly old friends have joined past critics in urging caution. I conclude that such advice is well taken.

PART THREE

Readings

SECTION ONE

Contending Evaluations

1
The Evolution of Research and
Development Policy in a Corporation: A
Case Study
W. G. Simeral

There are some of us who think of the history of research at Du Pont
as something unique in the industrial world.

That is understandable since Du Pont's Central Research and Development Department—our basic science laboratory—is one of the
oldest organizations of its kind in America. It was the forerunner of
basic research in the chemical industry, and Du Pont benefited very
substantially from that early research. The most famous discovery,
nylon, is a $5 billion-a-year business today.

Du Pont pioneered cooperative relationships with university research. Some of our products—a very early one, neoprene, and a very
recent one, the Automatic Clinical Analyzer—benefited from such
cooperative efforts.

The story of these successful developments, which I will discuss
further, supports the message that I would like to communicate,
namely, the nature of arrangements between industrial laboratories
and academic laboratories has not changed substantially in the last
forty years. The changes that have been made for the most part are
changes in degree or changes in emphasis—the latter usually following
general scientific trends.

However, there have been dramatic alterations in the social, politi-

From *Partners in the Research Enterprise,* Langfitt et. al., eds, University
of Pennsylvania Press, 1983.

cal, and economic environments in which research is conducted. These developments outside the research community have cast joint industrial and academic research in a new light. They have given rise to new concerns, and, in certain situations, politicized the goals and objectives of research.

With these points in mind, I would like to describe two examples of cooperative research between Du Pont and a university—which though separated by a generation were similar in essentials—and then compare and contrast current joint efforts to earlier ones.

But I must first interject a disclaimer. The examples I have chosen deal with collaborative research between industry and academe. I am not attempting to address such questions as university professors becoming active participants in and overseers of ventures closely related to their academic research. At Du Pont we have no experience with any of those situations. Suffice it to say that this is hardly a new phenomenon. The venture capital companies formed thirty years ago, based on the explosion of solid state physics and electronics technology, created the same questions. Today, the spotlight of media, public interest groups, and political institutions creates an impression that there is a dramatic new phenomenon to be dealt with.

The overall relationships between industry and university are extensive, complex, and far-reaching. While we at Du Pont consider research collaboration to be important, we consider as much more important the university as the principal source of basic research and of future leaders of our nations in all walks of life. We support universities extensively with grants having no quid pro quo as our way of encouraging excellence in the pursuit of these fundamental university objectives, especially in those fields of science, engineering, and business management of most direct concern to our corporation.

My first example is the discovery of neoprene, the first commercially produced synthetic rubber. When Du Pont introduced neoprene in 1931, more than a decade of investigations lay behind it. The early years of this research were not successful. Du Pont's research team under Elmer Bolton had pursued many avenues of investigation but had failed to come up with an acceptable polymer.

But in 1925, Bolton heard a paper read by Julius Nieuwland of the University of Notre Dame at the American Chemical Society's first organic symposium in Rochester. Neiuwland's paper discussed the discovery of divinylacetylene which had been made from acetylene gas using a new catalyst. Bolton recognized immediately that Nieuwland's work might be useful in bringing Du Pont's frustrated elastomer research to its desired end, especially since earlier that year Du Pont had initiated a project to make butadiene from acetylene in the hope that the butadiene could be converted to rubber.

Out of Bolton's early discussion with Nieuwland came two years of consultation and meetings between Du Pont and Notre Dame. The initial arrangement for Nieuwland's consultation fees was somewhat unusual because of his status as a Holy Cross Father. He had made a vow to poverty and therefore requested that he not be paid for his work. Instead he was authorized to purchase books for the university library and bill Du Pont for the costs.

As work progressed, however, it became apparent that a different arrangement would be necessary in the event of a patentable discovery. So in 1928, an agreement was reached to provide for royalties to Notre Dame in the event any commercial products resulted from one of Nieuwland's inventions.

Eventually, a polymer with the sought-after properties was synthesized. It did not come about as a result of the synthetic rubber experiments, but in the course of other investigations with the general goal of studying the "chemical possibilities" of divinylacetylene.

This separate project was under the direction of Wallace Carothers who came to Du Pont from Harvard in 1929. Carothers had a penchant for working with only high purity materials. Before he began studying DVA, he assigned one of his assistants, Arnold Collins, to prepare pure DVA from the mixture that resulted from reacting Nieuwland's catalyst with acetylene.

Collins's purification work separated both monovinylacetylene and a chlorine-containing product, chloroprene, from the DVA. Collins let the chloroprene stand in a test tube, and when he returned to it several days later he found that it had solidified. The solidified residue was determined to be a previously unknown material, polychloroprene. Polychloroprene had properties similar to natural rubber. It was patented by Carothers and Collins, dubbed "Duprene" and later given the generic name neoprene.

Although Nieuwland was not connected with the particular experiment that led to the discovery of neoprene, his earlier work had prepared the way. His catalyst was needed to make MVA, which in turn was reacted with hydrochloric acid to yield chloroporene, the monomer for neoprene. As a result, more than $2 million in royalties was eventually paid to Notre Dame.

The cooperative research between Du Pont and Notre Dame that led to the discovery of neoprene was the first undertaking of its kind for the company's Central Research and Development Department—which incidentally was only a few years old when neoprene was commercialized. But the experience was marked by several characteristics that were to show up repeatedly in later Du Pont—university collaborations.

First, the initial contact with the university was, to an extent, coincidental. I do not wish to make too much of this, but I want to mention that Du Pont was not out looking for a research partner. Nevertheless, once the opportunity presented itself, Du Pont was quick to seize it. This does not seem surprising today, but recall that in those years industrial research was still in its infancy. Du Pont was one of the few corporations in the U.S. developing a basic research capability. And one of the reasons for doing so was expressly to encourage contact between the company and university research scientists.

Second, Du Pont was drawn to Notre Dame because they were impressed by an individual's performance, in this instance, Nieuwland's. This was to characterize the company's interaction with university scientists from then on and remains important today; that is, we view successful Du Pont–industry collaboration as starting with an exceptional university scientist.

Third, university scientists did not invent the product that the company commercialized. The university provided scientific leads and concepts, and consultation over a period of several years, and Nieuwland was responsible for breakthroughs that provided valuable information. But the synthesis of the final compound was Du Pont's doing, as was the identification of its commercial potential. I would also stress that throughout the process Nieuwland's laboratory continued to do what it did best—basic research. All the applications work was done at Du Pont.

And fourth, Notre Dame was appropriately compensated for its role in the research. Admittedly, the initial arrangement of library books in lieu of consultation fees might seem quaint in light of today's practices. But the royalty arrangement was certainly normal and similar to current arrangements.

Another example of Du Pont working with a university research team dates from more than a generation later. By the 1960s, it was already evident that research was revolutionizing science as well as the everyday world. Scientific progress had changed some things in academic research, and many things had changed in industrial research. And the role of government in R&D was more pronounced than ever before.

But much about joint industrial-academic research had remained the same. In 1963, a Du Pont venture group entered into a consulting agreement at the University of Wisconsin for automating wet analytical chemistry. An outgrowth of this relationship was the Automatic Clinical Analyzer, the "aca." Today, the "aca" is an extremely successful product and the relationship with the University of Wisconsin continues.

Du Pont's interest in instruments dates to the forties and fifties. Many of the new materials we began producing then were manufactured by novel processes. Controls for those processes were not commercially available so we invented our own. In two decades we assembled an impressive array of instruments and began to consider opportunities to market some of them. From 150 candidates, 2 were chosen to be produced and sold. One was a process photometer, the other a thermal analyzer. Both were well received.

Encouraged by this success, we began to search out new opportunities that would provide the stimulus to develop completely new instruments. One area that offered promise was the automations of chemical analyses which typically involved the use of several kinds of glassware, liquid reagents, and several procedural steps. One market envisioned was the health care industry where the automation of standard clinical laboratory testing would prove a great contribution to efficiency.

During our early deliberations, we contacted Walter J. Bladel at the University of Wisconsin Department of Chemistry, who had for some time been investigating wet chemistry automation, and Bladel introduced us to his former student, G. Phillip Hicks. We extended our consulting agreement with Bladel to Hicks and eventually to his superior, Frank Larson. We also began to fund some of the research in Hicks's laboratory.

Despite the close relationship with Hicks, we did not adopt his equipment or his approach to wet chemistry automation. The basic concept we adopted for the "aca" came from our own research team under the direction of Don Johnson.

During two days of intense discussion in August 1964, Johnson and his colleagues hit on the central concept of the "aca": Chemical reagents and blood serum samples are placed in individual plastic envelopes; the reagents and serum are mixed by breaking certain seals; and the reaction mixture is measured photometrically through the envelope's transparent walls.

The conceptual breakthrough was only the beginning. Engineering was the next challenge, and it was not until 1967 that a satisfactory prototype was built that could accomplish the initial goal. During this time, the consulting relationship with Wisconsin continued, and late in 1967 the prototype was shipped to the University of Wisconsin Clinical Laboratories for evaluation.

The clinical tests provided us with valuable information, and offered the Wisconsin team the opportunity to prepare two widely publicized papers. In 1968, the "aca" was unveiled at the American Association for Clinical Chemistry in Washington. Rapid acceptance and use followed, and the impact of the "aca" on hospital clinical efficiency has been tremendous.

When first introduced, the "aca" performed eight tests; today it performs fifty. As our development of its potential continues, so does our relationship with the University of Wisconsin. At present we share interests in two patents not directly related to the "aca," which may result in commercial applications, and the university continues to test and evaluate new developments.

Although widely separated by time and clearly distinct in terms of research environment, our relationship with Wisconsin in the development of the "aca" shares some characteristics in common with the relationship between Du Pont and Notre Dame during the development of neoprene.

We were drawn to Wisconsin by the coincidence of research interests. We established consulting relationships with people there because we were convinced of their leadership in their field of expertise. As had been true when we worked with Notre Dame, the product was ultimately one that we conceptualized and invented, to which the university contributed valuable information and first-rate evaluation and assistance. And the compensation agreement was fair and equitable; both sides came out ahead.

With these two case histories as a background, I would like to describe a relationship that Du Pont is in the process of developing today, one generation after we began work on the "aca" and two generations removed from neoprene. I refer to our agreement to fund research in molecular genetics at the Harvard Medical School.

On the surface the scope and implications of our $6 million grant to Harvard's newly formed Department of Genetics would seem to dwarf our neoprene joint research and overshadow the partnership that worked on the "aca." But if we look behind this decision, we see that its foundation is formed by the same principles that have guided us in the past.

We begin with a coincidence of scientific concern. Du Pont has had an active interest in biochemistry for many years. Our existing businesses in agricultural chemistry and pharmaceuticals, for example, stand to benefit from developments in genetics and recombinant DNA technologies. And we are convinced that the Harvard staff under Phillip Leder constitutes one of the most talented research teams in the country.

It is, of course, premature to say whether or not any discovery made at Harvard will immediately lend itself to commercial applications. But based on our experience, we have come not to expect that, but rather to use the knowledge that their research will produce and apply it to our own ongoing investigations. In the event that patents arise from Harvard's research, we and the university feel confident that the agreement for licensing that we have established will cover any contingency. There are no provisions in our agreement that will in any way control, inhibit, or restrict the conduct of Harvard's research or the publication of its results.

I have consciously placed our latest joint research venture with a university squarely within the context of the history of research at Du Pont. That is how we see it. We do not believe that this latest development is in any sense a departure from the course that we have been following since the company established its basic research organization more than sixty years ago.

I realize that there is another context in which this development must be placed. Some have characterized joint university-industry research in the biotechnologies as a thoughtless rush to financial gain without regard for the university as primarily a teaching and fundamental research institution. Less informed people fear that the universities are losing control of their research; that somehow the "wrong" things will be invented and that science will be practiced for profit and not for the common good.

Such concerns are not completely unfounded; we live in an exciting era, things are moving quickly, and there is need for deliberate and controlled application of our hard-pressed resources for research.

Yet, many of the fears are exaggerated. In large part, the concern is based on popular, unfavorable, and largely erroneous caricatures of industry. The concerns also stem from lack of confidence in the integrity of our universities. We must address these concerns.

We must first deal with the concern that research carried out with public funds is improperly utilized by business concerns for private profit. Such a statement reflects a basic misunderstanding of the historic role of fundamental university research and the associated role of applied research, development, and commercialization in private companies. This division of effort is an essential part of the fabric of America. There is nothing wrong with it as long as the process is managed fairly and openly.

A university and its scientists should receive proper compensation for their contributions. And in those situations where a branch of government has sponsored research directed at a specific target, the government may well have an interest in further commercial applications. This, however, does not mean that only the government should enjoy the fruits of basic science results. The public depends on private companies to conceive of the practical applications of basic science— and to put new products on the market. The time and cost to move from a basic concept to a useful product is usually much greater than the uninformed person suspects.

We have a responsibility, therefore, to communicate to the public an understanding of how R&D is practiced. It is not generally understood that research for a corporation is a risk. And there are those who assume that university research can be made to order—that the company says to the university we need such and such a product and the university creates it.

However, while good basic science always produces something of academic value, it does not always produce something of commercial value. We need to emphasize this point, not in order to generate sympathy for corporations, but as a means of reminding people that it is a long road from test tube to commercialization with many costs and delays and not infrequent failures.

Moreover, it is ultimately the market—the purchases by the public— that decides which applications of science are useful. If it is to be successful, industrial research must lead to desirable, necessary, and useful products. Companies stay in business by fulfilling needs, not by ignoring them.

Research policy has become news and is much discussed in the media. This means that the formulators of research policy are now seeing their decisions treated to the same kind of news analysis that the actions of businessmen and legislators have received for many years.

Much of this analysis is first-rate; some of it reflects a lack of understanding. Moreover, it is inevitable that much of the analysis of research developments in the media will be political in nature. This is my final point and perhaps the one of chief concern. We live in an era when the resources available to research are subject to severe limitations. Because the costs of doing basic science have risen and because the funds for research support are limited, the decision about where the money goes will be subject to more intense political pressures than before.

The research community must demonstrate to the public its continuing concern to maintain the highest professional standards as well as increased openness to concerns of the type we are addressing here. We cannot afford to be insensitive to political and economic considerations, but that is not the same thing as capitulating to them.

As academic scientists and industrial scientists are drawn closer together by mutual interest and joint projects, more attention will focus on our aims and goals. Our work will be judged in part on how successful we are at establishing and communicating a consensus.

The nature of working relationships between academic and industrial research groups has not altered radically over the years, but the public perception of those relationships has changed. An important part of managing research in this decade and in the future will be to reassure our friends and our critics that we know what we are doing, and that our work is in the public interest.

2
The Commercialized University
Derek Bok

As all alumni know, universities are in chronic need of funds. They fill their ranks with creative people who have a continual stream of new ideas, most of which cost money. They compete vigorously with one another, but competition among universities—unlike corporations—means a constant struggle for the best students and faculty, which drives costs up rather than down. Meanwhile, research efforts in many fields grow steadily larger and more elaborately equipped, pushing up expenses faster than the cost of living.

For many years following World War II, Washington gladly met these mounting demands in order to help higher education build the world's leading research effort and accommodate larger fractions of the nation's youth. But federal outlays stopped growing at this pace two decades ago. Government officials now look for any way they can to force universities to pay more of their research and student-aid costs. As America's economic growth has slackened and federal deficits have increased, hopes for a quick return to the days of easy money have dwindled. Meanwhile, other sources of income have also fallen on hard times, as the general public has begun to complain increasingly about tuition increases, while competition for the philanthropic dollar has grown much keener.

These tendencies are gradually slowing the dynamism of our universities. In the 1950s and 1960s, government funding and endowment campaigns fueled a great expansion and a proliferation of new faculties and programs. By the mid-1970s, aggressive fund raising sufficed at best to allow modest expansion of existing programs, especially in "hot" areas of research, such as genetics and microbiology. By the end of the 1980s, new initiatives had pretty well ground to a halt, and ever more massive fund drives seemed to be needed simply to maintain existing programs at satisfactory levels of quality.

Caught in this financial squeeze, campus administrators have been looking hard for new sources of support. It has not escaped their notice that much of what universities do has monetary value, especially in a world where specialized knowledge is increasingly in demand. New scientific discoveries may lead to profitable products, while advances

From "Universities: Their Temptations and Tensions," *Journal of College and University Law*, 1991.

in electronics, materials science, and biotechnology can spawn entire industries. Advanced training, especially for affluent professions, may be worth a lot of money. The mere aura and prestige of a well-known university can have commercial value.

Like other universities, Harvard has moved aggressively in recent years to capitalize on these opportunities. Efforts to patent scientific discoveries and license them to corporations brought us over one million dollars in 1989–90. A venture capital fund—with Harvard to share in the profits—is now investing in new companies and development efforts that adapt medical discoveries to commercial use. Even our logo has proved an attractive source of profit, bringing several hundred thousand dollars to the University last year in return for using the Harvard name on sweat clothes, mugs, T-shirts, and other personal objects.

New opportunities for profit may be more lucrative still. With the aid of technology, the Harvard Business School has begun to sell instructional tapes on management topics taught by well-known members of its faculty. Not to be outdone, the Medical School has proposed a cable television series on cardiology with a corporate sponsor and commercial advertising.

There are important benefits from initiatives of this kind. Any profits or receipts are ploughed immediately back into education and research. In this way, Harvard diversifies its sources of support and helps to compensate for the steady erosion of federal funds. In addition, commercial rewards may bring forth valuable activities that would not otherwise exist. For example, the promise of royalties has already caused universities to make much greater efforts to transform their scientific discoveries into useful products and services. In the future, commercial sponsorship may prove important in attracting the funds required to finance the expensive computers that will allow students in our professional schools to learn in new and more effective ways.

Alas, however, there are no free lunches even for eleemosynary institutions. Efforts to turn university activities into money can easily distract the institution and cause it to sacrifice its most essential values. A glaring example is big-time university athletics, where the lure of television revenues has helped bring widespread corruption in admission practices, miseducation and exploitation of athletes, embarrassing compromises in academic standards, and even outright cheating and bribery.

Fortunately, Harvard has been largely free of these misadventures. But there are plenty of other dangers to guard against. Like other new activities, entrepreneurial ventures can burden the administration and divert the faculty. Graduate students may be drawn into commercial projects in ways that sacrifice their education for commercial gain. Research performed with an eye toward profit may lure investigators into conflicts of interest or cause them to practice forms of secrecy that hamper scientific progress. Ultimately, corporate ties may undermine the university's reputation for objectivity and, if foreign firms are involved, antagonize the Congress by seeming to favor America's commercial rivals.

Careful administration can contain many of these dangers, and Harvard has worked very hard to be careful. For example, our venture capital fund, like all of our corporate research agreements, contains elaborate safeguards against secrecy or the misuse of graduate students. The very existence of such a fund may serve academic values by keeping faculty members from wasting time looking for corporate sponsors and by channelling their commercial ventures through an organization under Harvard's observation and control.

Yet risks remain which are difficult to guard against completely. The benefits and risks of commercial activity are often intangible and hard to weigh. Our venture fund may indeed turn discoveries into useful medical products; it could even out the time that professors spend trying to patent and develop their inventions. But it is also possible that the fund will burden busy administrators with added supervisory tasks or seem to legitimate business ventures and thus encourage more professors to spend time commercializing their research. None of these conflicting possibilities can be measured. Amid the uncertainties, the only tangible result is the likelihood of added funds for research. Often, after much inconclusive argument, it is this alluring prospect that remains to carry the day.

For some commercial ventures, the typical cost-benefit analysis may actually produce absurd results. Consider a proposal to auction off the last fifty places in an entering college class. This procedure could raise a tidy sum for the university. It would be perfectly feasible to limit the bidding to a few thousand applicants, each possessing the intellectual and personal qualifications to be a worthy member of the class. Such a limited auction would do no perceptible damage to the quality of the class. The added funds could even be used to *raise* the level of the student body by increasing scholarship awards for exceptionally able applicants. Hence, the benefits would be clear and the drawbacks far from obvious. Yet the very thought of an auction is odious.

The point of this example is simply to show that ordinary forms of reasoning and evaluation not only fail to produce clear answers to some of the university's commercial dilemmas; they may even appear to justify grotesque conclusions. How then can we protect ourselves from folly? Clearly, some things in a university should not be for sale. But what things? And why, if they bring in money to be used for worthy academic purposes?

Some practices, such as charging tuition or billing the government for research, are obviously justifiable, since there is no way in which the institution could carry on basic academic activities without resorting to such methods to cover all or part of its costs. Certain other practices, such as licensing the use of the university's name on mugs and T-shirts, may be in questionable taste but do no even involve, let alone threaten, the central academic enterprise or its core values. Flashing yellow lights should appear, however, whenever the institution seeks to make a profit on basic academic functions—such as teaching, research, selecting students, or appointing faculty—in order to finance its other activities.

Occasionally, the profit motive will coincide with sound academic practice. For example, the promise of patent royalties may simply have the beneficial result of encouraging universities to work harder at finding opportunities to help turn scientific discoveries into useful products and devices.[1] But this justification does not apply to many other situations in which universities seek to profit from their normal activities. In these instances, the desire for profit can all too easily conflict with vital academic values. Take the sad case of intercollegiate athletics. Here, the promise of financial reward continually tempts campus officials to compromise admissions policies, distort grading practices, and lower academic standards in the classroom. Televising commercially-sponsored courses could likewise be dangerous, because campus officials might be led to alter the content of their educational material either to avoid offending their sponsor or to enlarge the viewing audience and thus increase their commercial rewards. Similarly, auctioning off places in the entering class would directly threaten basic academic values by constantly tempting university officials to expand the pool of eligible participants, even at the cost of lowering standards, in order to increase the take.

---

1. Granted, royalties could have unfortunate results if they diverted the labors of talented basic scientists into efforts to commercialize their ideas. But the potential rewards of patent licensing are too limited and uncertain to raise serious concerns of this sort.

In each of these cases, it is impossible for the outside world to know whether any university is actually compromising its standards to enlarge its income. All that the world can know is that the university has allowed another motive—the profit motive—to coexist with its desire to seek the truth and disseminate knowledge.[2] By so doing, even institutions that avoid all impropriety will have given the public cause to question their integrity. This is no small matter. One of the reasons that society accepts the policies of tenure and academic freedom is because it has been persuaded that the public will benefit in the long run if professors are insulated from pressures that could compromise their impartial search for knowledge. If universities themselves create pressures that threaten academic standards in order to obtain extra income, can they be as sure that the government will continue to have confidence in their work and maintain the conditions of freedom essential to its progress?

Beyond the risk of corrupting standards lies another, more subtle concern. Universities attract the loyalty of faculty and alumni and, to a degree, the respect of the public precisely because they act for reasons other than money and will not compromise certain values simply to gain immediate monetary rewards. As universities grow more aggressive in finding ways to turn their activities into cash, their image subtly changes. They appear less and less as a charitable institution seeking truth and serving students and more and more as a huge commerical operation that differs from corporations only because there are no shareholders and no dividends. Such an institution may still evoke pride and respect because of its intellectual achievements. But the feelings it engenders will not be quite the same as those produced by an institution that is prepared to forgo income, if need be, to preserve values of a nobler kind.

It is still not clear what effect these new commercial ventures will have on the feelings of constituencies whose loyalties are vital to the university: on faculty members, who must often do much more than their job description requires if the institution is to flourish; on the alumni, who must give generously of their time and money if the university is to progress; on the public, which gives various privileges to institutions of learning in the belief that they are not commercial

---

2. By agreeing to a commercially-sponsored TV program, the university also allows its good name to be joined with commercial products and sales techniques over which it can have but little control. In so doing, the university puts its reputation at risk in the eyes of the public.

ventures but organizations that subordinate money to other aims and values of distinct value to society.

If any change in attitude *has* occurred, it is probably in the eyes of the public and its official representatives. During the past two or three generations, universities have gradually lost their immunity from lawsuits and their protection from state regulation. Their tax exemption is under constant attack by local governments, their ability to borrow at tax-exempt rates has been limited, and Washington is beginning to interest itself in imposing a levy on their endowments. There are various reasons for these changes, and the ultimate status of universities under our laws is still unclear. Nevertheless, it would be myopic not to find some connection between the diminishing privileges of our institutions of learning and their increasingly commercial image. . . .

Opportunities for commercial profit come in many subtle and seductive guises, while the shape and contours of the university's values are often blurred by compromises previously made. The pressure for further concessions is especially intense because the university is caught between two of its most compelling interests. In large part, the progress and prosperity of the institution and the support of its faculty and alumni depend not only on preserving its academic values but also on its success in building needed facilities, mounting new programs, attracting outstanding faculty, and thereby gaining distinction in a highly competitive environment. The drive to succeed, or simply to keep up with the competition, generates strong pressure to find the necessary resources. In this atmosphere, it is hard to resist lucrative business ventures, especially if rival universities have already exploited them. The very competition that infuses so much energy and initiative into American higher education worked in this instance to hasten the process of commercializing our universities.

There is no reason to suppose that these pressures will diminish any time soon. On the contrary, massive federal deficits and a sluggish economy are likely to make the financial outlook for academe even chillier than in the past. If so, the search for new sources of revenue can only grow more intense, and universities will find themselves inexorably drawn into more and more commercial ventures. Should this trend materialize, it will take very strong leadership to keep the profit motive from gradually eroding the values on which the welfare and reputation of universities ultimately depend.

3
Technology Transfer at MIT
Paul E. Gray

Mr. Chairman, Members of the Subcommittee:

I am Paul E. Gray, President of the Massachusetts Institute of Technology. I was formerly Professor of Electrical Engineering at MIT and, before becoming President in July of 1980, I served successively as Dean of Engineering and Chancellor. I serve also as a director of several technology-dependent corporations, and I am Vice-Chairman of the Council on Competitiveness.

. . . I am pleased to have this opportunity to offer my observations on the process of technology transfer, because that issue has been one of my particular interests during my years as President at MIT. As I pointed out when I spoke before a committee of Congress in 1985, the university has traditionally been one of the primary sources of creative thought in society. But as all of us in the field of technology are aware, creative thought does not in itself ensure the transfer of discoveries and inventions to society in a meaningful way. It is therefore essential that we develop and maintain cooperative activities between basic research institutions and industry that will assure the rapid and effective transfer of new technologies, the relevance of our educational programs, and the necessary support for underlying research.

Since I offered those thoughts in 1985, the issue of technology transfer has assumed a new urgency, because of increasing concerns about America's competitiveness in the world marketplace. As Vice-Chairman of the Council on Competitiveness, I have had a special opportunity to compare the strengths, and weaknesses, of the American approach to technological development. I have become convinced that America has a unique advantage in its research universities, where exploration of the frontiers of science is supported by governmental and private funds, and where the channels between academia and commerce are well marked to permit the application of new discoveries to create products and processes of economic benefit to society. No

Congressional Testimony before the Committee on Government Operations, Subcommittee on Human Resource and Intergovernmental Operations, June 13, 1989.

other country has that capacity and linkage. It is incumbent on those of us with responsibility for guiding educational institutions, and on governmental leaders like yourselves, to make certain that this unique American strength is utilized and encouraged to help keep our country competitive.

While the fruits of basic research provide the basis for new products and new processes, much more is necessary to create reliable, desirable products that meet the test of the marketplace. The steps that lead from the conception of a new product through development and design, to market testing and manufacturing process development and manufacture of the product are extremely important. These steps do *not* occur in the university setting; they occur in industry.

. . . In the past decade the Congress has taken important steps to capitalize on the strength inherent in America's research universities by making more efficient the transfer of knowledge from theory to practice. The Patents and Trademark Amendments of 1980 (P.L. 96-517) decentralized the process of technology transfer by giving to universities, as well as other nonprofit organizations and small businesses, the first right of ownership to patentable inventions made with federal funds. That law balances the decentralization of the transfer process with assurances that the recipients of the patents must provide through open licensing for the prompt utilization of new inventions by industrial and commercial firms. The Federal Technology Transfer Act of 1986 (P.L. 99-502), expanding the Stevenson-Wydler Technology Innovation Act of 1980 (P.L. 96-480), extended this approach to federal laboratories, another important source of new discoveries with potential for practical applications.

With these advances have come new concerns. Any academic institution engaged in work that is "useful"—"useful" in the sense that its research has application to the practical world of commerce and industry—will naturally have a tension between the pursuit of research for the sake of expanding mankind's knowledge, and the time and effort necessary to transfer from the realm of the abstract to the realm of the practical the knowledge that has been achieved. This tension is heightened by the fact that the organizations that represent the practical world of commerce and industry—profit-making corporations—naturally seek a proprietary advantage, while universities have an essential commitment to openness in process and results.

Over the years the aspects of that tension that have seemed most critical have changed. In an early manifestation, it was concern that scientists would not devote proper time to research if they were also involved in the application of their findings to useful applications. After careful consideration, most research universities, including MIT, refined their policies to specify the level of outside professional or commercial activities permitted faculty members, and to monitor these activities on a regular basis, and those policies today generate little controversy because they appear to be working well.

More recently the inherent tension between research and the fruitful application of the knowledge gained from the research has focused on the issue of financial gain, and the appropriateness of permitting the researcher to share in the rewards that may flow from successful application of research findings. The manifestations of this tension today are various: Will the opportunity to share in the rewards improperly influence the course of the basic research? How should rewards be apportioned among the contributors to the scientific advances? Should the rewards be channelled back into the basic research effort, or should they flow in some measure to the individual researchers? And what is the proper treatment of rewards that are the result of research funded by a particular sponsor, either public or private?

Just as earlier issues in the tension between research and application presented opportunities for creative management by universities, and yielded to resolutions that are broadly accepted today, so will the issues now in the forefront benefit from thoughtful analysis and debate, so that the ultimate resolution serves the needs of society. . . .

Today M.I.T., and most major research universities, actively use a variety of strategies, first, to help link the academy with business and industry and, second, to encourage in particular, as does the Federal Government, technology transfer.

At MIT, these university-industry relationships take many forms.

First, the several departments in the MIT School of Engineering participate in a number of cooperative work-study programs with industry. About one-quarter of our junior and senior engineering students are enrolled in cooperative internship programs.

Second, we have a variety of degree programs that are specifically designed to meet perceived industrial needs. One brand new initiative of this kind is the MIT Leaders in Manufacturing program, which focuses on the education of engineers and managers who will bring their interests, knowledge and skills to bear on manufacturing, indeed on the entire process which begins with the conception of a product and ends with its marketing and continual improvement. This new program evolved from discussions between MIT faculty and industry leaders about how MIT could help improve the competitiveness of American manufacturers in the global market. Today this program is a partnership between MIT's Schools of Engineering and Management and 11 major American manufacturing firms[1] that are seeking to discover and codify the principles that should be taught and practiced in the future. The goal is both to develop manufacturing leaders through the program's graduates and to establish manufacturing principles and a curriculum to convey them.

Third, in this array of strategies, the Institute offers, through its summer session and its Center for Advanced Engineering Studies, several score short courses each year, both on and off the campus and on video tape, designed to keep practicing professionals in industry abreast of technical developments in their fields.

Further, there is significant industrial participation in, and support of, research and education programs at the Institute. . . . [One] interesting partnership is MIT's Project Athena, a large-scale program undertaken by MIT in collaboration with DEC and IBM to integrate networked computers with advanced computational and graphics capabilities into undergraduate education throughout the Institute.

One very practical and unexpected development that has arisen from this collaboration in education is the X-Window System, which is a method of managing access to multiple-task environments within a computer work station and which has gained broad acceptance worldwide as a standard method. MIT makes X-Window Source Codes available at virtually cost without licensing fees or restrictions.

MIT also operates, as you noted specifically in your letter to me, Mr. Chairman, a large Industrial Liaison Program (ILP). In existence for more than 40 years, the MIT ILP has today a membership of almost 300 companies. These companies represent a wide spectrum of industry sectors, almost all of which, including most recently the banking sector, rely extensively on technology. As the industrial democracies move more-and-more toward closer economic relationships, our membership rolls have included more and more multinational firms. We have seen this as a development that recognizes and accommodates to changes in the global economy.

Representatives of the member firms of the ILP visit the campus, speak with our faculty and research staff, attend MIT conferences on technology and management subjects, and have ready access to a range of publicly available MIT research reports and student theses.

---

1. Alcoa, Boeing, Chrysler Motors, Digital, Eastman Kodak, General Motors, Hewlett Packard, Johnson & Johnson, Motorola, Polaroid, and United Technologies Corporation.

To help each member firm identify areas of interest to it, ILP publishes yearly a directory entitled "Research at MIT." The Subcommittee has received copies of this compendium, going back a number of years, as well as a compilation of other data it requested.

Since our faculty are regularly involved in conferences and other professional activities away from our campus, we also arrange faculty visits to company locations through the ILP. Normally, the visiting professor will deliver a lecture presenting the state of his research.

We see the Industrial Liaison Program, including visits to the campus and to corporations, as a two-way street because it offers faculty a special opportunity to observe and understand industrial practice. Many of our young faculty, in particular, view this program as an effective way to become grounded in the industrial environment into which a majority of our graduates will eventually be placed. By this means, connections with industry have a leavening effect not only on our research but also on our educational programs. This vital linkage thus helps shape the MIT environment.

Corporations that participate in the ILP pay an annual fee that scales with size. These fees comprise a stream of unrestricted revenues for the Institute. The program is expensive to operate, so that a large fraction of the fee income is required to meet the direct expenses of the program. I wish to express my view that MIT would not operate this program were its only benefit a stream of revenue. The educational and research functions of this science-based university *require* broadly-based understanding of industrial practice and industrial needs. The ILP is an important vehicle for developing that understanding, and this is its principal benefit to the Institute.

The faculty who participate in the ILP program receive some revenue return for their time and effort—but not, I emphasize, for their personal financial gain but in support, rather, of their professional and research activities. Thomas Moebus, who is a director of the ILP, has explained this system, and its avoidance of the financial conflicts of interest you inquired about, to staff of the subcommittee.

This system distributes 10% of the total of fees received from ILP member companies to the individual members of the faculty and senior research staff who interact with those member companies. The program distributes this portion of the fees to MIT participants on the basis of measures of activity, such as visiting a company, hosting visitors to the campus, or chairing or participating in one of the score of ILP symposia which are arranged each year.

In Fiscal Year 1988, distributions available to the faculty ranged from $3,600 on average for the top 100 faculty participants to an average of $665 for all participating faculty. As Mr. Moebus has reported to you "this amount is distributed in an account to the Administrative Officer of the faculty member's unit at the conclusion of the academic year. The money is then available to be used for professional activities, to supplement in a modest way other sources of research support for the faculty. Approval for expenditure is by the Administrative Officer, which assures that MIT policies regarding these expenditures are upheld. Funds may be used, for instance, to purchase equipment or pay for travel to professional conferences. They may not be used for personal purposes. The faculty have often told us that while the points are valued, they are not at all the main motivation for participation in Program activities."

Let me turn now to an entirely distinct set of activities, and perhaps one where it is easiest to track MIT's direct connection to the commercial sphere, namely, the direct licensing of technologies invented at MIT and protected through the patent process. . . .

Over the past few years, the increasing pace of technical developments in many fields have brought a heightened interest on the part of industry in university research and the potential for new and useful technology. In the last few years, MIT has responded to this heightened interest in a number of ways, including strengthening of the technology transfer function within the Institute so that it is better positioned to take advantage of the decentralized technology management encouraged by recent changes in Federal policy and to utilize effectively the incentives that national policy provides.

The recent experience of the MIT Technology Licensing Office embraces interesting examples of how promising technology is moving toward commercial production and I will cite some of these in a moment. That experience also indicates that technology transfer has certain risks and dangers that we must learn to identify and to manage. These include conflicts of interest in various forms, including financial conflicts, and I will also cite some examples of these and indicate how we have addressed them.

Presently, MIT's Technology Licensing Office licenses technology to major new start-ups in which MIT people are involved at a rate of eight-plus per year, accounting for 10% of MIT license agreements. Last year, these companies averaged over two million dollars in first round investment and included some of the largest such investments in the country. Among these start-ups were such firms as American

Superconductor and Immulogic Pharmaceutical, to cite two examples which I think you will find interesting.

American Superconductor was founded in 1987 by two MIT professors and a venture fund, American Research and Development Co. The core technology is an invention that makes new high-temperature superconductors more flexible and therefore more practical for commercial applications. It allows, for instance, the making of superconductor wires that are sufficiently flexible to wrap around a golf ball without breaking. Without this approach, wires of comparable diameter would break if wrapped around a basketball. This technology could obviously have a major impact in those applications that require high-temperature superconductors in the form of wire.

My second example, Immulogic Pharmaceutical, was founded in 1987 by an MIT professor and a venture fund, Rothschild Ventures. The core technology here is a basic new understanding of the human immune system. From this understanding, the company can increase or decrease the immune response to a cell, virus, protein, etc. This means that the body can be "programmed" to reject or accept a foreign substance. Clearly, there is a remarkable potential here in this field.

Let me turn next to the potential conflicts inherent in licensing, and particularly in spin-off companies. Obviously they are numerous. Of these potentialities, the ones that give us the greatest concern are the following:

First, if a faculty member holds equity in a small closely-held company, we might be concerned that these holdings could (a) bias his research at MIT toward work that has higher commercial merit; (b) alter his openness toward others in the scientific community or in industry; (c) lead to abuse of students through biased grades or thesis topics based on the students' involvement with the company; and (d) encourage abuse of the time allowed for outside activities, which at MIT is one day a week.

Taking the next level of involvement, what if the university held equity in a similar company? We then should be concerned that these holdings might (a) bias promotions of our faculty based on our hopes of making money from their inventions; or (b) bias future technology transfer in favor of companies in which we have a vested interest.

We attempt at MIT to manage such potential conflicts head-on. Each time we license technology to a company in which an MIT employee holds a significant stock interest, we require that employee to sign a conflict-avoidance statement that confirms his recognition of these potential problems. He is forbidden from taking a line management position in the company or taking research funding at MIT from that company. He must differentiate his activities at the company from his continuing activities at MIT to the satisfaction of his department chairman. Our concern is to preserve openness and the integrity of the scientific mission at MIT. Occasionally, we will supplement the department chairman's oversight with two or three of the entrepreneur's peers to monitor his activities and to offer advice on conflict-avoidance.

The policies that MIT enforces on itself to manage conflict include a bar from MIT investing its own funds in the first round of financing of an MIT spin-off company. If we take equity as partial or full payment for a license agreement, that agreement must be approved at the highest level of the Institute. In such cases we will always have a share less than 20% of the company and will avoid participation on the board of directors of the company. We will avoid any favoritism toward the company regarding future inventions and regarding enforcement of milestones in the license.

Our policy fosters the commercialization of MIT technology and takes into account the need to support American industry and commerce. It encourages, I believe, the application and practical use of some of the fruits of federally-sponsored research at MIT, and it contributes to our national competitiveness in global markets. In accordance with law and our own practice, about 95% of our licenses are issued to U.S. companies. And whether our licenses are to either U.S. or foreign companies, we require substantial manufacture in the U.S. for products sold in the U.S.

. . . We believe that our MIT policies and procedures strike an appropriate balance between utilizing the unique American resource of a research institution that fosters practical applications of new technologies, and the need to assure that proper constraints are imposed to avoid the conficts, whether in time, research effort, or finances, that are inherent in the process of technology transfer. . . .

4
Technology Transfer at MIT: A Critical View
David Noble

Good morning, I am David Noble, a professor of history at Drexel University and a founding member of the National Coalition for Universities in the Public Interest. I am grateful for this opportunity to present my views on academic conflict of interest. I have spent nearly two decades examining the social history of science and technology, with a special interest in the evolving relations between the academic world of science and the world of commerce and industry. In the course of writing several books and numerous articles, I came to understand that the close connection between science and industry decisively influences the direction of scientific research and technological development. Given the enormous federal investment in academic science, I am convinced that private influence over publicly created university resources poses a grave danger to the public interest.

Despite the massive public investment in university research, government funded university officials and researchers are functioning as self-interested private agents, with little or no concern for the public interest. In 1982, Vincent Fulmer, then Secretary of the governing board of MIT, wrote to me that "Anyone who believes that (public) support equals proprietary entitlement ought to have recourse to a library. . . . MIT is a privately controlled, privately owned, privately managed institution operating in the public interest." The view that what's good for the university is good for the country—the implicit thesis in Fulmer's remark must now, unfortunately, be challenged.

While university officials and researchers have been entrusted with the disposition of invaluable public resources, they are free to make undisclosed arrangements with private corporations in which they often have equally undisclosed personal roles as owners, investors, consultants, directors, or advisors. They are free to shape and profit from the public investment in research, and many have done so. While university-industry collaboration may be useful, with proper disclosure

Congressional Testimony before the Committee on Government Operations, Subcommittee on Human Resource and Intergovernmental Operations, June 13, 1989.

and procedural safeguards, there is simply too much room for private gain at public expense to permit such arrangements to go unregulated.

The public has had no control over the use and disposition of these resources (though footing the bill), and has simply accepted the assurances of university CEO's that there would be widespread economic benefits from the large public investment in the universities. For example, in the late seventies, as American productivity lagged, many academic leaders lobbied Congress as part of a concerted effort by CEO's of major research universities and multinational corporations. United in a new organization especially created for this purpose, the Business Higher Education Forum, they successfully urged tax breaks for corporate investment in university research, together with outright patent ownership by universities of new inventions financed with federal money. They explicitly asked that multinational corporations be permitted to get exclusive licenses to market products invented with federal funds.

In return for this indirect subsidy, universities promised Congress that they would help America become more "competitive," that jobs would be created, and that our economic ills would disappear. This promise was disingenuous and self-serving.

In 1985, Paul Gray, president of MIT, and an important participant in this persuasive effort, testified before Congress and said that "the most obvious national advantage to the fostering of wider university-industry relations is clearly the quicker and more effective application of the fruits of research to industrial operations. We need to facilitate and accelerate this process. In recent years, the Japanese have not often seized from us positions of scientific leadership, but they have often succeeded in superior implementation. Thus, stronger relationships that bridge between U.S. industry and basic research can be seen as matters of national interest to be encouraged and fostered by Congress."

Gray went on to offer MIT's Industrial Liaison Program as a model for such publicly supported technology transfer. In exchange for a membership fee to the university (currently a maximum of $50,000 per annum), the ILP's member firms gain privileged access to MIT's largely government funded research (half a billion dollars annually). Using the ILP catalogue, member firms get research publications and, much more exciting in this age of high speed technology transfer and competition, *pre-published* materials. They also get on site visits to MIT labs and professors, while faculty and staff are encouraged to visit the plants of member firms. Gray said that members "gain a window through which to view the developments of technological research . . . which assists them in leapfrogging over the technical achievements of their foreign competitors."

What Gray failed to point out to Congress was that nearly all the member corporations of the ILP were multinationals with no necessary allegiance to the United States, that fully half of them were foreign, that 57 of them were major Japanese competitors, and that the ILP had for nearly a decade been operating an overseas sales office in downtown Tokyo.

A clear illustration of the consequences of such service is the current state of the computer electronics industry, a symbol of the multinational high tech economy. Drawing upon publicly-funded research of the postwar period, U.S. firms first developed the semi-conductor, integrated circuit, and microprocessor, and initially dominated the global computer marketplace. In 1985, the Japanese multinational NEC produced not only more microprocessors than any other firm but was also the world's leader in semi-conductor production and runner-up in the production of integrated circuits.

NEC, it turns out, is one of the Japanese members of MIT's Industrial Liaison Program and, as *Business Week* reported recently, "NEC Corporation Chairman Koji Kobayashi credits access to MIT research for much of NEC's success in computers." In 1987 46.6 percent of U.S. patents were issued to foreign companies, with nearly one fifth going to Japanese firms. The top two recipients of U.S. patents were the Japanese firms Canon and Hitachi, both of which are members of MIT's Industrial Liaison Program.

MIT is not alone in this. Many of our research universities are engaged in programs of technology transfer, even smaller "mid-sized" research universities like the Ohio University at Athens and the University of Florida at Gainesville, not to speak of Stanford. All show a similar indifference to the source and purpose of funds granted by Congress. The universities are currently selling publicly funded research generated and paid for by American taxpayers on the explicit assurance to Congress that such research would be of direct benefit to the American economy. By doing so, MIT and the other universities, who have indeed accepted MIT's ILP as their model, are betraying the public trust. In the interest of a short term gain, rather than improving American productivity and "competitiveness," they are subsidizing foreign competition and productivity with taxpayer supported research, and instead of retaining control of inventions crucial to the health of the American economy, they are contributing directly to the alienation of increasing numbers of patents held by foreign corporations who are members of the ILP and similar programs.

Unfortunately, conflicts of interest have grown remarkably in the past decade and have engulfed not only unprecedented numbers of professors, but now extend to the institutions themselves.

Moreover, with the advent of the corporate bottom line rationale as a major goal of universities, its administrators and chief CEO's can be similarly compromised by their own multinational corporate connections. For example, many university presidents sit on corporate boards (often two or three) and receive in compensation for each of these posts as much as one academic salary for a professor.

Such a president may choose to encourage the development of some portions of the university research agenda that benefit companies he directs, and may be forced to raise tuition costs to improve the labs in which corporately sponsored research will take place. The effect is to deny access to the university for those students who cannot pay, while tuition from those who can, is used to make investment in universities more attractive to particular corporations.

Who can say whether there is a real or only a perceived conflict of interest here? Who can judge whether or not the "honoraria" a university president receives from his corporate connections may not have influenced his choices? His priorities, focused by his corporate links, may now entail cutbacks in commercially less promising scientific fields, and in the liberal arts. And as tuition costs continue to escalate, and minorities, the poor, and the otherwise disadvantaged lose any chance of gaining a university education and breaking the cycle of poverty these new priorities will be challenged. Middle class families, too, are feeling the pinch, and many are going deeply in debt simply to maintain what they have achieved through years of hard work. Rutgers, CUNY and other universities have begun to see huge student demonstrations against such increases in tuition and the trend is likely to continue.

Under these circumstances the credibility of the university as a democratic institution, serving the many as well as the few, is bound to be tested. The public is already beginning to wonder about higher tuition rates even as universities are receiving more income from corporations, the federal government and other donors. We predict that the public will soon ask for more accountability from universities, and will soon demand to know whose interests are being served by publicly supported institutions that are so central to democratic values and purposes.

The past decade has witnessed an unprecedented expansion of the university-industry relationship, a relationship which has been applauded and developed with too little attention given to harmful consequences. The great expansion in consulting and other entrepreneurial activities of government-supported academic scientists and administrators, the increasing density of interlocking directorates between academic and industrial organizations, the remarkable growth in taxpayer subsidized university-industrial collaborations, together with the growing public attention to issues of scientific fraud and conflict of interest in the universities, is creating a crisis of public confidence in the impartiality of the universities.

There is a growing cynicism about the disinterested pursuit of knowledge and science which is troubling. Congress must now face the possibility that the objectivity and impartiality of the testimony offered by administrators and faculty on important issues of public policy may also be seriously compromised by these developments.

Many of my concerns are shared by others, including the National Science Foundation which in a 1980 letter to the presidents of grantee institutions encouraging closer university-industry collaboration, warned against potential abuse of the public trust which might result from conflict of interest; the diversion of public resources to private gain, the proprietary restriction on access to research findings, and possible distortion of the research agenda and results. Two years later, the Investigation and Oversight Committee of the House Science and Technology Committee held hearings on the issue of academic conflict of interest and witnesses provided ample evidence of actual and potential abuse and offered recommendations for policies.

Since this first wave of alarms, there has been enough experience to confirm that such concerns were warranted, as the experience with MIT suggests. Given the documented record of university conflicts of interest, it has become clear that universities and academic researchers are neither disposed nor able to police themselves.

Thus, some have already moved beyond speculation and suggestions to actual government oversight and regulation of academic conflict of interest. The experience of California merits special attention. In 1982, the California Fair Political Practices Commission (FPPC) extended its conflict of interest regulations to university personnel. FPPC regulations require, among other things, full disclosure by university decisionmakers, including scientists, of any financial interests they have in private corporations involved in taxpayer supported research projects. In the last half-dozen years, the FPPC has accumulated a mass of data on academic conflict of interest which, I am sure, would lay to rest once and for all simple claims to academic and scientific purity.

Moreover, the FPPC has formulated a uniform code of ethics, and regulatory mechanisms which are useful models for the nation. In light of the California experience, Congress should consider legislation conditioning the receipt of federal research grants by American universities—public and private alike—on the adoption of a code of ethics including full disclosure of potential conflicts of interest on the part of individuals and the institution itself. University personnel who hold decision-making power over the use of public funds are acting in the public trust. Such people should be held accountable to the same ethical standards as, say, members of Congress.

Toward this end, I would recommend that

1. administrators and researchers should be required to disclose individual income and assets, equity ownership, directorships and partnerships in all private corporations involved in publicly supported academic research projects to avoid any suspicion of self-interest in their decision-making. In addition, grantee institutions should disclose any private arrangements with corporations, such as those of MIT's ILP, involving the use and dissemination of taxpayer supported research. These requirements pose no danger to academic freedom, but only to the misuse of academic freedom to conceal private interests. Indeed, with controls upon proprietary tendencies, academic freedom will be enhanced, not diminished.

2. a federal code of ethics regarding academic conflict of interest should be formulated and adopted by grantee institutions. Such a code would bar those with conflicts of interest from participation in decisions regarding the use of public research resources.

3. conflict of interest review committees should be established in all grantee institutions on the model of existing committees on the experimental use of human beings. They should review all grants to insure that they satisfy the disclosure and code of ethics requirements.

4. as a final safeguard of the public interest, the Whistleblower Protection Act just signed should be extended to university personnel who learn about abuses, and try to alert the public and the government about them.

Here it is appropriate to add a personal note. In 1980, I closed an article in the *Nation* magazine entitled "Business Goes Back to College," with a description of the atmosphere of self-censorship and intimidation that was beginning to take hold on the nation's campuses in the wake of commercialization. I could see that my colleagues were learning to keep their mouths shut about the growing number of private deals, both to avoid administrative disfavor and in the hope of getting in on the action themselves. "Meanwhile," I wrote, "administrators intent upon maintaining the lucrative industrial connection, discipline, isolate or eliminate those few who refuse to go along."

I did not know then that four years later I would myself be fired for airing my views on these matters. Convinced that the exercise of my rights as a citizen had cost me my job, I filed suit against MIT on first amendment grounds. Documents and depositions secured during this suit amply demonstrate the pivotal role played by conflicts of interest in my firing.

These documents offer a rare insight into what is now going on in academia, the seamy underside of campus commercialization, and I recommend them to those concerned about academic freedom. Unfortunately, despite my efforts to make them public, MIT has used the courts to deny the information to the press and the Congress, but this Committee can get the documents if it wishes.

The extensive academic freedom litigation experience of the National Coalition for Universities in the Public Interest, meanwhile, attests to the fact that my experience is not unique.

Because of my own personal experience, as well as my work with NCUPI, I repeat for emphasis that it would serve the public interest if the Whistleblower Protection Act, recently signed, could be extended to university personnel who participate in federally funded research. Were I still at MIT, my "blowing the whistle" on the ILP program in testimony here today would cost me my job. The public interest can not tolerate the intimidation of responsible academic citizens any more than it can tolerate the continuation of unregulated academic conflicts of interest. This is an issue whose time has come. It is time not merely to talk about such real and potential abuse of the public trust, but to begin doing something practical about it. Thank you very much.

5
Technology Transfer in Biotech
Howard A. Schneiderman

I am Howard A. Schneiderman, Senior Vice President, Research and Development, at Monsanto Company, which is headquartered in St. Louis, Missouri. . . .

I should like to outline briefly my company's experience with university/industry research partnerships and why I believe they can be useful to companies, to universities and to the larger society.

Our nation's economy is rapidly changing from a resource-intensive economy to a knowledge-intensive economy. In agriculture, for example, the acres one could cultivate were once the dominant economic factor. Today, it is the knowledge-intensive methods used to manage those acres that determines the success of a farmer. Both agriculture and industry are learning how to substitute knowledge for resources. It is largely technological change, *not* access to natural resources that will drive America's and the world's economy in the future.

I am absolutely convinced that America can remain the leading productive economic force on this planet for the rest of this century and the next. But to secure this, this nation must be continuously positioned on the leading edge of technological change so that we can be the low-cost, high-quality producers of generation after generation of innovative and important products. For many industries in this country, the choice is clear: either be innovative or compete with a company in Japan, Korea, France, or elsewhere, which is innovative.

Many informed people believe that technological disadvantage has been a key factor in America's loss of economic competitiveness in industries like steel, automobiles, and much of electronics. Not the only factor, to be sure, but a key factor. There is reason to believe that unless we do something creative quickly this loss of competitiveness may damage other industries as well, such as pharmaceuticals, agriculture, telecommunications, and emerging industries such as those based on biotechnology, information science and new materials.

Congressional Testimony before the Committee on Sciences, Space, and Technology, Subcommittee on Science, Research, and Technology. Field Hearing on University/Industry Alliances, February 8, 1988.

In my brief remarks I will suggest that one way to greatly enhance industrial competitiveness is to couple the talents of America's research-driven industries with those of America's research universities. Each year this nation invests more than $6.5 billions in university research. How can we use more effectively the knowledge base and the skill base created by our research universities to improve the economic competitiveness of the nation's research-driven businesses?

I will draw on the experience of Monsanto Company, but I believe that our experience can be relevant to other companies, both large and small, who are contemplating university-industry ventures. Although my viewpoint is that of someone who is presently in industry, you will have a chance later today to hear the views of some of Monsanto's university partners.

Last year, Monsanto spent about $625M on research and development, of which between 15 and 20 million was spent on university research collaboration. This amounts to about 3 percent of our total R&D budget.

Let me emphasize that I am not talking about philanthropic gifts to universities nor about clinical trials of drugs conducted in research hospitals or field tests of new herbicides conducted in land grant colleges. I am talking about genuine research partnerships aimed at discovery.

Monsanto's largest research partnership is with Washington University Medical School in St. Louis. Washington University scientists work together with Monsanto scientists to discover new facts of nature such as what causes abnormal heart beats, as well as to discover new biologically-active molecules such as a small protein produced by the human heart that regulates blood pressure.

This joint research is *discovery research,* the kind of research that is appropriate to universities. It is not *drug development* research, the kind of research that is done in industry and is *not* appropriate for universities. Monsanto's partnerships with universities are in the area of discovery, some times very long-term discovery. Nothing that we do with Washington University or with our other university partners encourages the universities to pursue to short-term utilitarian goals. We see the university as a great source of discovery, and we see our company as a full partner in discovery. We are able to bring new skills, new ideas, whole new technologies to the research programs we conduct together. Indeed, the money Monsanto provides to Washington University Medical School is far less significant than the scientific insights and skills that our scientists contribute to solving major problems of medicine.

Beyond this, Monsanto develops these discoveries into new products that benefit people, new products that preserve and create jobs for our employees and strengthen this nation's economy, new products whose commercial success encourages pension funds and individual investors to invest in us.

But be assured that everyone in Monsanto and everyone in Washington University Medical School involved in our joint program knows that the missions of research universities and of companies are different: the objective of a research university is to teach and to advance knowledge; the objectives of a company is to advance knowledge *and* to use the knowledge gained to develop useful and profitable new products.

The joint discovery program between Monsanto and Washington University Medical School has had wonderful consequences for both institutions. Today hundreds of Monsanto scientists are part of a powerful team that includes about 120 Washington University scientists. Together we are able to solve some enormously difficult but important scientific problems that Monsanto can develop into new therapies for major diseases. We are convinced that our research collaboration with Washington University accelerates the rate at which our biomedical discoveries are translated or developed into new pharmaceutical products that benefit people. It is important to emphasize that the university is *not* in the pharmaceutical business. It remains in the knowledge business. The actual conversion of our joint research into new drugs that help people, the actual *development* of a new drug for hypertension, leukemia, osteoporosis, Alzheimer's disease or psoriasis is done by Monsanto. Today five new therapeutic products based on the Washington University/Monsanto research are being developed by G. D. Searle, Monsanto's pharmaceutical subsidiary.

Since Monsanto began the program with Washington University in 1982, more than 50 patents have been granted or applied for, largely for new drugs based on our joint research. Who owns the patents on those new discoveries? Let's answer that question and a number of other questions which loomed large at the outset of our joint research ventures with universities but turned out to be of no practical consequence.

In the case of patents, the university owns the patents. Monsanto has the exclusive right to license any patents that may come from the research and we provide the support needed for the university to obtain patents. The university can expect conventional royalties from a patentable discovery when the product based on that discovery is commercialized.

Do we delay publication and prevent the diffusion of knowledge? We have asked for 30 days to review papers for patentability before publication. This has proven satisfactory for more than 100 papers, no delays, no problems, no being "scooped" by a competitor. Knowledge has been advanced and made available.

Do we "direct" the university's research. As a former dean, I can attest that no one tells a professor in an American university what to do.

What about the fear that a contract between a company and a university will encourage the university to pursue excessively utilitarian goals and to neglect the long-term fundamental questions upon which the advance of science depends? This simply hasn't happened in any of the more than 50 research projects Monsanto has underway with universities. Indeed, Monsanto support has often encouraged university scientists to attack extremely difficult problems of long-term duration which do not produce immediately publishable results and which were much less likely to be supported by a traditional federal grant mechanism.

What about the fear of the loss of confidentiality? When Monsanto shares private research information with an academic colleague, we expect him or her to keep the information private. When an academic colleague shares a private research result with us, we keep the information private. Our behavior in this regard is precisely what one would expect of research scientists in universities who share confidential information with each other.

What special advantages are there to the university from university/industry research collaborations? For the universities there are a variety of advantages. For example, industry places a higher premium on progress and results than on process and paper work. Industrial grants tend to be simpler to apply for and are often awarded in a month or two rather than the 9 plus months required for most government grants. Universities can gain important insights from companies into the relevance and applicability of a particular piece of research.

But the most important advantage to the university is partnership with an exciting group of industrial research scientists, with complementary skills, new viewpoints, fresh ideas, urgency and results orientation. Industrial partners can help university scientists win their races for discovery and advance knowledge.

For both universities and industry there are some common advantages. For example, research partnerships between university and industry can accelerate research in both institutions. Some important questions require large research groups and enormous outlays for equipment that are often far beyond the resources of a single laboratory or department and often exceed a given industrial or academic institution. A joint university-industry research program in plant molecular biology, with 60 scientists with diverse skills drawn from both the industrial and the university community, is far more likely to tease secrets from protoplasts, chloroplasts and plant chromosomes than are several mini-teams.

Also, research is increasingly expensive: big science is certainly not restricted to high energy physics. Institutional competitiveness has given way to regional competitiveness. University-industry partnerships not only enhance the research competitiveness of the individual scientists and the institutions involved, but may also enhance the technological and economic competitiveness of the regions in which they are embedded. . . .

One of the issues upon which this Subcommittee has focused concerns foreign companies. Since university-industry partnerships can provide real economic advantage for the companies involved and for our nation, should government or universities seek to limit the involvement of foreign companies with university research? I believe that in most cases it would be a mistake to limit their involvement. Consider the following: Monsanto Company's second largest partnership in university research is with Oxford University in the United Kingdom where we support a major research program on the chemistry and biology of the sugars that decorate many important proteins in the human body. Why Oxford University? Because it is the leading center in the world for that special kind of research. Access to Oxford University technology will accelerate rapidly Monsanto's ability to introduce new drugs for presently untreatable diseases. It would be a great blow to both human medicine and to Monsanto if Monsanto scientists were prevented from collaborating with their British colleagues. It seems to me that fairness requires that if British companies like ICI or Glaxo decided to conduct joint research with a university in the United States, we should not hinder their programs.

In the case of Japan, it depends on whether American scientists can have ready access to the major research and engineering laboratories in Japan. Manufacturing technology is Japan's strong suit and one of the keys to Japan's economic competitiveness. If the Japanese will allow American engineers to collaborate with Japanese engineers in Japan at their great engineering research centers to design and improve manufacturing technology, and will allow American scientists and engineers to collaborate with their counterparts in Japan in designing new gene sequencers and other new instruments for biotechnology and will welcome American scientists into their world-famous ceramics research laboratories, then I have no problem with Japanese scientists and Japanese companies gaining access to America's strong suit, basic research and discovery. However, it should be a two-way street. More than 300 Japanese scientists conduct research at NIH in Bethesda, Maryland. I wonder how easy it is for American engineers to spend two years in manufacturing technology research centers and ceramic technology research centers in Japan.

. . . I do not believe we should limit the involvement of foreign companies with American research universities. But we should insist on equal access for America's scientists, engineers and companies to the best research and engineering centers of other countries.

To conclude, if the United States is to remain the leading economic power in the world, it must consciously position itself on the leading edge of technological and industrial change. These technological changes are occurring in the pharmaceutical, agricultural, telecommunications and micro-electronics industries, production of new materials, industrial control systems and also in many of our mature manufacturing industries. I see opportunities for hybrid technological vigor and exciting intellectual advance as the result of thoughtfully selected joint research programs between industries and universities. It is a way to "rustproof" America. I see whole new industries and new jobs emerging. In my view, university-industry partnerships are a vital national necessity. . . .

6
The Erosion of the Academic Ethos:
The Case of Biology
Nicholas Wade

The biological revolution has been slow to gather momentum. Though now firmly under way, it has taken an unexpected and troubling turning. The first efforts to commercialize the new technology have drawn so heavily on the research universities and their scientists that the line between campus and marketplace has become blurred; a substantial number—some say almost all—of the leading researchers responsible for creating the new knowledge are also involved in commercial attempts to apply it. The scientist's primary goal, the disinterested pursuit of truth, has become encumbered by other motives.

This novel situation presents potential risks to science, to universities, and to the public. For science, the dangers are that the direction of academic research will be diverted toward short-term applied objectives and that the traditionally open character of scientific inquiry will become veiled in secrecy. For the universities, the new links with industry may weaken their central role of creating and conserving knowledge, and alter the outside world's perception of their credibility and independence. For the public, the most serious threat is the loss of impartial and farsighted advice as the new technology probes the biological basis of life and creates new tools for the mastery of nature.

Innovation is essential to a healthy economy. The transfer of technology from universities to the marketplace is an undoubted social benefit, and, in the case of molecular biology, industry is so keenly aware of its potential that there is no danger of the transfer failing to occur. But the transfer of technology should be accomplished without harming the university.

That the commercialization of molecular biology presents scientists with conflicts of interest does not necessarily mean that harm will result. Many will be capable of handling such conflicts so that their

From *The Science Business: Report of the Twentieth Century Fund Task Force on the Commercialization of Scientific Research*, Priority Press, 1984. Reprinted by permission of the Twentieth Century Fund.

academic research is not impaired by their commercial interests. But potential conflicts of interest have become so widespread in molecular biology that without routine oversight there is a distinct possibility that some of these potential conflicts will become real. Academic biologists may gradually invest increasing amounts of their intellectual energy in profit-making ventures; university departments dependent on corporate funds may find the nature of their research shifting from pure to applied projects, with a consequent decline in equality.

Some observers assert that the situation will resolve itself spontaneously in a few years when the pure and applied aspects of molecular biology grow further apart. They argue that the commercialization of molecular biology is no different from what has occurred in other academic disciplines such as chemistry or engineering. Unfortunately, there is reason to doubt these sanguine appraisals. . . .

Biology: A Special Case

Universities have had close ties with industry in the past, and consulting is nothing new to academic electrical engineers or organic chemists. But for several reasons the commercialization of molecular biology is a unique case. First, the scale of the enterprise is unprecedented: never has a whole discipline, or at least the vast majority of its leading practitioners, become involved in commercial ties. Second, the separation that usually exists between the making of a discovery and its reduction to a salable commodity is almost completely absent in molecular biology. The traditional pattern of innovation has two distinct phases: one theoretical, in which pure research is conducted with public funds in the open manner of academic science; the other applied, in which a company works on the invention in its own laboratories, protecting its investment as trade secrets or with patents. The two phases are usually kept distinct by institutional barriers and by the length of time, often up to twenty years, that it may take for an idea to become a product. In molecular biology, however, an idea can have value from the instant it is validated in the research laboratory; biologists are filing for patents even before publishing their experiments in the scientific literature. A third reason for the unaccustomed speed of commercialization in molecular biology is that to some extent off-the-shelf equipment can be used. In other high-technology fields, many years must often be spent to develop equipment for even pilot operations. And finally, the commercialization of molecular biology is unique in its range of applications. Its impact seems likely to be felt in the pharmaceutical and health care industries, in agriculture, in mining, and in certain aspects of the chemical industry such as waste management.

Some contend that industry's dependence on university research is a temporary phase that will end as soon as companies have developed their own in-house expertise and the basic techniques have become commonplace. One exponent of this view is Walter Gilbert, an academic biologist who recently left Harvard to become chief executive officer of Biogen, Genentech's leading competitor. "In the short term there are stresses. We will go through these growing pains for five years or so, after which the pure and applied aspects of the field will be further apart," he states.[1] But predicting how a technology will develop, let alone its exact development timetable, is hazardous. No doubt certain aspects of biotechnology, such as the recipes for inserting useful genes into bacteria or yeast, will eventually become established techniques that can be handled in industrial laboratories. But the spate of findings from academic biology laboratories is only just beginning. It is hard to see how industry can relinquish its close association with universities if it wishes to remain abreast of this continuing stream of discovery. This is evidently the belief of companies like Hoechst and Monsanto, which have established long-term agreements with academic departments.

The commercialization of molecular biology is unique because of the nature of its subject matter. The new tools may well suffice to dissect the living cell into its finest components. It is already possible to state precisely the chemical composition of certain viruses, the simplest forms of life. It is probably only a matter of time before the material basis of human existence is understood to an almost equally thorough degree. The new knowledge will assuredly present extraordinary opportunities for manipulating both man and nature. Society will need as never before to rely on the advance of independent experts if it is to make informed decisions. Should inheritable alterations in the human gene set be permitted? If such alterations are allowed for the repair of genes that cause hereditary disease, should they also be permitted in order to enhance normal qualities, such as health, longevity, beauty, and intelligence? If genetically engineered crop plants are allowed into the environment, what guarantees should be sought to ensure that they will not become pests like the gypsy moth or water hyacinth? Should the enhancement of the intelligence of animals be permitted?

Even to frame such questions is to make fallible assumptions as to how the technology will develop. All that is certain is that no limits to the powers of the new techniques can yet be discerned. They appear to offer a general method for shaping and reworking the biological material of the planet, for shuffling genes from one species to another, and eventually for designing new genes. Maybe some vitalist force will emerge to emancipate living things from the laws of physics and chemistry, but there is no sign of it yet. The new tools will probably enable biologists to understand completely any biological machinery of interest, and within wide limits to change it.

No one can deny that molecular biology represents a special kind of knowledge. That is why its commercialization gives special cause for concern. . . .

The commercialization of biotechnology has already affected academic science. There has been an abrupt shift in the attitude of researchers, from open disdain for commercial involvement to implicit acceptance of it. This transformation of opinion has been accompanied by subtle changes in the morale of academic scientists and their standards of collegial behavior. Such changes have alarming implications for science, for if the academic ethos is seriously attenuated, universities may ultimately be unable to resist the diversion of pure research to industrial goals.

The threat to academic values that has materialized over the last several years has been little remarked, perhaps in part because molecular biologists have been reluctant to admit that there are differences between academic and industrial science. A scientist may work on a single research problem in both campus and company labs, and may assume that science is science whatever its venue, but in fact academic and industrial science differ significantly in their methodology.

According to the logical empiricist school of philosophy, science differs from other systems of knowledge in that its results are verifiable. This critical feature is a product of the communal nature of academic science: a scientific fact draws its legitimacy not merely from its discoverer's assertion that it is true but also from its verification by the community of specialists in the field.

The verification process incorporates three kinds of checks, the first of which is peer review. Applications for funding, usually to federal agencies, are carefully assessed and rated by impartial specialists in the field, who recommend only the most highly regarded applications for funding. A second check occurs after experiments have been completed and their results readied for publication; the scientific journals to which articles are submitted send them out to expert referees who assess their methodology and theoretical rigor. Failing this test, an essay is rejected or returned to its author for improvement. Finally, experimental results are checked for replicability. Any experiment described in the scientific literature must be presented in enough detail to permit other scientists to duplicate its results. Exact replication is rare in science, but it remains a cardinal principle of scientific reporting that replication must be possible.

It has been argued that these checks are not as effective as they might appear, since they frequently fail to flush out instances of scientific fraud,[2] but the fact remains that this is how quality control in science is achieved, however imperfectly. These dry procedures lie at the heart of academic science. They are less important in industrial science, except insofar as industrial scientists may choose to publish papers in academic journals to gain academic credentials. Industrial science typically rests on secrecy; it has little need for the verification process. The industrial scientist need not face the hurdle of peer review, since he is supported by his company, and rather than publish his discoveries, he seeks either to patent them or to keep them as trade secrets. The validation of industrial research is not intellectual collaboration but a product that succeeds in the marketplace.

While the industrial way of doing science is appropriate for its purpose, it is inappropriate in the academic setting. Yet it threatens to obstruct the methodology of pure research in several ways. First, the work of university biologists who receive funds from private companies (or share in corporate funds given to their departments) does not undergo peer review. Some industry-university contracts specify the supervision of projects by administrative committees, but these have little in common with peer review boards except in name.

Second, universities and biologists with industry ties commonly insist that freedom of publication is guaranteed in contracts with their industrial sponsor. But freedoms are not always exercised. A scientist might decide, or be persuaded, to keep his findings secret. Corporations that have gained the right of prior review of academic scientists' work are particularly well placed to induce such restraint should they perceive that a trade secret would be more advantageous than a patent. There is no sign that this has happened, but it is difficult to see what mechanisms would bring it to light if it did.

A more direct threat to the validation procedure of academic science is the tendency of some researchers to withhold certain details in the publication of experiments. Since these are often subtle points of technique, their absence is hard for journal referees to spot, yet without them, the work cannot be repeated. "People aren't putting all the information necessary for the science in the papers, and the reviewers aren't picking it up," comments Sidney Pestka of the Roche Institute of Molecular Biology.[3] Similar obstacles were reported to a congressional committee in June 1981 by Stanford President Donald Kennedy:

> There are at least three or four incidents during this past year in which at scientific meetings—at which the traditional valuation of basic research had always been expected to prevail—there were communications in which a scientist actually refused on questioning to divulge some detail of technique, claiming that, in fact, it was a proprietary matter and that he was not free to communicate it.
>
> If you are not free to communicate it, then somebody else can't repeat your experiment, and whatever enterprise you are involved in it is not the one that traditionally moves science forward.[4]

The Social Ethos of Science

Another fundamental difference between academic and industrial science lies in their different sustaining values. In his well-known 1942 essay, sociologist Robert Merton described modern science as being characterized by four institutional imperatives: universalism, "communism," disinterestedness, and organized skepticism.[5] Universalism is the principle of accepting or rejecting ideas on their merits, regardless of their author's standing. Communism, in Merton's sense, implies that all intellectual property is held in common: "Property rights in science are whittled down to a bare minimum. . . . The scientist's claim to 'his' intellectual 'property' is limited to that of recognition and esteem." Disinterestedness, the eschewal of personal gain in professional activity, is enforced by peer expectations. Finally, because of its bent for questioning everything (including the beliefs held by other social institutions), science institutionalizes doubt, a phenomenon that Merton refers to as organized skepticism.

Merton's four norms are ideals rather than descriptions of actual scientific practice. Nonetheless, they accurately describe the ways in which scientists believe it is appropriate for members of their community to behave, and they are almost universally accepted by sociologists and scientists who take an interest in such matters. The fact that the four norms are often breached does not diminish either their importance as guidelines or the seriousness of the threat of their erosion by the commercialization of molecular biology.

Academic scientists quite regularly depart from the norms of universalism, communism, and disinterestedness—usually in the pursuit of personal recognition. Vigorously asserting one's claim to a discovery, even at the expense of others' legitimate claims, is surely not disinterested, and may not even be justified, but it is probably not in itself a serious threat to the purity or progress of science. Indeed, such behavior is part of the competitive attitude that characterizes many of the fastest-moving arenas of scientific inquiry. And the intensity of glory-seeking is sometimes moderated by the need to observe at least the appearance of Mertonian norms; thus *The Double Helix,* James Watson's account of the competition to discover the structure of DNA, occasioned a major stir within the scientific community not so much because it described unusual behavior but because it publicly acknowledged motives that scientists usually reserve for private confessions.

Commercialization imposes constraints on scientific behavior quite different from those engendered by the pursuit of fame. Seeking recognition is for the most part a spur, not a deterrent, to the pursuit of pure knowledge; the profit motive, on the other hand, may induce a scientist to change his research goals or at least to divide his attention between pure and commercially relevant research. Secrecy was not of course unknown in science before the advent of business opportunities, but academic secrecy is quite different from commercial secrecy. The academic scientist traditionally keeps a finding or technique secret only for as long as it takes to prepare it for publication; even in the least competitive fields, a substantial delay increases his risk of being scooped. A trade secret, on the other hand, typically remains undisclosed for as long as its proprietor deems this to be in his commercial interest. Academic secrecy is a short-term expedient instituted to ensure first publication, but commercial secrecy is long-term. There are of course exceptions; academics can sometimes be inordinately secretive, and industrial scientists can sometimes discover what their colleagues are working on. But despite some degree of overlap, the academic and industrial milieus are essentially different, since they are designed to serve very different objectives.

The Scientist's View of Patents

The adjustment of academic biology to the demands of industrial science has occurred over a period of only about five years. When Stanley Cohen and Herbert Boyer invented the gene-splicing technique in 1973, they had no thought of patenting it; Cohen even resisted the suggestion of the Stanford University patent officer to do so. One reason was the prevalent notion that in science intellectual property should be held in common. "My initial reaction . . . was to question whether basic research of this type could or should be patented and to point out that our work had been dependent on a number of earlier discoveries by others," Cohen explains.[6] Since the cumulative nature of scientific knowledge means that even the most outstanding discovery is heavily dependent on the work of others, to patent a discovery would be to lay claim to the freely given intellectual property of others. Academic scientists thus have a strong bias against applying for patents on their work.

Finally persuaded that a patent would be to their universities' benefit, Cohen and Boyer agreed to let their institutions apply for one, but stipulated that they not receive the inventor's share of any royalties. Cohen assigned his share to a fund for supporting postdoctoral researchers. Boyer also assigned his share to his university. Some outsiders might view this renunciation of royalties as altruistic, others as useless self-denial. But to the community of which Cohen and Boyer were a part it was normal, almost instinctive, behavior.

Half a world away, but following the same ethos, the inventors of the other great biological technique of the 1970s proceeded in a similar manner. Cesar Milstein did apparently ask British government authorities whether the hybridoma technique should be patented, but received no encouragement. "We were too green and inexperienced on the matter of patents," Milstein now says. The policy of the Medical Research Council, his sponsor, was to make new methods freely available. "We were influenced by that psychology. We were mainly concerned with the scientific aspects and not giving particular thought to the commercial applications."[7]

This attitude, justified or not, was prevalent among molecular biologists in the mid-1970s. The subsequent reshaping of the scientific ethos under the pressures of commercialization was revealed in several incidents that, although minor in themselves, suggest the possibility of a community beginning to drift from its sustaining values.

Breaking the Rules in the Insulin Race

One of the earliest practical projects made possible by gene splicing was the programming of bacteria to synthesize insulin. A team at Harvard, the young biotechnology company Genentech, and researchers at the Department of Biochemistry and Biophysics at the University of California at San Francisco (UCSF) all set out to isolate the insulin gene in rats, with the UCSF team establishing a nonprofit corporation known as the California Institute for Genetic Research. It happened that Genentech's Herbert Boyer was associated with another laboratory in the same department at UCSF. With commercial pressures added to the normal desire to publish first, the secrecy maintained by the UCSF team grew to conspicuous levels. "People would stop talking when you came into the room, or change the subject if you tried to make conversation about how the insulin project was going," noted a member of the department.[8]

The commercial potential of the research caused considerable divisiveness. "Capitalism sticking its nose into the lab has tainted interpersonal relations. There are a number of people who feel rather strongly that there should be no commercialization of human insulin," one scientist remarked. Relations were not improved when the UCSF insulin team held a press conference in May 1977 to announce their success; their departmental colleagues resented the fact that they too were hearing the news for the first time.

Colleagues' feelings were not the only casualty of the rush to success. It later emerged that the successful team had been in such a hurry that they had breached government safety rules on gene splicing by using certain biological material before it had been certified as safe. Moreover, misleading entries were made in the laboratory logbook to conceal this fact. When the incident was reported to the departmental committee charged with overseeing recombinant DNA safety procedures, the ensuing investigation failed to bring to light any facts in the case except those critical of the National Institutes of Health (NIH), the agency that had instituted the guidelines.

Press Conference Science

Academic scientists were at the time engaged in a vigorous lobbying effort to dissuade Congress from passing legislation enforcing the NIH safety rules. The breach of the rules at UCSF, although minor, threatened to hinder these efforts. When a Senate subcommittee held a hearing on the incident, scientific leaders sought to counter its adverse effect by announcing a new scientific breakthrough based on gene splicing: the cloning of the gene for the hormone somatostatin. Philip Handler, then president of the National Academy of Sciences, informed the senators that the achievement was a "scientific triumph of the first order."[9] Paul Berg, a Stanford biochemist who had helped organize the Asilomar conference, called the advance "astonishing."[10] But the experiment in question was at best an interesting minor extension of the gene-splicing technique, for no major therapeutic role for somatostatin had yet been found.

Besides the hyperbole, another departure from the scientific ethos was the fact that at the time of its announcement the experiment had not been published. Because other scientists cannot comment on the validity of unpublished claims, pre-publication announcements are traditionally frowned upon as an illegitimate means of manipulating the press. More seriously, unpublished manuscripts have not been subject to review by journal referees. Since such checking procedures are part of the organized skepticism separating scientific claims from mere personal assertions, most academic scientists observe the convention that experiments not be described at press conferences or other public forums until published in the scientific literature. That the rule may be breached from time to time does not alter its importance.

To mold congressional opinion, Handler and Berg were prepared to flout this strict convention. The incident was perhaps insignificant in itself, but where the leaders of the scientific community had led, others followed. Press conference science became almost routine, as scientists attempted to stimulate interest in companies with which they were affiliated. Although acting as businessmen, researchers sought enhanced credibility for their announcements by presenting themselves to the press as academic scientists. Typically the experiments announced at these events had not been published, and the claims asserted were overblown.

Thus scientists from the City of Hope National Medical Center in Los Angeles and from Genetech held a press conference on September 6, 1978, to announce the cloning of human insulin. Because of hopes that human insulin would prove better for diabetics than the pork or cattle insulin in current use, the declaration made front-page news. Congressman Paul Rogers, a leading health legislator, hailed the achievement as "one further example of the pioneering research typical of American science." But when details of the experiment were published three months later, it emerged that the newly cloned human insulin had no biological activity. "Buried in the news accounts," notes Spyros Andreopoulos in a caustic review of the event, "was a clue to the significance of this news event. Eli Lilly and Company had entered into an agreement with Genetech for eventual commercial application."[11]

On a single day in July 1980, rival scientists from both Genetech and the University of California at San Francisco sent out press releases claiming priority for synthesizing human growth hormone in bacteria. When the work was published in the scientific literature several months later, neither group was able to show that its product was biologically active. The race between the two teams had been made even fiercer by the defection to Genetech of a key UCSF scientist, Peter Seeburg. Seeburg had started work on the project when his UCSF laboratory chiefs were traveling. "When they came back," Seeburg claims, "we told them what we had done and the next thing we knew they had drafted a patent without even including my name. This clinched it. I felt exploited so much I couldn't work there anymore."[12] Seeburg moved to Genetech, taking samples of all his growth hormone project materials with him. As in other laboratories, commercial incentives had engendered ill will that exacerbated the already fierce spirit of scientific competition.

The acme of press conference science was reached on January 16, 1980. A large crowd of reporters was summoned to the Boston Park Plaza Hotel by cables promising that Walter Gilbert, chairman of the scientific board of Biogen, would make "a major announcement . . . concerning molecular biology." Gilbert, a Nobel Prize winner and a leading biologist at Harvard, handed out copies of an unpublished paper co-authored with Charles Weissmann, a prominent Swiss biologist and fellow board member of Biogen, announcing the cloning of interferon. This natural antiviral substance, which one day may prove effective against viral diseases and possibly cancer, was touted by Gilbert and Weissmann as "a protein of dramatic medical interest." According to the *New York Times,* the pair "said they believed the research group was the first to get the gene for interferon into bacteria," and they remarked, "All of us regard it as a very significant advance."[13] "This is a tour de force, a demonstration of the power of the technique," Weissmann asserted.[14]

What neither chose to mention was that the same feat had already been accomplished and published by a Japanese research team.[15] Nor was it in any way a "significant advance" or "tour de force" in molecular biology, but merely the first of the many steps required to obtain efficient commercial production of interferon. Biogen's announcement, commented one of Wall Street's few knowledgeable analysts at the time, "should not be interpreted to mean that [the company] has any significant advantage in either technology or patent protection."[16]

Gilbert and Weissmann's announcement caused the stock of Schering-Plough, owner of 16 percent of Biogen and the rights to its interferon process, to rise by eight points, temporarily adding some $425 million to the company's value. But the real purpose of the press conference was to enhance Biogen's public image in preparation for an eventual public offering of its stock. According to the company's president, Robert Cawthorn, "the intent was to draw attention to Biogen. The day may come when we want to go public; so it is better that the public knows something about Biogen." The company's paper value, previously $50 million, rose to $100 million. . . .

Commercial Interests versus the Disinterested Pursuit of Truth

The incidents described above represent a marked change in the atmosphere surrounding academic science. Though few in number, their significance is as examples of behavior that is now apparently tolerated by the academic community. Only a few years ago an affront to the unwritten rules of the academic ethos would have received quick rebuke. Things are now very different. Researchers withhold information, a practice that undermines the principle of experimental replicability. They bend the gentleman's rules governing the use of the ideas and materials of others, thereby stifling open communication among researchers. The hallmark of pure research has always been the *disinterested* pursuit of knowledge, yet many academic biologists now have sizable commercial interests. . . .

The contracts made between universities and industries have been exhaustively analyzed for their likely effect on academic departments of molecular biology. The details of these contracts discussed below are significant, but what will determine whether they are upheld or not are the actual patterns of behavior among scientists. If the academic ethos remains robust, no amount of financial enticement will divert university scientists from their primary goals. If that ethos is abandoned, written contracts will not save university departments from becoming mere appendages to industrial laboratories. . . .

Preserving Academic Values

The commercialization of molecular biology need not necessarily lead to disaster, but the possibility of damage to scientific research, to universities, and to the public interest is certainly present. Steps to safeguard against such dangers are primarily the responsibility of universities, but the academic scientific community and government must also play a part.

For universities, the following actions might be considered:

• *Faculty members should be required to make full public disclosure of all commercial activities and interests relevant to their own research.* Without such an inventory, it is impossible to assess the extent of the problem or to keep track of its development. The findings of the California Fair Political Practices Commission suggest that potential conflicts of interest have already become sufficiently frequent to require monitoring. Unless a university insists on disclosure, faculty members may lack the objectivity to impose it on themselves. Yale's requirement of full disclosure should be widely copied.

• *When necessary, universities should take more assertive action to control faculty members' traditionally unregulated outside activities.* MIT's rule that no professor may hold an executive position in a company is a measure other universities should consider adopting. Another is Harvard's position that it will not grant exclusive licenses to any firm in which a Harvard researcher has a financial interest. To prevent all outside money-making activities by faculty would be excessively punitive, and on balance harmful. But universities need to intervene in situations where commercial temptations are so powerful that a scientist may neglect or divert his academic research. Some researchers might be lost to industry under such restrictions, but their numbers will probably be far fewer than those who threaten to leave.

• *No university, in its direct dealings with corporations, should allow a company to gain a position from which it may influence the course of the university's research,* although it may permit firms to take fair advantage of academic research. The danger is particularly acute when a corporation is the sole or even a major source of a department's funds. Universities should consider refusing to accept single-source funding for a department, or limiting contributions to some fraction, say, 20 percent, of a department's budget. They should in any case conduct independent reviews of corporate-sponsored research, to make sure that such research is not being diverted to applied goals and that quality is not deteriorating.

• *Universities should avoid making concessions to corporations that they would not readily grant to other parties, such as government.*

Giving outsiders a voice in faculty appointments and allowing corporations prior review of manuscripts are privileges that if extended to government would represent a severe erosion of university autonomy. If a corporation is allowed prior review of manuscripts, a university representative should see the manuscripts, too, and verify that all are published without change after a mutually acceptable waiting period.

For academic scientists, the following actions may be necessary:

• *Faculty members should support university initiatives to control commercialization,* for without faculty support the formal steps taken by universities are unlikely to be successful. In particular, faculty should press for full disclosure of outside commercial activities, which is the first step in ascertaining the dimensions of whatever problem may exist.

• *Researchers should fully endorse the academic ethos.* Those who breach the informal rules regarding the exchange of data or materials should be made to pay some price, even if it is only the disapproval of their peers, lest the ethos of disinterested research suffer a largescale breakdown.

For government, these specific roles are suggested:

• *Washington should ensure that the public's long-term investment in molecular biology is not turned to unfair private advantage.* The General Accounting Office's review of the MGH-Hoechst contract is an example of this kind of scrutiny.

• *Congressional oversight to ensure that the academic community follows its own best interests should be close and continuous.* Only if the academic community fails to cope with the issues surrounding academic research should government consider intervention, since any government-prescribed cure is likely to be worse than the malady.

The Uniqueness of Discovery

The new techniques of molecular biology have initiated an explosive new phase of scientific discovery. Whatever practical benefits may ensue, and there will doubtless be many, these developments will bring science to the threshold of a long-sought if often implicit goal: the complete understanding of Man as a physiochemical system. That journey of discovery can be made only once. It would be better undertaken by people whose only dedication is to the pursuit of pure knowledge, and who can offer detached advice about its consequences. The journey's course should not be set from the very start by those with short-term, private interests. Rather than risk contamination of science's most important endeavor, it would be better to ensure that those who resolve the ultimate mysteries of life have the disinterested quest for knowledge as their only guide.

Notes

1. Nicholas Wade, "Cloning Goldrush Makes Basic Biology Big Business," *Science,* May 16, 1980, p. 688.
2. William Broad and Nicholas Wade, *Betrayers of the Truth* (New York: Simon & Schuster, 1983).
3. Hal Lancaster, "Profits in Gene Splicing Bring the Tangled Issue of Ownership to the Fore," *Wall Street Journal,* December 3, 1980.
4. U.S. Congress, House Committee on Science and Technology, Subcommittee on Investigations and Oversight and Subcommittee on Science, Research, and Technology, *Commercialization of Academic Biomedical Research,* 97th Cong., 1st sess., June 8 and 9, 1981 (Washington, D.C.: U.S. Government Printing Office, 1981), p. 8.
5. Robert K. Merton, "The Normative Structure of Science," in *The Sociology of Science* (Chicago: University of Chicago Press, 1973), pp. 267–78.
6. Stanley N. Cohen, "The Stanford DNA Cloning Patent," in *From Genetic Engineering to Biotechnology—The Critical Transition,* ed. W. J. Whelan and Sandra Black (New York: John Wiley, 1982), pp. 213–16.
7. Nicholas Wade, "Inventor Omits to File for Patent," *Science,* May 16, 1980, p. 693.
8. Nicholas Wade, "Recombinant DNA: NIH Rules Broken in Insulin Gene Project," *Science,* September 30, 1977, pp. 1342–45.
9. U.S. Congress, Senate Committee on Commerce, Science, and Transportation, Subcommittee on Science, Technology, and Space, *Hearings on the Regulation of Recombinant DNA,* 95th Cong., 1st sess., November 2, 8, and 10, 1977 (Washington, D.C.: U.S. Government Printing Office, 1978), p. 13.
10. Ibid., p. 36.
11. Spyros Andreopoulos, "Gene Cloning by Press Conference," *New England Journal of Medicine* 302 (1980), pp. 743–46.
12. William Stockton, "On the Brink of Altering Life," *New York Times Magazine,* February 17, 1980, p. 19.
13. Harold M. Schmeck, "Natural Virus-Fighting Substance Is Reported Made by Gene-Splicing," *New York Times,* January 17, 1980.

14. Julie Miller, "Interferon: Gene-Splicing Triumph," *Science News* 117 (1980), p. 52.

15. T. Taniguchi et al., "Construction and Identification of a Bacterial Plasmid Containing the Human Fibroblast Interferon Gene Sequence," Proceedings of the Japanese Academy, 55, Series B (1979), pp. 464–69.

16. Nicholas Wade, "Cloning Goldrush Makes Basic Biology Big Business," *Science,* May 16, 1980, p. 688.

SECTION TWO

Historical Documents

1
Pajaro Dunes Conference—
Draft Statement

Preamble

Research of the past several decades, through enlightened public support, has profoundly advanced the understanding of life processes. A new biotechnology of extraordinary promise has emerged. While much of great importance remains to be learned at the most fundamental level about living organisms, applications of present knowledge can be foreseen that are likely to be of far-reaching benefit to people everywhere. These useful applications may well improve health, enhance food and energy supplies, improve the quality of the environment, and reduce the cost of many industrial processes and products.

With such beneficial possibilities at least dimly foreseeable, it becomes a matter of urgent concern to take constructive steps toward their fulfillment. Most of the basic research which made these applications possible has been done in universities in the United States, mainly with federal government funding. The development of these findings

From a Biotechnology Conference held at Pajaro Dunes, California, March 25–27, 1982. The presidents of Stanford University, the California Institute of Technology, the University of California, Harvard University, and Massachusetts Institute of Technology convened the meeting. The 35 invited participants included university presidents, administrators, faculty scientists, and industry representatives. Permission to publish granted by Robert M. Rosenzweig, Vice President for Public Affairs, Stanford University.

Published in *Journal of College and University Law*, 1982–3.

into useful processes and products is already vigorously underway in American industry. The chain of progress from basic research to useful applications necessarily involves universities and industry. For the promise to be fulfilled, all links in the chain must be strong.

The translation from opportunity to reality is not simple or easy. Serious problems are involved. These problems center on the preservation of the independence and integrity of the university and its faculty, both faced with unprecedented financial pressures and complex commercial relationships. Universities are a repository of public trust, and, in many cases, of public funds as well, and they have an obligation to the public as well as to their students and faculty to ensure that they remain devoted to their primary goals of education and research, and that their resources be properly used in their pursuit of these goals.

Therefore, leaders from five of the universities that have engaged heavily over many years in research in the life sciences met to explore problems and clarify the considerations essential to wise policy-making in this area. Each university invited members of its own faculty and people from the business community to attend as discussants and resources. These considerations must be viewed from the perspective of individual scientists, universities and institutions, industry large and small, and the general well-being of people everywhere who can someday benefit from the uses of biotechnology. The social consequences of the technologies are an integral part of research in this field.

There are several strong motivations for academic institutions and their faculties to seek industry support for research. First, there is a genuine interest in facilitating the transfer of technology—from discovery to use—to contribute to the health and productivity of society; second, there is interest in ongoing dialogue between academia and industry which could improve the level of applied science by close association with industry applications; and, third, academic institutions and their faculty members are feeling particularly hard-pressed financially and see such cooperation with industry as a way of compensating for a small but important part of the support lost from federal sources.

Although biotechnology is at the center of today's news, we have considered it appropriate to discuss a broader range of university-industry relationships without regard to subject area.

From industry's point of view, a competitive position is critical. Each high-technology company seeks to develop the "best technology" and to use it productively. The development by a business of a cooperative research relationship with a university is likely to be based on the presumption that "best technology" can most readily be created by "best people," access to whom is one objective for the business which finances the program. As long as the conditions which surround access to a university's "best people" are not too onerous, business will continue to make new agreements with universities to enhance their opportunities to achieve competitive advantages.

But the appropriate development of new opportunities in academic-industrial relations presents universities with a host of problems. The most important of these is the potential distortion such relationships may cause to academic objectives. While this issue may vary in degree from one academic institution to another, it is shared by most research-based universities and institutes. If not carefully managed, these patterns of affiliations among university faculty, universities and industrial firms, beneficial though they may be to the transfer of technology, may lead to serious difficulties.

The purpose of the meeting was to contribute usefully to a more fruitful process of policy-making—but not to make policy. This responsibility rests with the individual institutions. The focus of the conference was to define the areas of difficulty or potential conflict and to develop suggestions for guiding the growth of industry-university cooperation in research. It has long been felt that university administrators, faculty and industry leaders have not been communicating enough about the problems arising within the universities in connection with the commercialization of basic research. Equally important, the problems and objectives of industry have been often ignored. As a result, different institutions have been engaged in ad hoc policy formulation, without the benefit of sharing their experience and discussing their common problems.

The overriding concern of the participants was to explore effective ways to satisfy the university community and the public that research agreements and other arrangements with industry be so constructed as not to promote a secrecy that will harm the progress of science; impair the educational experience of students and postdoctoral fellows; diminish the role of the university as a credible and impartial resource; interfere with the choice by faculty members of the scientific questions they pursue, or divert the energies of faculty members and the resources of the university from primary educational and research missions.

Relationships Between Universities and Industry

Research Agreements

It is important that universities and industries maintain basic academic values in their research agreements. Agreements should be constructed, for example, in ways that do not promote a secrecy that will harm the progress of science, impair the education of students, interfere with the choice by faculty members of the scientific questions or lines of inquiry they pursue, or divert the energies of faculty members from their primary obligations to teaching and research.

Universities have a responsibility not only to maintain these values but also to satisfy faculty, students and the general public that they are being maintained. One way of accomplishing this result might be to make public the relevant provisions of research contracts with industry. Another method may be to allow a faculty committee or some other competent body to examine all research contracts with industry and assure that their terms are consistent with essential academic values. Reasonable people may differ on the choice of methods to be used, and we propose no single solution. What is essential is that each university establish some effective method.

The traditions of open research and prompt transmission of research results should govern all university research, including research sponsored by industry. Those traditions require that universities encourage open communication about research in progress and research results. However, as discussed below, it is appropriate for institutions to file for patent coverage for inventions and discoveries that result from university research. This action may require brief delays in publication or other public disclosure.

Receipt of proprietary information from a sponsor may occasionally be desirable to facilitate the research. Such situations must be handled on a case-by-case basis in a manner which neither violates the principle stated above nor interferes with the educational process. Any other restrictions on control of information disclosure by institutions are not appropriate as general policy.

Patent Licensing

Patents and patent licensing provide valuable incentives to facilitate the process of translating scientific discoveries into useful processes and products. By protecting the rights of the inventor, patents also encourage inventors and institutions to make public their discoveries, thus promoting the progress of science and technology. These advantages are fully applicable to universities, which need an incentive to identify potentially useful discoveries and to seek companies that have the resources and capabilities to bring these ideas to the marketplace. The federal government has recognized these advantages by amending the law to allow universities to own and license patents on discoveries made in the course of research financed by government grants and contracts.

Universities are now developing more effective programs to identify and patent potentially useful discoveries and to license them to interested firms. With few exceptions, such programs have not resulted in significant financial gains to universities though greater gains may come in the future. However, regardless of the uncertainty of the economic return, as recipients of public funds, universities have a responsibility to initiate and maintain effective patent and patent-licensing programs to encourage technology transfer.

It is important that universities administer patent programs in a manner that conforms to the public interest and to the universities' primary commitment to teaching and research. One important question is whether universities should grant exclusive or non-exclusive licenses. Some people fear that allowing a single firm the sole right to develop a patent will necessarily remove competition, slow the development of the patent or even prevent development altogether. This fear is exaggerated. Although, in some cases, multiple licenses will undoubtedly speed development, in other cases, exclusive rights are essential if development is to take place since no firm will expend large sums for development that will primarily benefit others.

Thus, universities should be able to negotiate exclusive licenses provided that exclusivity seems important to allow prompt, vigorous development of the patent to occur. The desirability of exclusivity in certain cases is recognized under current federal law. When exclusivity is allowed, however, it should be permitted for only the interval necessary to encourage the desired development. In addition, the university should insist upon a requirement of due diligence on the part of the licensee in developing and using the patent. In exercising these responsibilities, universities should seek to insure that their patents are vigorously developed—not only to promote the public interest but also to further the universities' rights to royalty income.

While the foregoing policies seem acceptable for licensing patents on discoveries already made, greater difficulties arise in corporate research agreements where the sponsor requests the right to exclusive licenses on all discoveries made [as] a result of the research funded by the company. Some of us believe that such exclusive rights are an appropriate *quid pro quo* for the funds provided for research. Others believe that the university should be willing to agree to provide instead non-exclusive royalty-free licenses to the sponsor, but should not give up its right to examine the appropriateness of exclusivity for each invention on a case-by-case basis. This question needs to be addressed by universities on a continuing basis in light of their experience.

It is important that universities not influence the nature of the research proposed by professors, postdoctoral fellows, or students by pressing them to do work of potential commercial importance or to become involved in other commercial activities. Professors may choose to delay publication of research findings for a brief period to permit the timely filing of patent applications, but, absent a contractual obligation, universities should not try to prevent faculty members from publishing or disclosing their research findings to preserve the universities' patent rights.

Universities should not be improperly influenced in choosing a licensee by the fact that a faculty member, or the university itself, is a substantial stockholder or has other significant ties with a particular company.

Licensing agreements between a university and a company are intended to accomplish the transfer of technology in an effective way. In those rare instances where a faculty member or the university has a major financial interest in a company seeking such an agreement, and where the technology to be licensed has been, in whole or in part, developed by the faculty member, licensing should ordinarily be on a non-exclusive basis. Exceptions might arise if the transfer of technology is best accomplished through an exclusive arrangement for a limited period, as, for example, in the case of companies possessing unique skills necessary to such transfer on a timely basis.

The University and Its Faculty

University professors have long associated with companies through consulting and other types of relationships. Such interaction can have significant advantage to the university, to the faculty member, to the company, and to the public. In many fields, faculty involvement with the commercial world provides valuable material for teaching and research, career opportunities for students and support for institutional activities.

Notwithstanding these benefits, professors' relationships with commercial firms should not be allowed to interfere with their overriding obligation to the university to fulfill their primary responsibilities of teaching and research.

In recent years, the problems of achieving this goal have assumed greater urgency by virtue of the growing tendency, especially in the biotechnology field, for professors to own significant blocks of stock in commercial enterprises, to assist in the formation of such enterprises, or even to assume substantial executive responsibilities. Conflicts of interest may arise through combinations of public funding, private consulting, and equity holding in companies engaged in activities in a faculty member's area of research. These developments underscore the need for universities to consider the rules and procedures needed to insure that faculty members fulfill their responsibilities to teaching and research, and to avoid conflicts of interest.

At times, the research or entrepreneurial efforts of a faculty member may have the potential materially to affect the economic condition of a company. (In such cases, the faculty member is often a substantial stockholder in the firm.) Under these conditions, investment by the professor's own university in the firm gives the institution a financial stake in the activities of its faculty member. This situation may cause others to believe that the university encourages entrepreneurial activities by its faculty. Moreover, it may cause, or appear to cause, the university to extend preferential treatment to the professor, for example, in such matters as promotion, space, or teaching loads and thus undermine the morale and academic integrity of the institution. Hence, it is not advisable for universities to make such investments unless they are convinced that there are sufficient safeguards to avoid adverse effects on the morale of the institution or on the academic relationship between the university, its faculty, and its students.

Many approaches have been used by different universities to address these problems. We make no effort to specify the proper rules and procedures to be used for this purpose. The development of these rules is a matter internal to each university and extends to all faculty members—scientists and non-scientists alike. Hence, this conference does not provide a proper forum in which to resolve such issues. Different rules and procedures may well be appropriate to suit the special circumstances and traditions of different institutions.

Although we see no single "right" policy, we do believe that each university should address the problem vigorously and make efforts to publicize widely and effectively the rules and procedures it adopts to avoid compromising the quality of its teaching and research. Our institutions are committed to such an undertaking.

We also feel that faculty members have an obligation not only to abide by the prevailing rules but to make these restrictions known to the companies with which they have a relationship.

Finally, we suggest that firms ask for copies of applicable rules in hiring university consultants and act in conformity with these regulations.

We do not view this summary statement as the end of the process of deliberation on these important issues. Rather, we offer it as a contribution to further consideration in meetings of other groups and in many individual institutions. We emphasize again that what we have produced is not policy, but an agenda of issues that may be a useful framework for the development of policy.

2
Diamond, Commissioner of Patents and Trademarks *v*. Chakrabarty

Mr. Chief Justice Burger delivered the opinion of the Court.

We granted certiorari to determine whether a live, human-made micro-organism is patentable subject matter under 35 U. S. C. § 101.

I

In 1972, respondent Chakrabarty, a microbiologist, filed a patent application, assigned to the General Electric Co. The application asserted 36 claims related to Chakrabarty's invention of "a bacterium from the genus *Pseudomonas* containing therein at least two stable energy-generating plasmids, each of said plasmids providing a separate hydrocarbon degradative pathway." This human-made, genetically engineered bacterium is capable of breaking down multiple components of crude oil. Because of this property, which is possessed by no naturally occurring bacteria, Chakrabarty's invention is believed to have significant value for the treatment of oil spills.

Chakrabarty's patent claims were of three types: first, process claims for the method of producing the bacteria; second, claims for an inoculum comprised of a carrier material floating on water, such as straw, and the new bacteria; and third, claims to the bacteria themselves. The patent examiner allowed the claims falling into the first two categories, but rejected claims for the bacteria. His decision rested on two grounds: (1) that micro-organisms are "products of nature," and (2) that as living things they are not patentable subject matter under 35 U. S. C. § 101. . . .

II

The Constitution grants Congress broad power to legislate to "promote the Progress of Science and useful Arts, by securing for limited

U.S. Supreme Court Decision, June 16, 1980. Citations and footnotes omitted.

Times to Authors and Inventors the exclusive Right to their respective
Writings and Discoveries." Art. I, § 8, cl. 8. The patent laws promote
this progress by offering inventors exclusive rights for a limited period
as an incentive for their inventiveness and research efforts. The authority of Congress is exercised in the hope that "[t]he productive
effort thereby fostered will have a positive effect on society through
the introduction of new products and processes of manufacture into
the economy, and the emanations by way of increased employment
and better lives for our citizens."

The question before us in this case is a narrow one of statutory
interpretation requiring us to construe 35 U. S. C. § 101, which
provides:

> "Whoever invents or discovers any new and useful process, machine,
> manufacture, or composition of matter, or any new and useful improve-
> ment thereof, may obtain a patent therefor, subject to the conditions and
> requirements of this title."

Specifically, we must determine whether respondent's micro-organism
constitutes a "manufacture" or "composition of matter" within the
meaning of the statute.

III

In cases of statutory construction we begin, of course, with the
language of the statute. And "unless otherwise defined, words will be
interpreted as taking their ordinary, contemporary, common meaning." We have also cautioned that courts "should not read into the
patent laws limitations and conditions which the legislature has not
expressed."

Guided by these canons of construction, this Court has read the
term "manufacture" in § 101 in accordance with its dictionary definition to mean "the production of articles for use from raw or prepared
materials by giving to these materials new forms, qualities, properties,
or combinations, whether by hand-labor or by machinery." Similarly,
"composition of matter" has been construed consistent with its common usage to include "all compositions of two or more substances and
. . . all composite articles, whether they be the results of chemical
union, or of mechanical mixture, or whether they be gases, fluids,
powders or solids." In choosing such expansive terms as "manufac-

ture" and "composition of matter," modified by the comprehensive "any," Congress plainly contemplated that the patent laws would be given wide scope.

The relevant legislative history also supports a broad construction. The Patent Act of 1793, authored by Thomas Jefferson, defined statutory subject matter as "any new and useful art, machine, manufacture, or composition of matter, or any new or useful improvement [thereof]." The Act embodied Jefferson's philosophy that "ingenuity should receive a liberal encouragement." Subsequent patent statutes in 1836, 1870, and 1874 employed this same broad language. In 1952, when the patent laws were recodified, Congress replaced the word "art" with "process," but otherwise left Jefferson's language intact. The Committee Reports accompanying the 1952 Act inform us that Congress intended statutory subject matter to "include anything under the sun that is made by man."

This is not to suggest that § 101 has no limits or that it embraces every discovery. The laws of nature, physical phenomena, and abstract ideas have been held not patentable. Thus, a new mineral discovered in the earth or a new plant found in the wild is not patentable subject matter. Likewise, Einstein could not patent his celebrated law that $E = mc^2$; nor could Newton have patented the law of gravity. Such discoveries are "manifestations of . . . nature, free to all men and reserved exclusively to none."

Judged in this light, respondent's micro-organism plainly qualifies as patentable subject matter. His claim is not to a hitherto unknown natural phenomenon, but to a nonnaturally occurring manufacture or composition of matter—a product of human ingenuity "having a distinctive name, character [and] use." The point is underscored dramatically by comparison of the invention here with that in *Funk*. There, the patentee had discovered that there existed in nature certain species of root-nodule bacteria which did not exert a mutually inhibitive effect on each other. He used that discovery to produce a mixed culture capable of inoculating the seeds of leguminous plants. Concluding that the patentee had discovered "only some of the handiwork of nature," the Court ruled the product nonpatentable:

"Each of the species of root-nodule bacteria contained in the package infects the same group of leguminous plants which it always infected. No species acquires a different use. The combination of species produces no new bacteria, no change in the six species of bacteria, and no enlargement of the range of their utility. Each species has the same effect it always had. The bacteria perform in their natural way. Their use in combination does not improve in any way their natural functioning. They serve the ends nature originally provided and act quite independently of any effort of the patentee." 333 U. S., at 131.

Here, by contrast, the patentee has produced a new bacterium with markedly different characteristics from any found in nature and one having the potential for significant utility. His discovery is not nature's handiwork, but his own; accordingly it is patentable subject matter under § 101.

IV

Two contrary arguments are advanced, neither of which we find persuasive.

(A)

[omitted]

(B)

The petitioner's second argument is that micro-organisms cannot qualify as patentable subject matter until Congress expressly authorizes such protection. His position rests on the fact that genetic technology was unforeseen when Congress enacted § 101. From this it is argued that resolution of the patentability of inventions such as respondent's should be left to Congress. The legislative process, the petitioner argues, is best equipped to weigh the competing economic, social, and scientific considerations involved, and to determine whether living organisms produced by genetic engineering should receive patent protection. In support of this position, the petitioner relies on our recent holding in *Parker* v. *Flook,* 437 U. S. 584 (1978), and the statement that the judiciary "must proceed cautiously when . . . asked to extend patent rights into areas wholly unforeseen by Congress." *Id.,* at 596.

It is, of course, correct that Congress, not the courts, must define the limits of patentability; but it is equally true that once Congress has spoken it is "the province and duty of the judicial department to say what the law is." Congress has performed its constitutional role in defining patentable subject matter in § 101; we perform ours in construing the language Congress has employed. In so doing, our obligation is to take statutes as we find them, guided, if ambiguity appears, by the legislative history and statutory purpose. Here, we perceive no ambiguity. The subject-matter provisions of the patent law have been cast in broad terms to fulfill the constitutional and statutory goal of promoting "the Progress of Science and the useful Arts" with all that means for the social and economic benefits envisioned by Jefferson. Broad general language is not necessarily ambiguous when congressional objectives require broad terms.

Nothing in *Flook* is to the contrary. That case applied our prior precedents to determine that a "claim for an improved method of calculation, even when tied to a specific end use, is unpatentable subject matter under § 101." The Court carefully scrutinized the claim at issue to determine whether it was precluded from patent protection under "the principles underlying the prohibition against patents for 'ideas' or phenomena of nature." *Id.,* at 593. We have done that here. *Flook* did not announce a new principle that inventions in areas not contemplated by Congress when the patent laws were enacted are unpatentable *per se.*

To read that concept into *Flook* would frustrate the purposes of the patent law. This Court frequently has observed that a statute is not to be confined to the "particular application[s] . . . contemplated by the legislators." This is especially true in the field of patent law. A rule that unanticipated inventions are without protection would conflict with the core concept of the patent law that anticipation undermines patentability. Mr. Justice Douglas reminded that the inventions most benefiting mankind are those that "push back the frontiers of chemistry, physics, and the like." Congress employed broad general language in drafting § 101 precisely because such inventions are often unforeseeable.

To buttress his argument, the petitioner, with the support of *amicus,* points to grave risks that may be generated by research endeavors such as respondent's. The briefs present a gruesome parade of horribles. Scientists, among them Nobel laureates, are quoted suggesting that genetic research may pose a serious threat to the human race, or, at the very least, that the dangers are far too substantial to permit such research to proceed apace at this time. We are told that genetic research and related technological developments may spread pollution and disease, that it may result in a loss of genetic diversity, and that its practice may tend to depreciate the value of human life. These arguments are forcefully, even passionately, presented; they remind us that, at times, human ingenuity seems unable to control fully the forces it creates—that, with Hamlet, it is sometimes better "to bear those ills we have than fly to others that we know not of."

It is argued that this Court should weigh these potential hazards in considering whether respondent's invention is patentable subject matter under § 101. We disagree. The grant or denial of patents on microorganisms is not likely to put an end to genetic research or to its attendant risks. The large amount of research that has already occurred when no researcher had sure knowledge that patent protection would be available suggests that legislative or judicial fiat as to patentability will not deter the scientific mind from probing into the unknown any more than Canute could command the tides. Whether respondent's claims are patentable may determine whether research efforts are accelerated by the hope of reward or slowed by want of incentives, but that is all.

What is more important is that we are without competence to entertain these arguments—either to brush them aside as fantasies generated by fear of the unknown, or to act on them. The choice we are urged to make is a matter of high policy for resolution within the legislative process after the kind of investigation, examination, and study that legislative bodies can provide and courts cannot. That process involves the balancing of competing values and interests, which in our democratic system is the business of elected representatives. Whatever their validity, the contentions now pressed on us should be addressed to the political branches of the Government, the Congress and the Executive, and not to the courts.

We have emphasized in the recent past that "[o]ur individual appraisal of the wisdom or unwisdom of a particular [legislative] course . . . is to be put aside in the process of interpreting a statute." Our task, rather, is the narrow one of determining what Congress meant by the words it used in the statute; once that is done our powers are exhausted. Congress is free to amend § 101 so as to exclude from patent protection organisms produced by genetic engineering. Cf. 42 35 U. S. C. § 2181 (a), exempting from patent protection inventions "useful solely in the utilization of special nuclear material or atomic energy in an atomic weapon." Or it may choose to craft a statute specifically designed for such living things. But, until Congress takes such action, this Court must construe the language of § 101 as it is. The language of that section fairly embraces respondent's invention.

Accordingly, the judgment of the Court of Customs and Patent Appeals is

Affirmed.

Mr. Justice Brennan, with whom Mr. Justice White, Mr. Justice Marshall, and Mr. Justice Powell join, dissenting.

I agree with the Court that the question before us is a narrow one. Neither the future of scientific research, nor even the ability of respondent Chakrabarty to reap some monopoly profits from his pioneering work, is at stake. Patents on the processes by which he has produced and employed the new living organism are not contested. The only question we need decide is whether Congress, exercising its authority under Art. I, § 8, of the Constitution, intended that he be able to secure a monopoly on the living organism itself, no matter how produced or how used. Because I believe the Court has misread the applicable legislation, I dissent.

The patent laws attempt to reconcile this Nation's deep-seated antipathy to monopolies with the need to encourage progress. Given the complexity and legislative nature of this delicate task, we must be careful to extend patent protection no further than Congress has provided. In particular, were there an absence of legislative direction, the courts should leave to Congress the decisions whether and how far to extend the patent privilege into areas where the common understanding has been that patents are not available.

In this case, however, we do not confront a complete legislative vacuum. The sweeping language of the Patent Act of 1793, as re-enacted in 1952, is not the last pronouncement Congress has made in this area. In 1930 Congress enacted the Plant Patent Act affording patent protection to developers of certain asexually reproduced plants. In 1970 Congress enacted the Plant Variety Protection Act to extend protection to certain new plant varieties capable of sexual reproduction. Thus, we are not dealing—as the Court would have it—with the routine problem of "unanticipated inventions." *Ante,* at 316. In these two Acts Congress has addressed the general problem of patenting animate inventions and has chosen carefully limited language granting protection to some kinds of discoveries, but specifically excluding others. These Acts strongly evidence a congressional limitation that excludes bacteria from patentability.

First, the Acts evidence Congress' understanding, at least since 1930, that § 101 does not include living organisms. If newly developed living organisms not naturally occurring had been patentable under § 101, the plants included in the scope of the 1930 and 1970 Acts could have been patented without new legislation. Those plants, like the bacteria involved in this case, were new varieties not naturally occurring. Although the Court, *ante,* at 311, rejects this line of argument, it does not explain why the Acts were necessary unless to correct a pre-existing situation. I cannot share the Court's implicit assumption that Congress was engaged in either idle exercises or mere correction of the public record when it enacted the 1930 and 1970 Acts. And Congress certainly thought it was doing something significant. The Committee Reports contain expansive prose about the previously unavailable benefits to be derived from extending patent protection to plants. Because Congress thought it had to legislate in order to make agricultural "human-made inventions" patentable and because the legislation Congress enacted is limited, it follows that Congress never meant to make items outside the scope of the legislation patentable.

Second, the 1970 Act clearly indicates that Congress has included bacteria within the focus of its legislative concern, but not within the scope of patent protection. Congress specifically excluded bacteria from the coverage of the 1970 Act. The Court's attempts to supply explanations for this explicit exclusion ring hollow. It is true that there is no mention in the legislative history of the exclusion, but that does not give us license to invent reasons. The fact is that Congress, assuming that animate objects as to which it had not specifically legislated could not be patented, excluded bacteria from the set of patentable organisms.

The Court protests that its holding today is dictated by the broad language of § 101, which cannot "be confined to the 'particular application[s] . . . contemplated by the legislators.' " But as I have shown, the Court's decision does not follow the unavoidable implications of the statute. Rather, it extends the patent system to cover living material even though Congress plainly has legislated in the belief that § 101 does not encompass living organisms. It is the role of Congress, not this Court, to broaden or narrow the reach of the patent laws. This is especially true where, as here, the composition sought to be patented uniquely implicates matters of public concern.

3
Pennsylvania Statutes Creating
Ben Franklin Partnerships

Article XVII. Economic Revitalization Tax Credit

§ 8702. Legislative intent

The General Assembly of the Commonwealth of Pennsylvania hereby finds that:

(a) Whereas, in certain regions of this Commonwealth, industries and other businesses important to the economic well-being of this State suffered substantial losses during the recent recession and because of these losses closed plants and other facilities and laid off thousands of Pennsylvania workers; and

(b) Whereas, many of these distressed industries have not yet sufficiently returned to profitability to recover their losses and either rehire laid-off workers or expand their employment in Pennsylvania; and

(c) Whereas, new capital investments for the economic revitalization of these distressed industries during the current economic expansion are crucial in order to rehire laid-off workers, expand employment and avoid even more serious economic dislocations within this Commonwealth in any future economic recessions;

(d) Therefore, it is in the public interest to provide tax credits to distressed industries and other businesses for new investments above threshold investment levels which will cause the rehiring of laid-off Pennsylvania workers or will result in the retention of existing jobs or the creation of expanded permanent employment opportunities in these distressed industries within Pennsylvania. . . .

§ 8710. Application procedures

(a) Applications for credits pursuant to this article shall be filed with the Secretary of Revenue not later than February 1 or August 1 based upon planned expenditures for qualified investment projects to be made in the current tax year or an upcoming taxable year. In addition to any other information as may be required pursuant to this article, the application shall include:

From *Purdon's Statutes*: 72 P.S. §§ 8702, 8710, 8712; and 71 P.S. §§ 158, 607.1; 1990.

(1) a five-year history of the applicant's investment and employment activities in this Commonwealth;

(2) a detailed description of the qualified investment projects in excess of the threshold level for which a credit is requested;

(3) an explanation of how the investments for which the credit is claimed will result in the rehiring of laid-off workers, the retention of existing jobs in Pennsylvania or the expansion of employment within this Commonwealth, and a quantitative estimate of the impact of such investment upon employment; and

(4) the identification of other forms of Federal, State and local economic development assistance being utilized by the taxpayer, including, but not limited to, industrial development loans, Pennsylvania Industrial Development Agency loans, job training assistance and other low-interest loans or grants being received by the taxpayer.

(b) The secretary shall review all applications received and shall certify whether or not expenditures for which credits are requested will meet the requirements for qualified investment projects set forth in section 1704(a), (b) and (c) and whether or not all or a specified portion of the expenditures will be in excess of the threshold level and shall certify the portion of excess net loss claimable as credit and the amount of credit for which the taxpayer may be eligible pursuant to section 1707. The secretary shall forward all such certifications, together with all such applications submitted by taxpayers, to the Board of the Ben Franklin Partnership Fund. Information forwarded to the Board of the Ben Franklin Partnership Fund by the secretary shall constitute "public records" pursuant to the act of June 21, 1957 (P.L.390, No. 212), referred to as the Right-to-Know Law.

(c) The Board of the Ben Franklin Partnership Fund shall review all applications received from the Secretary of Revenue and approve, in whole or in part, those applications which, in the judgment of the board, will best contribute to the purposes and objectives of this article. The board shall certify to the Secretary of Revenue the amount of credits approved, and the secretary shall notify the taxpayer that appropriate credits will be entered upon the accounts of the taxpayer upon the submission of evidence to the secretary that expenditures for which the application was approved have been made by the taxpayer.

(d) In the review of applications, the Board of the Ben Franklin Partnership Fund shall make its decisions on the basis of criteria, including, but not limited to:

(1) the long-term employment potential resulting from the investment, including projected jobs retained and created over a five-year period;

(2) the market demand for products resulting from such investments;

(3) the anticipated increase in Pennsylvania's share of domestic and international markets from new markets captured from out-of-state or foreign competitors due to such investments; and

(4) the utilization by the taxpayer of new and advanced technologies in such investments which are likely to permanently enhance the taxpayer's competitive position within its industry or business.

(e) The Board of the Ben Franklin Partnership Fund shall limit total credits approved for any taxpayer, together with any credit awarded to a subsidiary corporation of the taxpayer, to an amount not in excess of six million two hundred and fifty thousand dollars ($6,250,000) and shall limit total credits approved pursuant to this article to an amount not in excess of twenty-five million dollars ($25,000,000). A subsidiary corporation shall be defined in the manner provided by section 601.

(f) On or before the fifteenth day of the fourth month following the end of any taxable year for which credits are requested, the taxpayer shall file a report with the Secretary of Revenue showing the actual amount of investment made during such period. If expenditures for qualified investments for which credits have been approved plus other expenditures for manufacturing, processing or research and development investments within this Commonwealth exceed the threshold level, the secretary shall enter such credits as the taxpayer may be entitled to pursuant to section 1707 upon the account of the taxpayer. If actual investments made are less than the amount upon which any credits approved were based, the secretary shall reduce the amount of credits awarded to that taxpayer by an appropriate fractional amount of the deficiency of such investment.

(g) The Secretary of Revenue and the Board of the Ben Franklin Partnership Fund shall jointly establish procedures for the application by taxpayers for credits pursuant to this article, the review and approval or disapproval of such applications, and the calculation, award and utilization of such credits. The secretary and the board may jointly promulgate rules and regulations, statements of policy, forms and other rulings and interpretations necessary to implement this article. . . .

§ 8712. Annual reports

(a) On or before November 1, 1986, and for each year thereafter, the Board of the Ben Franklin Partnership Fund, in cooperation with the Secretary of Revenue, shall provide the General Assembly with a report showing the following information for the period beginning with the effective date of this article and ending on the last day of September:

(i) The amount of tax credits approved for each taxpayer pursuant to this article.

(ii) The name of each such taxpayer.

(iii) A description of the qualified property, including its location, for which the credit was granted.

(iv) The number of workers to be rehired at each location, the number of jobs to be retained at each location and the number of new jobs created at each location, as certified by the board.

(v) The amount of tax credits utilized by each taxpayer pursuant to this article.

(vi) The information contained in the applications, whether approved or rejected, as specified in section 1710.

(b) The provisions of section 408(b) of this act relating to confidentiality of information, and any other provisions of law preventing the disclosure of information required pursuant to subsection (a) of this section, shall not apply when the information is divulged for the purposes of subsection (a) of this section. . . .

§ 158. (Adm. Code § 448). Advisory boards and commissions

The advisory boards and commissions, within the several administrative departments, shall be constituted as follows: . . .

(n) There is hereby created in the Department of Commerce a Board of the Ben Franklin Partnership Fund which shall consist of the Secretaries of Commerce, Environmental Resources and Agriculture, the Director of the Governor's Office of Policy and Planning and the Executive Director of the Pennsylvania Energy Office, the chairman of the Milrite Council, two members of the Senate appointed by the President pro tempore of the Senate, one of whom shall be a member of the majority party of the Senate and one of whom shall be a member of the minority party of the Senate, two members of the House of Representatives appointed by the Speaker of the House of Representatives, one of whom shall be a member of the majority party of the House of Representatives and one of whom shall be a member of the minority party of the House of Representatives, and five additional members to be appointed by the Governor at least one of whom shall represent organized labor and at least one of whom shall be an owner of a small business. The Secretaries of Commerce, Environmental Resources and Agriculture, the Director of the Governor's Office on Policy and Planning, the Executive Director of the Pennsylvania Energy Office, the chairman of the Milrite Council and the members of the General Assembly shall be authorized to designate officers or employees from their respective agencies to act in their stead in the conduct of the business of the board. The chairman of this board shall be the Secretary of Commerce.

All members shall be appointed for terms of four years, such terms to run concurrent with that of the Governor. Any member appointed to fill a vacancy created otherwise than by expiration of term shall be appointed for the unexpired term of the member whom he is to succeed.

The board members shall receive no compensation for their services but shall be reimbursed for their expenses actually incurred by them in the performance of their duties under this act.

The Department of Commerce shall provide an executive director and all other staff services to the board, including liaison between the board and science and engineering research, business, labor, development and education agencies and related organizations, and between the foundation and other agencies of the Commonwealth. The board may adopt bylaws dealing with the organization, meetings, activities and other such considerations as it may deem appropriate and consistent with its powers and duties. . . .

(n.1) There is hereby created the Pennsylvania Academic Commission on Technological Development as an advisory body to the Board of the Ben Franklin Partnership Fund, which shall consist of the Chairman of the Ben Franklin Partnership Fund, or his designee, who shall serve as chairman of the commission, the Secretary of Education, or his designee, three representatives from universities within the Pennsylvania State System of Higher Education, to be appointed by the chancellor of the system, and one representative from each of the following institutions, to be appointed by the chief executive officer of the institution:

The Pennsylvania State University
The University of Pittsburgh
Temple University
Lincoln University

The University of Pennsylvania
Hahnemann Medical College
Thomas Jefferson University
The Medical College of Pennsylvania
The Philadelphia College of Osteopathic Medicine
Drexel University
The Pennsylvania College of Optometry
The Pennsylvania College of Podiatric Medicine
The Lancaster Cleft Palate
The Pittsburgh Cleft Palate
The Franklin Institute
The Academy of Natural Sciences
Buhl Science Center
The Pittsburgh Home for Crippled Children
Carnegie-Mellon University, so long as the institution is participating in the Ben Franklin Partnership Fund Program as an advanced technology center.

Lehigh University, so long as the institution is participating in the Ben Franklin Partnership Fund Program as an advanced technology center.

In addition, the chairman of the commission may accept for membership representatives from any other educational, scientific or research institution located within the Commonwealth, to be appointed by the respective chief executive officer thereof.

The Chairman of the Ben Franklin Partnership Fund and the Secretary of Education shall serve for the duration of their tenure of office. If designees are chosen, such designees shall serve at the pleasure of the Chairman of the Ben Franklin Partnership Fund or the Secretary of Education, whichever appointed said designee. Members from the State System of Higher Education shall serve at the pleasure of the chancellor of the system. The remaining members shall serve at the pleasure of the chief executive officer of their respective institutions.

Members shall receive no compensation for their services but shall be reimbursed for expenses actually incurred by them in the performance of their duties by the Ben Franklin Partnership Fund in the case of the Chairman of the Ben Franklin Partnership Fund or his designee, by the Department of Education in the case of the Secretary of Education or his designee and by the respective institutions in the case of other members. Technical, managerial and other assistance required by the commission in the performance of its powers and duties shall be provided by the Ben Franklin Partnership Fund staff. Actual and necessary expenses incurred by the commission shall be paid from the Ben Franklin Partnership Fund Program. . . .

§ 670.1. (Adm. Code § 2503–B). **Duties and powers of the Board of the Ben Franklin Partnership Fund**

(a) The Board of the Ben Franklin Partnership Fund is authorized to promote, stimulate and encourage (i) basic and applied scientific research and development in Pennsylvania and (ii) scientific and technological education in Pennsylvania, which may reasonably be expected to advance the Commonwealth's economic growth and welfare. In addition, the board shall, upon request, provide advice to the Governor and the executive agencies concerning scientific, technological and engineering matters, which relate to the economic growth and the health, safety and welfare of the Commonwealth and its citizens; and may establish advanced technology centers which shall serve as university-based consortiums between business, universities and government to provide advanced technology research and development, training, education and related activities which show significant potential in diversification of Pennsylvania's economy and the State's economic growth.

(b) With the approval of the Governor, the board is authorized to enter into mutually satisfactory contracts, agreements or grants with educational institutions, nonprofit institutions and organizations, business enterprises and other persons concerned with scientific and technological research, and development in the Commonwealth, as well as any State or Federal agency, to foster and support scientific and technological research, development, education and promotion of applied advanced technological activities. The board may, subject to the approval of the Governor, make grants to educational institutions, nonprofit institutions and organizations, and other persons for the same purposes. The board may sponsor and conduct conferences and studies, collect and disseminate information, and issue periodic reports relating to scientific and technological research, development, and education in the Commonwealth, including grants for Governor's chairs to Pennsylvania colleges and universities in the field of new materials; maintain registers and inventories of scientific and technological personnel and facilities, including but not limited to scientific libraries and data centers. It may receive gifts, grants, bequests or devises from any source, including funds from the Federal government.

(c) The board may enter into a matching grant program, involving consortiums of college or university and private sector organizations for the purposes of establishing, operating and promoting advanced technology centers throughout the Commonwealth. Such centers shall receive no more than fifty per centum (50%) of their financial support from this board. Applicants for funds provided under this section shall secure financial commitments from profit and nonprofit groups and organizations, including the Federal government or local political subdivisions and shall be required to submit applications in accordance with policies and criteria issued by the board. The board shall utilize adequate financial controls, including a program of audits, to implement the matching grant program. Such centers shall utilize to the extent possible, existing or new private businesses operating or willing to operate in the fields of expertise needed to accomplish the purposes of the center. Eligible purposes which the board may fund under this matching grant program include, but are not limited to:

(1) Development and strengthening of joint research and development efforts including facilities for advanced technologies activities, equipment, personnel, land and related activities, which will lead to new technologies which will create or preserve jobs.

(2) Providing training and curriculum development related to advanced technology in order to provide a skilled work force to secure employment in advanced technology industries.

(3) Technical assistance and technology transfer activities on an area-wide or Statewide basis to transfer research and development activities into the marketplace.

(4) Assistance through small business incubators, including, but not limited to space, services and technical assistance.

(5) Market development, feasibility studies and other activities related to increasing jobs in advanced technology industries.

(6) Staff support for advanced technology councils or other mechanisms to encourage labor, business, university and governmental linkages in promoting advanced technology industrial diversification.

(7) Facilitate establishment of technology parks, which will serve as locations for facilities devoted to research and development and technology-intensive light manufacturing. . . .

4
Government-University-Industry Research Round Table: Model Agreements for University-Cooperative Research (1988)

Research Agreement*

THIS AGREEMENT effective this ____day of _____, 198____, by and between _____(hereinafter referred to as "Sponsor") and the UNIVERSITY OF _____, a non-profit educational institution (or its agent) of the State of _____(hereinafter referred to as "University").

WITNESSETH:

WHEREAS, the research program contemplated by this Agreement is of mutual interest and benefit to University and to Sponsor, will further the instructional and research objectives of University in a manner consistent with its status as a non-profit, tax-exempt, educational institution, and may derive benefits for both Sponsor and University through inventions, improvements, and/or discoveries;

NOW, THEREFORE, in consideration of the premises and mutual covenants herein contained, the parties hereto agree to the following:

Article 1—Definitions

As used herein, the following terms shall have the following meanings:

1.1 "Project" shall mean the description of the project as described in Appendix A hereof, under the direction of Dr._____ as principal investigator.

1.2 "Contract Period" is _____, 198____ through _____, 198____.

---

*Brackets ([ ]) have been placed in the text where appropriate to indicate variable time frames that can be used in an agreement. In some cases, ranges of time have been placed in the brackets to suggest reasonable lengths of time.

1.3 "University Intellectual Property" shall mean individually and collectively all inventions, improvements and/or discoveries which are conceived and/or made (i) by one or more employees of University, or (ii) jointly by one or more employees of University and by one or more employees of Sponsor in performance of Project.

Article 2—Research Work

2.1 University shall commence the performance of Project promptly after the effective date of this Agreement, and shall use reasonable efforts to perform such Project substantially in accordance with the terms and conditions of this Agreement. Anything in this Agreement to the contrary notwithstanding, Sponsor and University may at any time amend Project by mutual written agreement.

2.2 In the event that the Principal Investigator becomes unable or unwilling to continue Project, and a mutually acceptable substitute is not available, University and/or Sponsor shall have the option to terminate said Project.

Article 3—Reports and Conferences

3.1 Written program reports shall be provided by University to Sponsor every [_____] months, and a final report shall be submitted by University within [forty-five (45) days] of the conclusion of the Contract Period, or early termination of this Agreement.

3.2 During the term of this Agreement, representatives of University will meet with representatives of Sponsor at times and places mutually agreed upon to discuss the progress and results, as well as ongoing plans, or changes therein, of Project to be performed hereunder.

Article 4—Costs, Billings, and Other Support

4.1 It is agreed to and understood by the parties hereto that, subject to Article 2, total costs to Sponsor hereunder shall not exceed the sum of _____Dollars ($_____). Payment shall be made by Sponsor according to the following schedule: [_____].

4.2 Sponsor shall loan/donate the following equipment to University under the following conditions: [_____]. University shall retain title to any equipment purchased with funds provided by Sponsor under this Agreement.

4.3 Anything herein to the contrary notwithstanding, in the event of early termination of this Agreement by Sponsor pursuant to Article 9 hereof, Sponsor shall pay all costs accrued by University as of the date of termination, including non-cancellable obligations, which shall include all non-cancellable contracts and fellowships or postdoctoral associate appointments called for in Appendix A, incurred prior to the effective date of termination. After termination, any obligation of Sponsor for fellowships or postdoctoral associates shall end no later than the end of University's academic year following termination.

Article 5—Publicity

5.1 Sponsor will not use the name of University, nor of any member of University's Project staff, in any publicity, advertising, or news release without the prior written approval of an authorized representative of University. University will not use the name of Sponsor, nor any employee of Sponsor, in any publicity without the prior written approval of Sponsor.

Article 6—Publications

6.1 Sponsor recognizes that under University policy, the results of University Project must be publishable and agrees that Researchers engaged in Project shall be permitted to present at symposia, national, or regional professional meetings, and to publish in journals, theses or dissertations, or otherwise of their own choosing, methods and results of Project, provided, however, that Sponsor shall have been furnished copies of any proposed publication or presentation at least [_____] months in advance of the submission of such proposed publication or presentation to a journal, editor, or other third party. Sponsor shall have [_____] months, after receipt of said copies, to object to such proposed presentation or proposed publication because there is patentable subject matter which needs protection. In the event that Sponsor makes such objection, said Researcher(s) shall refrain from making such publication or presentation for a maximum of [_____] months from date of receipt of such objection in order for University to file patent application(s) with the United States Patent and Trademark Office and/or foreign patent office(s) directed to the patentable subject matter contained in the proposed publication or presentation.

Article 7—Intellectual Property

7.1 All rights and title to University Intellectual Property under Project shall belong to University and shall be subject to the terms and conditions of this Agreement.

7.2 Rights to inventions, improvements and/or discoveries, whether patentable or copyrightable or not, relating to Project made solely by employees of Sponsor shall belong to Sponsor. Such inventions, improvements, and/or discoveries shall not be subject to the terms and conditions of this Agreement.

7.3 University will promptly notify Sponsor of any University Intellectual Property conceived and/or made during the Contract Period under Project. If Sponsor directs that a patent application or application for other intellectual property protection be filed, University shall promptly prepare, file, and prosecute such U.S. and foreign application in University's name. Sponsor shall bear all costs incurred in connection with such preparation, filing, prosecution, and maintenance of U.S. and foreign application(s) directed to said University Intellectual Property. Sponsor shall cooperate with University to assure that such application(s) will cover, to the best of Sponsor's knowledge, all items of commercial interest and importance. While University shall be responsible for making decisions regarding scope and content of application(s) to be filed and prosecution thereof, Sponsor shall be given an opportunity to review and provide input thereto. University shall keep Sponsor advised as to all developments with respect to such application(s) and shall promptly supply to Sponsor copies of all papers received and filed in connection with the prosecution thereof in sufficient time for Sponsor to comment thereon.

7.4 If Sponsor elects not to exercise its option or decides to discontinue the financial support of the prosecution or maintenance of the protection, University shall be free to file or continue prosecution or maintain any such application(s), and to maintain any protection issuing thereon in the U.S. and in any foreign country at University's sole expense.

Article 8—Grant of Rights

Pursuant to Article 7.3, University grants Sponsor the first option, at Sponsor's sole selection, for either a non-exclusive, royalty-free license or, for consideration, an exclusive license with a right to sublicense on terms and conditions to be mutually agreed upon. The option shall extend for a time period of [_____] from the date of termination of the Agreement.

Article 9—Term and Termination

9.1 This Agreement shall become effective upon the date first hereinabove written and shall continue in effect for the full duration of the Contract Period unless sooner terminated in accordance with the provisions of this Article. The parties hereto may, however, extend the term of this Agreement for additional periods as desired under mutually agreeable terms and conditions which the parties reduce to writing and sign. Either party may terminate this agreement upon ninety (90) days prior written notice to the other.

9.2 In the event that either party hereto shall commit any breach of or default in any of the terms or conditions of this Agreement, and also shall fail to remedy such default or breach within ninety (90) days after receipt of written notice thereof from the other party hereto, the party giving notice may, at its option and in addition to any other remedies which it may have at law or in equity, terminate this Agreement by sending notice of termination in writing to the other party to such effect, and such termination shall be effective as of the date of the receipt of such notice.

9.3 Subject to Article 8, termination of this Agreement by either party for any reason shall not affect the rights and obligations of the parties accrued prior to the effective date of termination of this Agreement. No termination of this Agreement, however effectuated, shall affect the Sponsor's rights and duties under Article 7 hereof, or release the parties hereto from their rights and obligations under Articles 4, 5, 6, 7, 8, and 10.

Article 10—Independent Contractor

10.1 In the performance of all services hereunder:

10.1.1 University shall be deemed to be and shall be an independent contractor and, as such, University shall not be entitled to any benefits applicable to employees of Sponsor;

10.1.3 Neither party is authorized or empowered to act as agent for the other for any purpose and shall not on behalf of the other enter into any contract, warranty, or representation as to any matter. Neither shall be bound by the acts or conduct of the other.

Article 11—Insurance

11.1 University warrants and represents that University has adequate liability insurance, such protection being applicable to officers, employees, and agents while acting within the scope of their employment by University, and University has no liability insurance policy as such that can extend protection to any other person.

11.2 Each party hereby assumes any and all risks of personal injury and property damage attributable to the negligent acts or omissions of that party and the officers, employees, and agents thereof.

Article 12—Governing Law

12.1 This Agreement shall be governed and construed in accordance with the laws of the State of _____.

Article 13—Assignment

13.1 This Agreement shall not be assigned by either party without the prior written consent of the parties hereto.

13.2 This Agreement is assignable to any division of Sponsor, any majority stockholder of Sponsor, and/or any subsidiary of Sponsor in which [_____] percent of the outstanding stock is owned by Sponsor.

Article 14—Agreement Modification

14.1 Any agreement to change the terms of this Agreement in any way shall be valid only if the change is made in writing and approved by mutual agreement of authorized representatives of the parties hereto.

Article 15—Notices

15.1 Notices, invoices, communications, and payments hereunder shall be deemed made if given by registered or certified envelope, postage prepaid, and addressed to the party to receive such notice, invoice, or communication at the address given below, or such address as may hereafter be designated by notice in writing:

If to Sponsor: SPONSOR
ADDRESS
CITY, STATE, ZIP CODE

If to University: UNIVERSITY
                      ADDRESS
                      CITY, STATE, ZIP CODE

If Technical Matter: PRINCIPAL INVESTIGATOR
                      TITLE
                      UNIVERSITY ADDRESS
                      CITY, STATE, ZIP CODE

IN WITNESS WHEREOF, the parties have caused these presents to
be executed in duplicate as of the day and year first above written.

(SPONSOR)   (UNIVERSITY)

_____   _____
By: By:
Title: Title:

_____   _____
Witness   Witness

5
National Science Foundation Program Announcement: Industry/University Cooperative Research Centers Program (1990)

Goals

The Industry/University Cooperative Research Centers Program is administered by the Engineering Centers Division in the Directorate for Engineering of the National Science Foundation.

The goals of the Industry/University Cooperative Research Centers Program are to:

• develop industry, state, and other support for industry/university interaction on industrially relevant fundamental research topics;

• promote university research to provide a knowledge base for industrial and technological advancement while training students; and

• promote research centers that become self-sustaining with industry, state, and other funding within a five-year period.

Background

The Industry/University Cooperative Research Centers (I/UCRC) Program was initiated by the National Science Foundation (NSF) in 1973 to stimulate the interaction of the university and industrial communities on fundamental scientific and engineering research important to technological innovation and industrial development. The vehicle for this interaction is a research center developed to create long-term interaction between the two communities on research topics pertinent to industry.

The National Science Foundation supports the initiation of these centers through a phased approach. The I/UCRC Program provides some support to study the feasibility of establishing an operating center. Once a center reaches the operational phase, the program provides seed funds; but, a significant proportion of a center's support comes from industrial, state, and other funds. As the center progresses, it becomes less dependent upon I/UCRC funds, until it reaches the point of self-sufficiency, and the program discontinues operational support. Most fully operational centers require funding of $300,000 annually from at least six firms to have a sufficient research base. All are expected to expand their base of support to include the university, state agencies, federal laboratories, or other organizations. Established centers have the opportunity for supplemental NSF funding to accomplish special activities such as cross-center collaborative projects, minority outreach efforts, etc. Centers are based in academic research institutions and some centers combine the research talents of more than one university or college.

The scientific and/or engineering research agenda is established by the researchers and firms participating in the center and is focused on topics important to the contributing firms. I/UCRC Centers may combine a range of disciplines and skills necessary to address the research issues posed by industry. Proposed centers should not significantly duplicate the research focus of other centers in the program.

The objectives of the centers are:

- to pursue fundamental engineering and scientific research having industrial relevance;
- to produce graduates who have a broad, industrially oriented perspective in their research and practice; and
- to achieve self-sufficiency from NSF support within five years of operation.

I. Concept Papers

Prior to submission of a formal proposal for a planning or operational center grant, concept papers describing a potential center should be submitted to the program office for comment. The concept papers will be reviewed by NSF staff. Comments will be furnished to the originator of the concept paper who may use this information for deciding upon the suitability of submitting a formal planning or operational center grant proposal *to* the National Science Foundation. . . .

II. Planning Grant Proposals

For a potential center where an operational plan, research agenda, and industrial support have not been developed, the I/UCRC Center Program accepts proposals to plan the joint industry/university research interests and to determine the feasibility and viability of developing a center. These planning awards typically are for $25,000. . . .

III. Center Proposals

NSF will accept proposals for I/UCR Centers without a planning phase only when operational plans have been fully developed, industry commitments of at least $300,000 funding for the first year have been made, and a concept paper has been approved. Where university and/ or state support is an added source of funding for the proposed center, the potential for NSF support is significantly enhanced. I/UCR Centers moving from the planning to operational phase must submit a new proposal when they have met the above criteria.

I/UCR Center awards generally are five year awards that start between $50,000 and $100,000 per year to augment existing center funding. I/UCRC operational support is subject to renewal criteria being met each year and phases out at the end of the award period. The Center is expected to become self-sufficient on other sources of funding at the end of the award period.

NSF requires that the progress of each center be independently observed and evaluated during its planning and operational phases. The evaluation normally is conducted by an evaluation expert, usually from within the university but not from the department receiving center funding. Guidance on this requirement is available from the program. Funds are provided by NSF to help cover operational support. . . .

Center Proposal Evaluation Criteria

The primary criteria for evaluating a center proposal are technical and managerial quality of the proposal, qualifications of the proposers, industrial involvement and the likelihood of achieving the goal of the I/UCRC program. As such the NSF reviewers will consider the extent to which there is evidence the center will:

1. Have aggregate industrial support of approximately $300,000/year (on a membership fee basis) and growth potential;
2. Focus on high quality, industrially relevant research that will involve students with industry and the research;
3. Have a strong leader;

4. Become self-sustaining by the end of the time period of the request (within a five-year period);

5. Have university, state, and other sources of support;

6. Have an effective structure and management plan with an industrial advisory board;

7. Proprietary rights, patent, and publication policies clearly defined in a university/industry membership agreement; and

8. Have an independent evaluation component to assess the progress of the center. . . .

Publication and Patent Policy

Prompt publication of research results is expected. Participating firms and universities, however, may wish to agree upon appropriate delays in publication to safeguard patentability or proprietary information. Awardees may retain the principal rights to and all income from NSF-supported copyrightable material, including software.

Awardees may elect to retain principal patent rights to any inventions made with NSF support, subject to the terms and conditions in the Foundation's Patent Rights clause (see the NSF Grant Policy Manual or 45 CFR Part 650). In previously funded centers, the participating university or the center itself usually has held the patents on NSF-supported inventions, with participating firms receiving some nonexclusive rights or options. . . .

6
Government-University-Industry Research Roundtable: New Alliances and Partnerships in American Science and Engineering (1986)

Part I: Historical Precedent and the Current Context[1]

The Historical Context

Commentators on recent industry-university relationships sometimes write as if these are new and novel and in some sense stain the otherwise pure fabric of academic science and teaching.[2] In fact, many of the recent programs have recognizable antecedents that go back in time. Many fields of science have traditionally been strongly applications-oriented, and teaching in these fields has for the most part been preparation for industrial careers.[3] Also, many universities have traditionally seen the fostering of local or state industry as one of their missions. This is not meant to minimize the potential for tension and conflict in industry-university relationships. While they have long been an intrinsic part of the academic enterprise, the present situation certainly involves a dramatic expansion in their number and an important change in their character. Whether these constitute fundamental changes in the participating institutions is a matter of dispute and one of the concerns of this inquiry.

---

1. Taken from a paper, "University-Industry Alliances," prepared by Dorothy Nelkin and Richard Nelson, with help by Casey Kiernan, for the Government-University-Industry Research Roundtable. The authors of that paper acknowledge the fount of useful information about university-industry cooperative arrangements contained in a study put out by New York University's Center for Science and Technology Policy. See *University-Industry Research Relationships,* National Science Board, 1982.
2. Irwin Stark, "The University Goes to Market," *Thought and Action* vol. 11, Fall 1984, pp. 9–21.
3. David Noble, *America by Design,* New York: Knopf, 1977; Henry Etzkowitz, "Entrepreneurial Scientists and Entrepreneurial Universities in American Academic Science," Minerva XXI, Summer 1983, pp. 198–233.

The constellation of research universities in the United States arose from several different sources. The group of east coast universities whose grounding predates the American revolution, were originally designed to educate American ministers and other members of the intellectual elite.

Many writers on "university culture" seem to have these institutions in mind. But the American university scene is marked also, and perhaps more prominently, by another group of universities which were formed for quite different purposes. We refer here to the land grant universities, put into place to train common citizens in the agricultural and mechanical arts. Still another strain of research universities, particularly prominent in the current context, grew up as "technical schools," and are now the great engineering-oriented universities such as MIT, RPI, California Institute of Technology and Georgia Tech.[4]

Modern science entered the curriculum of the old elite universities as "natural philosophy." These universities strongly resisted any notion that the training they provided was to be "practical." In contrast, the land grants and technical schools were inclined to stress the applied and the useful. Yet, these institutions were frequently ambivalent. On the one hand, their mandate emphasized applied science; on the other hand, their faculty and government officers looked toward the more traditional, and prestigious institutions for guidance. As theoretical science gradually became a central part of the curricula in the older institutions, the land grants tended to follow. A considerable diversity evolved.

Cutting across these differences in university cultures are significant variations among scientific fields in terms of their intimacy with practical applications. Some sociologists of science have used theoretical physics as an example of a field where there is a sharp split between the philosophical and intellectual concerns of academe, and the practical concerns of industry.[5] However, historians have pointed out that

---

4. The published literature on the history of American research universities is scattered. Roger Geiger's new book pulls much of it together. See his *To Advance Knowledge: Growth of American Research Universities 1900–1940,* Oxford University Press, Oxford, 1986.

5. While Derek Price often referred to science in general in his argument that science and technology develop independently of each other in terms of the purposes and agendas, his discussions almost always concerned physics. See for example, *The Nature of the Scientific Community,* Yale University Press, New Haven, 1980.

the field of thermodynamics arose largely out of curiosity about how engines worked. Certain important areas of contemporary theoretical physics, for example, the study of materials, are closely connected with practical concerns. Nonetheless, for many fields of physics the characterization of the sociologists does ring true.

Academic chemistry, however, has from the beginning been closely tied to industrial chemistry. Chemistry, as a field, took hold in universities in the United States at about the same time that the U.S. chemical industry was beginning to grow. From the late 19th century on, professors of chemistry have served as consultants to chemical firms, often moving back and forth between industry and academe. Chemistry undergraduates then and now have found their careers largely in industry. Arnold Thackray describes how Ph.D.-level training in chemistry in the east coast universities was initially a closed academic circuit. But he describes, as well, the training of industry-oriented Ph.D.s in the land grant colleges and technical schools.[6]

Much of modern biology is, of course, deeply rooted in the search for solutions to practical agricultural, medical, and industrial problems. Similarly, computer science, by the very nature of the subject, is closely tied to applications. And, of course, the set of applied scientific fields which call themselves "engineering disciplines" are directly oriented to applications.

This historical perspective is intended to stress two points. First, propositions about a natural chasm between academic science and industry science have often been drawn too sharply and too globally. Second, these cultures have been living together for a long time. Indeed, academic science and industrial science in the United States grew up together.

If scientific fields differ in their linkages with industry, industries also differ in the extent to which the development of their technologies is connected to academic research, and in the extent they are dependent on academic training of employees. In the 19th century, industries where "mechanical engineering" was the dominant technical skill depended mainly on practical on-the-job experience. Academically-trained mechanical engineers had a difficult time gaining acceptance in these industries. In contrast, from their beginning, the chemical-based industries and those concerned with electrical phenomena and appa-

6. Arnold Thackray, "University-Industry Connections and Chemical Research: An Historical Perspective" in National Science Board, *University-Industry Research Relationship: Selected Studies* USGPO.

ratus turned to universities for scientific training of their technical employees. Early on, both of these industries established close contacts with technical employees and close contacts with technical schools, like MIT.[7]

Industry interests in academic research are not static. While academic scientists played an important role in the early days of the modern electrical industry, the work done in industry later came to stand largely on its own. In the early days of semiconductor and computer technologies, university researchers were heavily involved in research relevant to industry. However, industrial R&D on transistors and later integrated circuits gradually became quite separate from work done at universities. In contrast, academic computer science departments continue to do work that is highly relevant to industrial R&D.

For the past quarter of a century, certain parts of academic biology and biochemistry have been very important to industry. University research has pointed the way to new drugs, and pioneered many of the important techniques in pharmaceutical R&D now employed by corporations. At the present time, corporate R&D in biotechnology draws heavily on university research, and the techniques and instrumentation developed at universities.

The nature and strength of university-industry connections vary with the traditions of the university in question, the scientific discipline involved, and the industry. They are also influenced by the sources of university funding, and prevailing attitudes about the appropriate roles of universities, business, and government.

During the 1920s and 1930s, private foundations were the dominate external source of university research funding. While those who made decisions about funding emphatically believed that the objective was to benefit mankind and made their decisions accordingly, they also believed that the appropriate role for universities was to do basic research. With few exceptions, the foundations looked askance at university work that was close to commercial interests, and at universities that seemed too cozy with industry. Their attitude reflected and sustained the notion that a relatively sharp line should be drawn between university laboratories and industrial R&D.

After World War II, funding for research increased dramatically. The federal government became the dominant external source of research funding at the universities. Industrial support also grew,

---

7. Noble, *op. cit.*

although at a more gradual pace. In the NSF and NIH, academic researchers themselves played a principal role in allocating funds. Although this arrangement reinforced university values calling for distance from business interests, government funds were often justified by the argument that focused academic science was the key to practical progress.[8]

University faculty members and facilities also played a major role in military research and development during both the first and second World Wars. During the post-World War II period, the Department of Defense, the Atomic Energy Commission, and, to a lesser extent, NASA, were major supporters of R&D at universities or of facilities associated with universities. The projects sometimes called for interaction between university and corporate research and development, and in a number of instances, the university researchers developed links with business firms, or set up firms of their own.

Thus, during the 1960s and 1970s, the sources of funding tended to support the notion of a separate academic research enterprise, but at the same time tended to pull parts of the academic enterprise into closer contact with business. As a result of the research funding patterns, certain universities came to be defined as research institutions, with long term consequences for the balance of interests within academe. These trends set the stage for the development of the new industrial alliances and also for the ambivalent reactions to them.

What lies behind the recent surge of new arrangements among universities and industry? During the 1970s, universities became increasingly aware that in many fields the cost of doing research was growing at the same time that federal support was in danger of decline.[9] It is natural that the attention of university administrators and researchers should be drawn to industry. The experience with Route 128 and Silicon Valley came into focus as potential models.

Developments on the industrial front led industry to reciprocate the interest in new and strengthened connections. During the 1970s there developed a growing perception and fear that the United States was losing its technological primacy in a variety of industries where we had become accustomed to unquestioned leadership.[10] At least two areas

8. Harvey Brooks, *The Government of Science,* Cambridge: MIT Press, 1968.

9. Donald Kennedy, "Government Policies and the Cost of Doing Research," *Science* 227, 1 February 1985, pp. 480–484.

10. President's Commission on Industrial Competitiveness, *Global Competition: The New Reality,* vol. II, Washington, D.C.: USGPO, January 1985.

of cutting edge technology—computers and biotechnology—were recognized as closely linked to academic science. It is noteworthy that a non-trivial fraction of the new industry-university arrangements are involved in these two fields.

The relative decline of American industry soon became a matter of wide spread popular concern, affecting both federal and state politics. The question of how to link industry and university research, and the presumption that this was a good thing to do, lay behind a variety of new policy departures. At the federal level, the Patent and Trademarks Amendment Act (1980) and the Stevenson/Wydler Technology Innovation Act (1980) are particular cases in point. The Patent Amendments allowed universities to own patents resulting from federally-sponsored research for the first time. Federal agencies such as the NSF developed programs with the objective of forming industry-university cooperative projects.[11] A number of states initiated programs to encourage universities to support the development of state and regional high technology industry.

While there has been a long history of interaction between universities and industry, the new situation involves an explosion in the number of alliances and qualitative changes in their form. They have been created for different reasons, but in every case they involve an element of faith that they will be good for business, helpful and appropriate to universities, and in the public interest. Whether or not this faith is justified remains an open question. It is apparent that the nation is engaged in an experiment, and the stakes are high. . . .

Dimensions of Variation

Activities. The partnerships vary considerably in the activities involved. Some are largely concerned with basic research. In other arrangements, the work is largely applied, intended to solve or illuminate a well-defined practical problem. Some involve very little research on the part of academics, but rather, are focused on providing consultation or other help to a company, under academic auspices. Many, but not all, are associated with the training of undergraduates or graduate students. In some cases, constraints are imposed to limit

---

11. National Science Foundation, *Cooperative Science: A National Study of University and Industrial Researchers,* November 1984; J.D. Eveland, "Communications Networks in University/Industry Cooperative Research Centers," National Science Foundation, March 1985.

faculty entrepreneurship, while in others, the arrangement is designed to channel and facilitate that entrepreneurship.

Goals and Expectations. The goals and expectations of industry and university participants reflect the nature of the activities. Some industry participants articulate their goal in terms of a "window" into a scientific field. Elsewhere, corporate interest is tied to particular product or process development.

There is similar variation in what academics are trying to achieve. Some simply want to augment funds for certain kinds of research or equipment. Some believe the arrangements will facilitate job-hunting by their students. Often faculty members indicate that better access to the world of corporate R&D enhances their own competence and knowledge. It may enhance their incomes as well through consulting arrangements. In fact, some of the new arrangements have been put in place to regularize or gain control over consulting and entrepreneurial activities of faculty, or to provide commercial and entrepreneurial opportunities for faculty to attract them to the university or to keep them from leaving for more lucrative jobs. In a number of cases, the university administration sees the activities as an effective way of carrying out their mandate of providing public service.

University Culture. Most of the arrangements we studied are located in parts of universities with strong applied interests; that is, engineering schools, medical schools, and chemistry or computer science departments. However, universities differ greatly in their attitudes towards what kinds of relationships with industry are or are not appropriate. Those with long-standing liberal arts traditions have customarily considered the sciences in terms of their contributions to knowledge rather than technology. They avoid relationships other than those which support basic research, and insist that university faculty preserve the lion's share of control. The technical universities like MIT and RPI have shown a greater willingness to engage in applied research with industry funding. And universities like Georgia Tech, which grew up with a strong commitment to community service, consider a range of activities, from business incubator programs to proprietary contract research, as part of their mandate. In other words, it is the university's culture that defines the range of activities considered appropriate.

Industry Culture. The nature of the alliances also is strongly influenced by the cultural characteristics of the companies involved. Companies with a strong research tradition are more likely to invest in the long-term potential of a window on particular fields of science—more likely to fund basic research in the knowledge that it may not yield direct economic benefits, or at least not quickly. Some may not want a window on a particular field, but are willing to fund academic research, perhaps through consortia of companies, to help maintain the scientific vitality of their industry and the supply of well-trained industrial scientists. Other companies may feel that basic research is not a sound risk for them, even if they can afford it, and prefer arrangements with academe that focus on work of more immediate commercial potential. Some may prefer to keep their R&D in-house, where they can control its pace and direction and need not be concerned about the division of whatever economic returns materialize. Companies tend to be quite sensitive to the antitrust laws and to avoid arrangements that may put them at risk.

Differences also exist across industry sectors as indicated by the differing objectives and operating styles of the Semiconductor Research Corporation and the Council for Chemical Research. Member companies of SRC pool their resources to support a multi-million dollar, highly organized research program in universities, while CCR encourages one-on-one diverse, decentralized, and smaller-scale research programs.

Organization and Governance. The arrangements we have considered differ significantly in terms of organization and governance. Those involving basic research are located in regular university departments or schools, and are closely connected with general academic activity. Others, for example, the incubators and the institutes for contract research, involve facilities outside the main academic organization.

The programs also differ in terms of the relative influence of the university and industrial participants. In some of the research partnerships, corporate sponsors often do little more than broadly define legitimate fields of inquiry at the time of funding. In others, corporate representatives sit on committees which screen, focus, and thereby influence the direction of research. In still others, the relationship is contractual, with the sponsor defining the objective quite closely.

Federal and state governments also are important players in some programs with roles ranging from simply providing funds, to actively stimulating university-industry interactions, to influencing program development, operations, and governance.

Funding. In many of the programs, corporations are the principal sources of financing. In a few cases, industry associations provide support. In some, university funds are up front, with hope that these can be recouped. In others, federal or state governmental funds are important.

Clusters

The nature of the activities, expectations, university and industry culture, and governance clearly are correlated. While one can find examples of partnerships in virtually all positions of the map, we tend to see certain recognizable clusters. Five are described below, but obviously there are overlaps between adjacent types.

Research programs or centers that support many research projects, and that are closely tied to general academic research and teaching activities. Included here are the Monsanto-Washington University partnership, the Cornell Biotechnology Program, the Stanford Center for Integrated Systems, the relationship between Massachusetts General Hospital Department of Molecular Biology and Hoechst, and the Exxon-MIT arrangement. These programs sponsor research that is germane to the disciplinary interests of the involved faculty, and is "basic" in the sense that it is expected to yield publishable scientific findings. Training of graduate students is part of these programs. While the sponsoring corporations may expect special benefits from the projects, and therefore may have some proprietary stake in the results, specific commercial product or process development is not involved. University units are protective of academic freedom, although they are also sensitive to the interests of the sponsor. Consulting activity and faculty entrepreneurship may result from work on a project, but are not integral to it.

There may be a single sponsor, multiple sponsors, or sponsorship through an industry consortium; however, there is an identifiable and stable clientele. Corporate influence is exerted through membership on project selection committees, but corporate funders do not directly or independently specify what is to be done. University faculty retains considerable, usually dominant, control.

Focused projects involving both a well-defined practical objective and intellectual goals. Projects of this sort engage a research team— often including both university and corporate scientists—working toward a well-defined goal of interest both to the sponsor and the faculty. The academics involved tend to be in fields like engineering, applied physics, or computer science, where advancing or confirming ideas is associated with creating or testing devices or systems. Only one of these is in the set of cases considered in detail—the relationship between Carnegie-Mellon University and IBM, which aims at developing a computer system appropriate for a university. There are, however, many such programs in universities supported by the Department of Defense.

Characteristically, the client, be it a corporation or a government agency, has a major proprietary interest in achieving certain results. The academic reputations of key faculty members are also on the line, with the project representing the testing of their ideas. The design of the project represents a combining of both interests. The project may be located in a university department or school, or at a research institute affiliated with the university, but regular university faculty are centrally involved in the endeavor.

Programs developed to help commercialize faculty research. The incubator program at RPI largely fits this mold, as does Case Western Reserve's University Technology Incorporated, and Engenics, (associated with The Center for Biotechnology Research, MIT, the University of California at Berkeley, and Stanford University). These organizations differ from traditional contract research operations within technical universities, in that their aim is to help faculty implement the fruits of their research; however, the two kinds of activities are related. For example, the Route 128 companies were first established by scientists and engineers who had been working at MIT on contract research projects. Centocor and Neogen also operate with this objective, but as freestanding, for-profit companies that reach into the universities to identify and develop commercially promising research and technology.

Programs or institutions organized to help clients, operating outside the university. This group includes certain incubator programs, for example at Georgia Tech, and university contract research laboratories. The service provided may be directed to industry or to a government agency.

The universities involved in this kind of activity tend to have a long tradition of public service and industrial collaboration, often associated with engineering schools. The programs are conducted in laboratories that have some administrative distance from the university, although access to university faculty and equipment may be important.

Free standing research institutes, linked to several universities. The Microelectronics Center of North Carolina and the Industrial Technology Institute of Michigan differ from the above organizations. While university officials are on their governing boards, they operate on their own, staffed largely by their own employees. In both of these cases, the distancing from a university culture was deliberate, with the purpose of making the operation more like a corporate laboratory or a contract research facility. However, both organizations depend on part-time participation of university faculty and other university resources. . . .

Post Conference Commentary

Funding of university-industry alliances should involve more than a commercial objective. Support must also be provided for maintaining the general university research capacity and for the growth of specific disciplines; industry must support research whose applicability is not readily apparent. The Group recognizes the difficulty that individual companies have in pursuing such a course of action, but feels that industry must contribute to the general advancement of science and engineering. Failure to do so may put the nation at risk. . . .

Members of the Working Group are not of one mind regarding how they read these affirmations that all is going beautifully. That the parties are getting along amicably is not in itself evidence that the work the parties are doing is proving valuable to both. Indeed in the judgement of many members of the Group, most of the new arrangements are too new to evaluate that matter. In terms of the value actually gained by the parties, some undoubtedly will prove very successful, but we suspect that a number of others will not. . . .

The Working Group warns that the impact of faculty entrepreneurship may change the ambiance of the university. Of particular concern is the student-professor relationship which is necessarily affected by the dual roles of faculty marketing their inventions. Universities must be prepared to address such issues in order to avoid the consequences. . . .

The Working Group expressed the impression that royalty streams over the next 25 years will be insignificant compared to the total amount of research support at any given university. For example, the University of Wisconsin receives approximately $150 million from federal sources and approximately $4 to $5 million from the Wisconsin Alumni Research Foundation (WARF). (WARF provides funds for development of technologically useful products from the university's research.) The roughly 3% of the budget that the university receives from royalties through WARF has an impact, particularly because the funds have no strings. However, in terms of quantity, the funds are quite small. The Group sees the Wisconsin paradigm as typical; royalty streams, although desirable, will not become significant. . . .

There is a growing mutual dependence among universities and industry for the conduct of research. For example, in the fields of biomedical research, engineering, and some of the physical sciences, the cost of instrumentation and facilities is becoming progressively prohibitive. In some fields, industry will never be able to attract and retain all of the talented investigators that they need. The only reasonable mechanism for research in the future will be increasing collaboration and the development of permanent alliances. From this perspective, the Working Group considers the alliances as essential to maintaining the strength of the science and technology base, and not solely as a vehicle for enhancing commercial development. . . .

Part III: Observations After the Conference

Dorothy Nelkin and Richard Nelson

We learned a considerable amount about the new alliances in the study we conducted prior to the conference. Our knowledge about them was enhanced significantly by the discussion at the conference. However, for the most part what we learned confirmed and strengthened our prior view of the current situation.

One striking observation from our earlier research was emphatically reinforced at the conference. That was the enthusiasm of the participants for these arrangements, and their strongly expressed beliefs that good things would come of them. There were a few critics as well. However, unlike the critics who have expressed themselves in print, often espousing a point of view that the new arrangements are quite dangerous, for the most part the critics at the conference simply expressed a cautionary note. Their view was that there were several important issues that had not been thought through adequately, that it was too early to judge the results of many of the new alliances. While appreciating the enthusiasm and energy of those involved in the current experiments, we here want to join the critics in stressing that what is going on is still very much an experiment. And the experiments have yet to be seriously winnowed by history.

Some critics of the new arrangements have stressed their concerns that they jeopardize the role of universities as open institutions, and repositories of public knowledge. We think that enough information is in now to reduce, if not eradicate, these fears. Most universities continued to be aware that their principal mission is public science and education. While certain of the new arrangements we have learned about give us cause for concern, in our view the current threat to the openness of American universities lies far less in the new industry-university alliances, than in the increase in Department of Defense funded classified work conducted at universities, and a potential tightening of governmentally imposed constraints on free exchange of information.

We are more concerned about the rhetoric if not the substance of corporate influence on the allocation of university research resources. We place high value in the understanding that research priorities in scientific fields should be set to some considerable degree by working scientists themselves, on the basis of criteria internal to that field. Of course, "to some considerable degree" does not mean exclusively, especially in fields that are driven by concern with applications. The university research funding system as has grown up in the United States since World War II, by working through a variety of different funding sources with different attitudes and mandates regarding the matter, has achieved a sort of balance between internal and external criteria for funding.

The current rhetoric surrounding the new alliances sounds to us like a call for a significant increase in the weight of external, and in particular commercial, criteria relative to internal criteria. We would argue that the evidence supporting this call is not persuasive. Indeed, to our knowledge, there has been no real study of the issue. However, as we indicated above, our concern here is with the rhetoric, not the substance. We agree with those at the conference who argued that corporate funding of university research inevitably is going to account for a very small fraction of the total.

We are more cautious than many of the participants at the conference regarding how valuable the new partnerships are going to turn out to be for the corporations involved. To what extent is it sensible and responsible business strategy to tie into academia for certain kinds of research instead of doing the work in-house? While business gains by access to top-flight university people, the academic route reduces corporate control over research and limits the ability to appropriate returns. Universities are inherently leaky places. If proprietary rights are important, does it make sense to finance the work in academia? But if corporations do not gain some sort of a special advantage through their funding of an activity in the universities, what is in it for them? Corporations can be philanthropic, but not to a large degree, and corporate philanthropy is highly vulnerable to hard times. Academics should not count on much of it. It should be well noted that many corporate executives, and prominent academics, during the 1920s and 1930s called for significant increased funding of basic research at universities, through the vehicle of corporate philanthropy. For reasons that should be well understood, that never came about. We only got large-scale external funding of academic research when the American people agreed that government should do that job.

Of the many different kinds of experiments that are going on, some will turn out to be successful for the corporate sponsors as well as for the universities. But a number of others, we believe just as strongly, are going to turn out to be worthless to sponsoring companies, and perhaps not very valuable for the universities involved. There is a lot of winnowing that will go on.

As our final observation we offer the following. The last half-decade has been a very unusual time. We have seen, first, huge government deficits, and then later clumsy and Draconian measures to get the deficits down. As a result, the conventional wisdom now is bearish on what government ought to and can be doing in the arena of research finance, as elsewhere. We also have seen a sharp rise in the value of the dollar which accounts for much of the perceived decline in the competitiveness of American industry, including our high technology industries. But sooner or later the government budget will come into balance, and the nation will again be able to discuss new government roles in the financing of the nation's research. And the dollar will get better into line, and American industry will not be as much burdened in the competitive struggle by its over-valuation.

When these things happen, interest in industry-university alliances will surely continue. But there is good reason to believe that a changed environment will significantly modify the way they are perceived.

7
Government-University-Industry Research Roundtable: Industrial Perspectives on Innovation and Interactions with Universities (1991)

Innovation and Technical Change

How innovation is viewed is important in thinking about how it occurs and what roles universities can play in the innovative process. For the purposes of these interviews with seventeen senior research managers, innovation was considered as the conception of an idea and its movement toward and embodiment in a commercially successful product or process. Technical change and technical advance are steps in and contributors to the process of innovation.

Breakthrough Discovery versus Incremental Advance

In many industries, technical advance occurs most often through small incremental improvements to existing products and processes rather than as large technical breakthroughs. It is the incremental technological advance that is the dominant step in the process of innovation that is related to competitiveness and international trade. This view—stressed by most interviewees as the most important perspective on the process of innovation—is one that affects industrial approaches to technical change and collaboration. Incremental advance most often occurs in industry; universities play a small role, according to interviewees, because university scientists often tend not to operate on or understand industry's short-term schedules or the tools involved in developing an incremental improvement.

The interviewed industrial officials stated that during the early stages of a large, breakthrough discovery, however, industries often need to interact closely with universities to gain a more thorough understanding of the science underlying the discovery. Thus universities sometimes play a major role following a major breakthrough, when it is necessary to establish a base of understanding on which the breakthrough can be bolstered and continue to grow. Industry looks to universities to fill this role but does not want universities to become oriented toward product development, according to interviewees.

The reputation of a research lab is often based on feats of invention rather than incremental improvement . . . in spite of the fact that most of its staff are involved in incremental development and, typically less than 10 percent are doing truly creative breakthrough research, according to Albert Westwood. Procter & Gamble also continuously works to change or improve products through a combination of evolutionary and revolutionary product improvements. Geoffrey Place feels this is fundamental to P&G's success.

Hubert Schoemaker noted that the basic research in biotechnology conducted at universities and the initial hybridoma products speak to the significant role for universities in this emerging field. As biotechnology matures and the focus turns more to product development and incremental improvements, Centocor and other biotechnology firms may rely less on universities than they currently do.

Sources of Innovation and Technical Change

Most industry officials interviewed believed that, whereas universities are at the forefront of scientific discovery, product- and process-oriented technical change occurs within industrial firms for most fields. Industry is the primary source of innovation because industry culture fosters entrepreneurial awareness of profitable emerging fields and ideas. In addition, industry scientists and engineers know more about a technology—its detail and its system—than do academic scientists and engineers. The limited role of universities in innovation has not been recognized because of the misconception that technological change generally occurs through a remarkable breakthrough that will revolutionize an industry, because of the excitement that accompanies such radical new ideas regardless of how infrequently they occur, and because university scientists tend to have a simplistic understanding of how product development and commercialization occur, according to interviewees.

Peter Boer believes that the forefront of innovation often comes from industry. Industrial scientists have a good nose for profitable emerging fields. They tend to be better at setting goals and at interdisciplinary research, and can assess what needs to be done to develop a field; they are better than academics at seeing the broader scope and the long-range outcome.

For new advance, Rodney Hanneman stated that Reynolds Metals adopts alternative materials where strategically appropriate and synergistic with existing materials and products using the existing infrastructure (e.g. Reynolds Plastic Wrap and vinyl siding). In-house experts conduct complex and expensive process-oriented R&D using full scale systems involving many disciplines to achieve such advance. Technical advance also tends to come from in-house research at Inland Steel. There, according to Howard Pielet, innovation develops out of specific needs for a better system or widget.

Centocor is oriented to look outward for its sources of technology and to rely heavily on academic collaboration. These collaborations provide access to a tremendous pool of government-funded basic research that is critical for small businesses. For small biotechnology companies like Genentech and Centocor, according to David Botstein and Hubert Schoemaker, advance requires close connection with universities. In this field, as in superconductivity, innovations come from universities. Allied-Signal also looks to universities for advances, but only those 20 years or so into the future; advances that are not even conceived of in the present. Lance Davis noted though that "next generation products" at Allied-Signal, like many other firms, are developed in-house.

Place noted that the foods business at Procter & Gamble, on the other hand, is an industry that is not driven by technology change; it is low technology and has a limited science base. There is a fair amount of research into food products at universities, but it is not at the cutting edge.

At the same time, an enormous amount of basic research is being conducted in universities to add to the knowledge base that supports both the processes of incremental technological advance and breakthrough discoveries. How much companies rely on universities, however, varies as a function of the technical field, the maturity of the industry, the stage of research, and the size of company.

For many reasons that will be discussed below, there are limits to the role that research divisions—from universities or industry—can play in the innovation process, according to industry officials. However, interviewees also noted that without university research there would be a considerable lack of depth in the level of scientific understanding about products and processes. The industry interviewees recognized the role of universities in providing understanding and techniques that enable companies to solve problems, invent, and design effectively.

Not much new product technology comes from universities unless Procter & Gamble leads a project on an innovation, according to Place.

University contribution is through access to knowledge, not access to technology. Universities do not have a sophisticated understanding of the commercial needs, so when they apply knowledge to a need, they are frequently off base.

Westwood considers that Martin Marietta has had few if any products come directly from university research. However, coupled university and company programs have often been very productive. Udo Axen agreed stating that Upjohn sees little that academics are doing directly that the company may want to buy into; universities generally have not been a source of new pharmaceuticals beyond biotechnology. Universities are not equipped to develop products through a multidisciplinary approach.

Much of International Paper's work is in process optimization and product design that involves such technological development, according to Keith Hall. Most work is done internally; universities do not have appropriate equipment. However, some R&D in the pulp and paper industry emphasizes "better" trees. This R&D is carried out in cooperatives run by universities.

Joel Birnbaum noted that in computing, new research is generally carried out by entrepreneurs and industrialists; universities can then take the time to search for fundamental understanding which leads to refinement and the second wave of innovation. A prototype then often comes out of university research with new experimental tools often calling for new measurement capacity. Universities do not need to carry out the initial breakthrough, but a relationship should be sought to take advantage of creating complete and correct systems.

Key Role for Universities in Training and Education

A key role for universities is the training and education of scientists and engineers. This message was highlighted and repeated throughout the interviews as the most important and significant role for universities. Most interviewees stated that U.S. colleges and universities are doing a good job of teaching science and engineering students the fundamentals, although educating students is not always a priority for faculty members. Many commented that there is room for improvement in certain areas, however, including management skills, communication skills, quality assurance, and a team approach to problem solving. Some interviewees noted that training students for academic careers does not fully prepare students for industrial careers—teaching focuses on the single investigator rather than on a team approach. . . .

Industrial Collaboration for Innovation

Although most firms look to themselves as a source of incremental technological advance, all industry interviewees acknowledged their reliance on other organizations and institutions for scientific and technological breadth and for in-depth understanding. Collaborative efforts are forged—with universities, other companies, federal laboratories, and in-house departments—to allow a firm access to new and emerging ideas, bright minds with varying perspectives, and financial leveraging for precompetitive R&D.

In general, industry interviewees stated that they find the most fruitful form of collaboration to be a "bottom-up" scientist-to-scientist approach with one-on-one relationships rather than "top-down" management decisions for collaborative arrangements. Although a number of interviewees indicated that they participate in collaboration that did not arise from a "bottom up" approach, primarily with university centers, consortia, or affiliates programs, all see these as mechanisms for accessing expertise—of consultants or recruits—or for promoting good will. Interviewees emphasized the importance of informal as well as formal interactions for collaboration; often long-term interactions begin as informal discussions among potential collaborators.

Most industry participants expressed skepticism about the results of generic research contributing to competitive advantage, and thus they are not willing to support it to a large extent. Many stated the belief that it is the role of the federal government to pay for the major share of this type of research. In the interest of the national welfare, many firms are willing to spend a small amount—less than 2 percent of their R&D budget—on precompetitive, generic research, although there is some variation by industry. In addition, precompetitive research is not generally pursued through company-financed consortial arrangements with universities either, according to industry interviewees. Companies would want to retain proprietary status for any discoveries that might emerge and would prefer not to lose competitive advantage through the sharing required in a collaborative program.

Procter & Gamble is less internally focused with respect to science and technology than it was a decade ago, Place noted. This change has been driven by two factors; the need for external expertise as the business moved into diverse areas of technology, and the movement of environment and safety issues and concerns into all areas. Environmental concerns are key to the paper industry, now and in the future according to

Hall. Research on environmental concerns at International Paper is conducted through cooperatives with vendors, competitors and with other industries.

Bell Laboratories research scientists, on the other hand, do not often need to collaborate because they usually have the capacity to do the work in-house. They consider the Laboratories to be a peer of universities, and as a "captive university" to AT&T, according to Robert Lucky.

According to the industry interviewees, the amount and type of collaboration that a company will undertake is based on the stage of the research, the scientific field, and the size of the company and R&D effort. For small companies, in particular, external collaboration is critical, because these firms often have limited R&D budgets and therefore need to maximize research capacity by leveraging work through collaboration.

Collaboration with Universities

Although industry does not rely on universities for commercially viable innovative technologies, all interviewees acknowledged the importance of collaboration with universities. Industry needs new knowledge from universities in order to build new technologies and to improve old ones. In fact, a company will occasionally support university research in an area that is new to the company and that also extends the university's research program into new topics. In addition, industry officials increasingly participate on advisory committees at universities to provide their perspectives on promising long-term research frontiers. Collaborations also occur with consultants from academia who provide perspective, analysis, and special expertise for many industry projects.

Smith pointed out that there are only a finite number of relationships with universities that a company can sustain. For every dollar spent on research, $10 needs to be spent on development, and $100 on design and building. Currently, Conductus is focusing on development and design and, therefore, can only participate in selected opportunities to leverage those developments in the best way possible. Collaboration with universities is also self-limiting by the number of in-house lab scientists who care about the research project and are willing to put in the time for collaboration as well as by financial constraints, according to Boer and others. A few interviewees noted that university contracts are a financial cost at the margin of the company's portfolio, and can be put on hold if need be during times of financial stress.

Martin Marietta prefers to fund university research that will stretch it into an area where the firm has only limited expertise, according to Westwood. Otherwise, the flow of information tends to be from the company to the university. This work at the margin of Martin Marietta's current capabilities will permit the firm to expand its know-how and understanding. Similarly, GM Research Laboratories funds only basic research on specific technology that is not close to the firm's proprietary research, Frosch noted. W. R. Grace also does not establish contracts with universities in technologies where the firm has a vested interest. Rather, it seeks to create relationships around emerging technologies in key scientific areas for the company. Boer believes that the company has no choice but to stay abreast with university research applicable to key areas for the company. A high percent of Procter & Gamble's drug discoveries or therapies will come from understanding underlying mechanisms, not primarily from a new drug structure, Place said. Therefore, it is important to work with universities whose scientists are highly competent in relevant research. Cost, talent, speed, and degree of protection dictates the amount of collaboration that P&G will seek from universities on any given project. In-house research can be done much faster at high cost if need be.

University Misconceptions about Commercialization and the Process of Innovation

According to a number of industry interviewees, many university officials erroneously believe that discovery of new ideas represents the most significant step in the process of innovation, and that universities are the key source. While the creative aspect of invention should not be minimized, even in the rare breakthrough event the development of an idea into a commercial product is a long, costly, and often unsuccessful process. Interviewees stated that many university officials tend to have an inflated view of the importance of university research efforts in innovation. Most often ideas from university scientists are too embryonic to be quickly or easily commercialized.

Some industry interviewees expressed the concern that universities in the wake of increasing financial constraints and limitations on the support of basic research will take on product discovery as part of their mission and research. They stated that this would be a mistake. Universities should not attempt to orient their research more closely to product discovery; this is not an appropriate role for universities, nor is it a task for which they are generally well suited, said the interviewees. Rather, they must continue to teach, to foster creativity, and to advance the frontiers of knowledge through long-term basic research. Most, if not all, interviewees commented that this role does not conflict with the need for university-industry collaboration. On the contrary, they explained that this role creates the underlying structure for the nature of collaborations and the expectations that universities should have when entering into cooperative programs with industry; universities can provide the trained manpower to address long-term basic research questions related to industrial goals. In addition, it was noted that for a few particular industries—not represented in the IRI-Roundtable study—applied research at universities is germane to industrial development.

Boer finds that 50 to 60 percent of the industry-university relationships have poor convergence of goals, i.e., typically where W. R. Grace is seen mainly as a source of money. In the other 40 to 50 percent, however, the relationship is successful, persists for a long time, and funding tends to increase. W. R. Grace is generally loyal to those who establish ideas and move them forward. Money spent at universities should be focused on long-term basic research, but universities also must understand the goals of industry: to link discovery and commercial reality. Boer views successful projects as those where convergence on a meaningful societal goal has occurred and both intellectual and commercial achievements are attained. Boer agreed that W. R. Grace contracts may cause a shift in direction of university research, but he pointed out that this is a voluntary process beginning with a proposal from a faculty member.

Heininger believes that since World War II, university research has tended to focus on the source of funds and has de-emphasized interaction with the users of the output of research. Government funding by peer-review decisions means that university scientists have played a key role in deciding what research to fund and this has emphasized the pursuit of scientific knowledge, while not necessarily providing a balancing input as to what society's needs are likely to be from other points of view. Heininger acknowledges that the needs of industry cannot be the only important criteria for the conduct of basic research, but he believes the selection process for investing in R&D may be part of the reason for our current competitiveness problem. Place believes that universities should continue to conduct basic research; that if industry and technical growth were the "customers" for the results of academic research, the use of discoveries and the education system would be drastically altered. . . .

Consortia, Centers, and Affiliates Programs

Consortia and centers that include the participation of several companies may be good at promoting basic science but are not effective at commercialization: they are too remote from the marketplace; they provide uncertain commercialization benefits given the generic nature of the work; and there is a strong motivation for individual industrial members to develop products in-house rather than share results, according to a number of industry officials interviewed. Consortia and centers may be effective in addressing generic issues in the development of new technologies and providing a networking source, interviewees noted, but they are unlikely to play a significant role in the process of innovation.

Generally, industrial affiliates programs are not profitable, according to industry interviewees, and generally, companies are less and less interested in participating. Those that continue to support such programs tend to do so either as good will gestures or to have access to students and faculty for recruitment.

W. R. Grace has joined a number of consortia, and subsequently has dropped out of most of them because they were not meeting W. R. Grace's needs for competitive advantage. In their primary form, university-based consortia are strong interdisciplinary faculty groups working on industrial issues of common interest to leverage financial investments. Boer believes that: the value for a company to join a consortium is inversely proportional to the amount of knowledge it has about the subject—creating the possibility of proprietary technology leaking to competition if one participates actively; often faculty do not collaborate actively with member companies; and it is time-consuming to find out what is going on in a consortium.

International Paper participates in consortia in forest research, according to Hall. The company does not expect proprietary information from consortia arrangements and sees no advantage other than that the firm is the largest landowner in the U.S. and, therefore, has the most potential for advance. For a modest investment, consortia provide the company with access to cutting edge research.

Place believes that sometimes creating a structure for interaction gets in the way of the potential when two individuals—one in-house researcher and one university researcher—want to work together to address a particular problem or system. The one-on-one approach is the vehicle of choice for collaborating with universities from the perspective of Procter & Gamble and other industries.

Large Multimillion-Dollar Alliances

In general, most firms do not opt for large multimillion-dollar partnerships with universities or university departments, according to industry interviewees. Indeed, only a few of the interviewees work in companies that are involved in large alliances.

From Heininger's point of view, both of the large university alliances in which Monsanto has participated—with Harvard and with Washington University—have not yet demonstrated success. He noted, however, that others within Monsanto view the alliances quite differently and believe them to be very successful. The bottom line is that products need to be eventually developed if a major collaboration is to be judged successful for both parties, Heininger believes. Otherwise, Monsanto's participation becomes a charitable donation to the university. No product leads emerged from the 12-year project with Harvard. The current interaction with Washington University cannot be judged yet, but to date no products have been developed. Primarily, those ideas touted thus far have been failures because the assumptions that a product was ready for development was premature. Heininger says that at this point in a well-run in-house project, Monsanto would have expected products by now.

Many of the interviewees noted that they had some skepticism as to the ultimate commercial success of these partnerships. Some commented that while the projects are viewed as great successes from the university perspective because they provide a large source of funds in support of worthwhile basic research efforts, the industry perspective is that their success in promoting innovation and commercialization remains to be seen.

Intellectual Property Rights

Industry interviewees complained about difficulties in negotiating intellectual property rights and patenting and licensing agreements in university-industry partnerships. The probability of any commercially viable product or process evolving from an alliance with a university is remote, according to a number of interviewees, because of the type of research that companies support at universities. Interviewees noted that, ironically, industry in general is becoming more flexible in the conditions of its support for university research while universities are becoming more stringent in negotiating intellectual property rights for potential discoveries based on the slim chance that a significant, commercially viable breakthrough will occur and hence will result in an opportunity for the university to reap great financial rewards. Industry interviewees stated that these expectations are, in general, unrealistic and arise from the views held by many university officials regarding the innovation process and the role of breakthrough discoveries in that process. Furthermore, these expectations on the part of university officials can cause divisiveness on the campus between university administrators adamant about claiming intellectual property rights and university scientists who wish to conduct the research without burdensome policies, and between the university and industry participants, according to interviewees.

Martin Marietta is not overly sensitive to how the intellectual property issue is handled in contracts with universities because, in Westwood's view, the probability of any moneymaking product being developed is very low. However, he resents any university lawyer or financial spokesman declaring that the company has no rights to outcomes of research that the firm has funded at a university. Westwood's opinion is that these people do not understand the R&D process, and are sometimes so rigid that further useful dialogue is not possible.

Hanneman observed that at Reynolds Metals, most patents from academia are usually not crucial from a business viewpoint. Internally generated technology is often sufficiently complex that it is unlikely that a competitor will stumble onto an exact replica. Because this industry is more mature than some, it is less likely that a competitor will develop a broad dominating patent.

Because Conductus and Centocor are small companies, they are more dependent on patents that come from outside the firm. Exclusivity is important in many technologies in order to limit others from doing the same work. Universities must find a way to grant exclusivity to firms in which faculty are involved, according to Smith. This is often viewed as a conflict of interest. Rather, it should be viewed as a mutuality of interests to maximize the chances of marketing the discovery. . . .

Summary

The purpose of this document is to add the perspectives of seventeen senior industrial officials to the ongoing discussions of how innovation occurs and how alliances with universities contribute to technical change and competitiveness within individual companies. It is important to note that the term innovation was considered by these industrial officials as the conception of an idea and its movement toward and embodiment in a commercially successful product or process.

The perspectives presented in this document are not intended to represent generalized conclusions for all of industry, but rather should be interpreted as a collection of opinions of the seventeen industrial officials interviewed. As is reflected in the text, diverse perspectives exist among these industry officials.

Four central themes emerged from the interviews:

• In many industries, innovation usually occurs through in-house incremental improvement to existing products or processes rather than the rarer breakthrough event that revolutionizes a product or process.

• Industry is the primary source for innovation. Universities play only a limited role in this realm. Interviewees noted that the role of universities varies depending on the maturity of the field, the type of innovation—incremental or breakthrough—and the "culture" of the company.

• The primary role for universities is as educator and provider of talent. This function is universities' greatest contribution to the process of innovation, according to interviewees. Providing in-depth, fundamental understanding of scientifically and technologically new or emerging ideas is another significant role for universities. According to interviewees product development should not be an academic role.

• The challenge for industry is to determine the adequacy of the knowledge base; to identify emerging technologies and barriers to knowledge transfer; and to define approaches to collaboration for maximum input of new knowledge. No company is large enough or smart enough to meet all of its knowledge needs within the firm. Interviewees stressed that industry must maintain relationships with universities, companies, and federal laboratories on topics relevant to their company's technological focus.

SECTION THREE

Conflicts of Interest

1

Case Study: Pharmatec and the University
of Florida: Intertwining Interests

In 1982, Dr. Nicholas Bodor, a Graduate Research Professor at the College of Pharmacy at the University of Florida, invented a chemical carrier system with the potential for delivering drugs directly to the brain. Dr. Bodor assigned the patent to the University of Florida, which issued an exclusive license to Loeb & Company. Loeb & Company agreed to raise more than $6 million for the development and testing of the new drugs, which became known as the chemical delivery system (CDS); a start-up company, Pharmatec, was incorporated to develop those drugs.

Dr. Bodor was listed as the sole inventor of the CDS, and the Vice President and Director of Pharmatec, while retaining his position at the university. The license specified that $1 million of the $6 million raised through sales of stock was to be spent on grants and contracts for development and testing of inventions and products at the University of Florida.

On July 6, 1983, a prospectus for Pharmatec stated that (1) Pharmatec was totally dependent on Dr. Bodor, the inventor, for the development of drug-carrier combinations, (2) Dr. Bodor was to spend 20 percent of his time working for Pharmatec, (3) Dr. Bodor was to spend an additional 10–20 percent of his time in his capacity as director of

From Nineteenth Report, Committee on Government Operations, ''Are Scientific Misconduct and Conflicts of Interest Hazardous to Our Health?,'' September 10, 1990.

221

employees of the university engaged in R & D activities for Pharmatec, and (4) Dr. Bodor owned about 5.1 percent of the total Pharmatec stock (subject to Dr. Bodor serving his 5-year commitment to Pharmatec). On April 4, 1984, the above statements were repeated in Pharmatec's 10-K tax form for the year 1983.

In addition to Dr. Bodor, Pharmatec hired three other University of Florida College of Pharmacy faculty members, paying each with 1,000 shares of stock, valued at $5,000 at the time, and additional stock options. Pharmatec also gave 1,000 shares of stock to the Dean of the College of Pharmacy, Michael Schwartz, and provided stock or stock options to several other key administrators. Dr. Bodor, Dean Schwartz, and several faculty members served on the company's scientific advisory board. These arrangements were made according to university guidelines, and with the assistance of the university.

In the fall of 1984, Dr. Kenneth Sloan, an Associate Professor at the University of Florida School of Pharmacy who was a member of the Advisory Board of Pharmatec, read two scientific articles that suggested to him that there was a structural similarity between CDS and a known neurotoxin called MPTP, and that CDS might cause symptoms similar to those for Parkinson's disease through skin contact or inhalation. Dr. Sloan became concerned that the CDS might be dangerous to the students and researchers studying CDS, so on December 12, 1984, he gave copies of the two scientific articles to Dr. Michael Schwartz, the Dean of the College of Pharmacy, who was also a member of the Pharmatec Advisory Board and a Pharmatec stockholder. Sloan asked Schwartz to show the articles to Dr. Bodor and Pharmatec without mentioning Sloan's name. At that time, Dr. Bodor, besides being a Vice President of Pharmatec, was also Chairman of the Department of Medicinal Chemistry, the department in which Dr. Sloan was also a member.

On January 25, 1985, Dr. Bodor asked Dr. Sloan, in his capacity as a member of the Pharmatec Advisory Board, to give his opinion of the two articles. Dr. Sloan responded in a memorandum, suggesting that since there might be risks associated with contact with the CDS, appropriate toxicity tests should be run and greater care should be exercised by everyone working with the CDS.

At about the same time, Dr. Sloan began to publicly question how Dr. Bodor could spend 20 percent of his time at Pharmatec and another 10–20 percent of his time working on Pharmatec projects at the university and still be considered a full-time faculty member. In March, the College of Pharmacy faculty were informed by the Dean that the description of Dr. Bodor's time commitment to Pharmatec in the prospectus and 10-K were errors. However, three days after the Dean's letter was sent, the same statements as in the prospectus and the 1983 10-K were repeated in the Pharmatec 10-K for 1984.

On April 1, 1985, Dr. Sloan resigned as a member of the Pharmatec Advisory Board because of the discrepancies between Dean Schwartz' letter of March 25, 1985, and the Pharmatec 10-K forms. He had concluded that either Dean Schwartz and the university or Pharmatec were not telling the truth about Dr. Bodor's time commitment to Pharmatec and the research being funded at the university by Pharmatec, or they were misleading the stockholders and the IRS.

Dean Schwartz and Dr. Bodor continued to claim that they had informed the Chairman of Pharmatec of the errors in the prospectus and 10-Ks in early 1984; however, similar statements regarding Dr. Bodor's time commitments were repeated in the 1985 10-K, which was filed in 1986, and the 1986 10-K, which was filed in 1987.

In 1985 and 1986, the question of the potential dangers of CDS was raised at student seminars at the university on CDS research. According to Dr. Sloan, Pharmatec and university officials defended the safety of CDS, and resisted suggestions that it should be tested on primates.

At the time that Pharmatec made its agreement with Dr. Bodor regarding his future ownership of 5.1 percent of Pharmatec stock, it was illegal for any State employee to own five percent or more of the total stock of a company doing business with the State. In July 1986, the State of Florida Attorney's office created an exemption to the State law for faculty entrepreneurial ventures. This exemption made it legal for Dr. Bodor to eventually own 5.1 percent of Pharmatec stock upon completion of his 5 years as Director of Pharmatec in January 1988.

Meanwhile, by the late 1980's consultants and officials associated with Pharmatec occupied most of the positions of authority in the College of Pharmacy, including the Associate Dean of Research, Chair of the Department of Pharmaceutics, and Chair of the Department of Pharmacodynamics. Dr. Bodor, Vice President for Pharmatec Research, was Chairman of the Department of Medicinal Chemistry in the College of Pharmacy, then stepped down to become a Graduate Research Professor in the university.

In September 1988, Dr. Sloan's accusations were described by Dr. Leonard Minsky of the National Coalition for Universities in the Public Interest, in testimony before the subcommittee. This testimony generated widespread media interest, which was followed by strong university criticism against Dr. Sloan, and a negative annual report of Dr. Sloan's academic performance. Subsequently, Dr. Sloan received a much lower salary increase than faculty with similar performance ratings; he has filed a complaint in response. . . .

[On another matter] in 1985, Dr. Sloan and other scientists raised questions regarding possible Parkinson disease-like symptoms from working with CDS, and Sloan asked that animal testing be conducted to make sure the CDS was safe for study by students and faculty. The university refused to do so. Instead, officials have claimed that after the School of Pharmacy turned to an outside scientist for advice, they decided that no precautions were needed, because the scientist concluded that the suggestion of toxicity based on chemical structure resulted from a "fallacy of reasoning that had to derive from individuals unfamiliar with chemistry or pharmacology, except in the most superficial sense."[1] However, the same scientist supported Sloan's advice, stating that it was not enough to look at chemical structures, because it is necessary to "do the animal testing to ascertain whether there is toxicity or not."[2]

Several years after Sloan made that request, Dr. Bodor, the Director of Pharmatec, finally conducted toxicity research on animals, publishing his results finding no toxicity in 1988. Assuming these findings are accurate, the story of Pharmatec demonstrates how the financial interests of universities and their faculty can conflict with such important scientific questions as the safe conduct of research, as well as the fair treatment of faculty.

---

1. Letter from Donald R. Price, Vice President for Research, and David R. Challoner, Vice President for Health Affairs, to *Science*, June 15, 1990, Vol. 248, p. 1280.

2. Response from Elliot Marshall to Donald Price and David Challoner, *Science*, June 15, 1990, Vol. 248, p. 1280.

2
Corporate Funding of Academic Research (AAUP Report)

The report which follows was prepared by a subcommittee of the Association's Committee A on Academic Freedom and Tenure. It was approved for publication by the Committee in September, 1983, for the information of the profession. Comments from chapters, conferences, and other interested persons are welcome and should be addressed to the Association's Washington Office.

A considerable amount of concern has been expressed about the recent increase in the amount of corporation-funded research that is conducted on university campuses by university personnel and about the variety of new institutional arrangements under which that research is carried out. At its meeting in June 1982, Committee A appointed the undersigned subcommittee "to identify the issues in this subject that are of Association concern and to advise as to how these issues might best be addressed."

The following report is divided into four parts. *Part I* gives a brief history of corporate-university funding relationships. *Part II* surveys the kinds of arrangements under which faculty members are currently cooperating with business. Some of these arrangements have generated concerns; *Part III* describes the concerns which are of special interest to the AAUP, mainly those that lie in the possible effects of these arrangements on academic freedom and on the employment and working conditions of faculty members and their students. *Part IV* makes recommendations.

Part I: History[1]

Corporations were a major source of university research funds before World War II. Their contributions were not large and were

---

From *Academe,* November–December, 1983.

1. The information contained in *Part I* comes largely from the following: Derek C. Bok, *Beyond the Ivory Tower: Social Responsibilities of the Modern University* (Cambridge, Mass.: Harvard University Press, 1982), ch. 6; Bruce L. R. Smith and Joseph J. Karlesky, *The Universities in the Nation's Research Efforts,* vol. 1 of *The State of Academic Science* (New York: Change Magazine Press, 1977), chs. 2, 3; and Robert M. Rosenzweig and Barbara Turlington,

aimed primarily at supporting applied research on specified practical problems; nevertheless, these contributions constituted a significant portion of the small amount of money available for campus-based research.

Federal support for university research began to grow slowly during the 1930s, but it was the nation's urgent wartime needs that made plain the great importance of university scientists, and federal support for their research began to grow dramatically. This growth continued after the war, with continued public concern about military preparedness during the cold war, and with postwar affluence making possible an increase in expenditure on health-related research and on basic research in a wide range of disciplines. "In 1940, total funds available for scientific research in universities from all sources were $31 million. In fiscal year 1979 . . . total government support for university-based research surpassed $3 billion."[2]

Not surprisingly, corporate funds for university research occupied a less and less significant place in university budgets during those years. At the same time, universities were expanding, so that the better graduate students could look forward to careers in the university, doing academic research, rather than in industry. Moreover, industry's own investment in basic research was declining during those years, and the scientist in industry therefore had less and less to talk about with the scientist in the university. In short, the links between the corporation and the university grew progressively weaker.

By the late 1970s, a reversal of this trend was clearly under way. In the first place, federal funds for university research, having grown (in constant 1972 dollars) at an annual rate of between 12 and 14 percent between 1953 and 1968, dropped to no growth at all between 1968 and 1974, and grew at an annual rate of only 4 percent from 1974 to 1978. The shock to university budgets was severe. Second, the universities themselves were no longer expanding; they would have to train their graduate students for careers in industry, and that required attending to industry's needs. And third, industry had its own problems—increasing competition from abroad, and slowing productivity at home—and it became increasingly interested in the possible benefits

---

The Research Universities and Their Patrons (Berkeley: University of California Press, 1982), chs. 1, 3. See also "University-Industry Research Relationships: Myths, Realities, and Potentials," Fourteenth Annual Report of the National Science Board, 1982.

2. Rosenzweig and Turlington, p. 16.

to itself to be derived from closer cooperation with the university. The federal government encouraged that cooperation.

The extent to which industry is currently supporting university research should not be exaggerated, however. Industry's support of university research grew slowly during the 1970s; but its share of the total funds currently entering the university for support of research is just under 4 percent.[3] Moreover, that percentage is not generally expected to increase very much. The federal government has been, and is certain to remain in the foreseeable future, the dominant source of funds for university research.

On the other hand, industry's support for university research is by and large entering a relatively small number of universities; and it is entering those universities in a fairly narrow range of disciplines— primarily in biology, chemistry, and engineering. So its impact on those universities has been greater than its total quantity might have led one to expect.

Part II: Current Industry-University Relationships

Corporations are in contact with universities and their faculties in a wide variety of ways. We survey six kinds of contact, in order of increasing involvement of the corporation in the life of the university.[4]

Faculty Consulting

Many faculty members, in a wide variety of disciplines, serve as part-time paid consultants to corporations. Under such arrangements, the faculty member usually leaves the campus and goes to the corporation; and the university is implicated in such arrangements only by virtue of the fact that its policies permit them.

---

3. Cf. Herbert I. Fusfeld, "Overview of University-Industry Research Interactions," in *Partners in the Research Enterprise: University-Corporate Relations in Science and Technology,* ed. Thomas W. Langfitt, *et al.* (Philadelphia: University of Pennsylvania Press, 1983), 10–19. But see also "University-Industry Research Relationships: Myths, Realities, and Potentials."
4. Much of the information in the following survey comes from Denis J. Prager and Gilbert S. Omenn, "Research, Innovation, and University-Industry Linkages," *Science,* 25 January 1980, 379–84.

Industrial Associates Programs

Several universities have worked out programs under which a variety of corporations pay a yearly fee to the university, in return for which they receive publications and attend on-campus briefings, seminars, and conferences on research in the areas of interest to them. The university is at liberty to use the funds so generated for any purposes it chooses.

Research Consortia

One or more universities may arrange with several companies to do research in an area of interest to the companies. The member companies pay a yearly fee to support the research, and they share in its results. The Massachusetts Institute of Technology's Polymer Processing Program is an example of such an arrangement. MIT's staff meets regularly with company representatives to identify research needs; MIT then selects the projects to be worked on, and the work is done by MIT's own staff and students. MIT owns all patents, and can license member or nonmember companies to develop the patented processes. No constraints are imposed on publication of research results.

Research Centers

These differ from research consortia chiefly in scale: they are larger and more heavily funded. Stanford University's Center for Integrated Systems is an example of such an arrangement. It will be supported partly by a consortium of corporations which will jointly contribute $12 million, partly by a grant of $8 million from the federal Defense Advance Research Projects Agency. The Center will be staffed largely by Stanford's faculty and students; but member companies may also send their own scientists to work at the Center. Final decisions as to the research programs to be carried out will be made by Stanford. Patents will be owned by Stanford; and, according to Stanford's current regulations, royalties will be divided as follows: one-third to the investigator, one-third to his or her department, and one-third to the school that houses the department—the university having first taken 15 percent for administration and overhead.

Research Partnerships

A true research partnership involves joint planning and joint implementation of the research program. Harvard University's relationship with Monsanto is an example of such an arrangement. Monsanto has agreed to pay $20 million over a twelve-year period to support research in those areas of biochemical and biological research in which Monsanto is interested. Harvard personnel conduct the more basic scientific research and contribute to the training of Monsanto scientists, who carry out the research required for developing marketable products out of the results of the basic research. The charter agreement provides that some patents are to be held by Harvard, some by Monsanto; and Monsanto has limited-term exclusive license to develop all Harvard intentions in the areas of research covered by the agreement. No constraints are imposed on publication of the research results beyond the requirement that the other party be informed prior to publication.

Corporation Formation

There has been discussion on a few campuses of the possibility that the university might itself participate in the formation of a for-profit corporation to exploit the discoveries of its own faculty members. The details of the various ideas discussed differ widely, but all would involve the university's becoming a stockholder in the new corporation in return for a relatively small investment by the university (plan approved by the University of Michigan Senate Assembly) or no investment by the university at all (plan rejected by Harvard).

Part III: Concerns Generated by Industry-University Relationships

Many people have expressed concern about the possibility that corporate-academic linkages of the kind here surveyed may generate pressure on universities and their faculties to shift attention from basic scientific and engineering research toward applied research into product development. It is arguable that this source of concern should be taken seriously: certainly it is the rare corporation that is large enough and farsighted enough to be able and willing to invest in pure research. On the other hand, it is also arguable that the increasing closeness between industry and the universities is of sufficient benefit to them, and to the nation as a whole, to outweigh that risk. Many people believe that one source of the nation's decline in productivity is the decline in recent years in the pace of technological innovation; and corporate-university linkages are thought to be likely to stimulate transfer of pure research results into new technologies and products.

We shall not address ourselves to any of the broader issues hinted at in the preceding paragraph. What will interest us is only the sources of concern that lie in the possible effects of corporate-academic linkages on academic freedom and on the employment and working conditions of faculty members and students.

Some of those sources of concern have long been familiar on university campuses. Others resemble those that were pointed to during the 1950s and 1960s, the years of dramatic increase in the federal government's investment in academic research.[5] We shall point to some similarities and differences as we proceed. It may perhaps be said by way of general summary at the outset that the differences are largely quantitative, and that they issue from the profits—to individuals and to universities—which the new corporate-academic linkages make possible.

Conflict of Interest

It has been argued that corporate-academic linkages of the kind we have surveyed constitute a standing invitation to faculty members to divert their time away from their proper academic duties—academic research and teaching—toward work for the corporations with which they are associated.

The possibility that faculty time may be diverted to off-campus activities is certainly not a novel idea. All universities encourage their faculty members to participate in such off-campus activities as may enrich their research and teaching; all universities discourage excessive involvement in off-campus activities which make no obvious direct or indirect contribution to the faculty member's capacity to carry out his or her proper academic duties. Faculty consulting, in particular, has long been regarded as a source of concern. Some consulting surely

---

5. The AAUP's statement of principles governing federally sponsored research, formulated jointly with the American Council on Education, may be found in "On Preventing Conflicts of Interest in Government-Sponsored Research at Universities," *AAUP Bulletin* 51 (Spring 1965): 42–43.

does contribute to the faculty member's work; but there are limits to what can be regarded as compatible with the holding of a full-time academic position. For this reason, most universities do place limits on the time that may be devoted to consulting: many now permit a maximum of the equivalent of one day a week.

Such limits cannot be policed, however; and where the financial rewards are great—for an extreme example, where faculty members serve in a management capacity, or own a substantial share of stock, in the corporation to which they are consultants—it would be no surprise if they were tempted to exceed the limit.

It is not clear how serious this source of concern is. Surveys conducted in 1969 and 1975 show that only 6 percent of the respondents devoted more than one day a week to consulting, and that paid consultants generally taught as much as, and published more than, their colleagues.[6] But it is entirely possible that faculty consulting has greatly increased in recent years, with the relative decline in faculty salaries and the increasing corporate interest in acquiring academic consultants.

Diversion of faculty time is only one of the possible products of a conflict of interest. Some commentators have claimed that faculty members' corporate associations may affect their assessment and treatment of their junior colleagues and graduate students: they may favor those whose work would be valuable to the corporate associate, and they may channel their graduate students into work that is potentially profitable to the corporate associate but that is not educationally valuable. Moreover, they may be tempted to exploit those whose research they direct: they may be tempted to make private profit from ideas generated in the university's laboratory by their junior colleagues and graduate students.

The availability of funds from external sources—funds targeted to research on topics chosen at least in part by the funding source—may be expected to provoke concern about the ways in which principal investigators assess and direct the work of their juniors; senior faculty members who exploit the work of their juniors did not arrive at the university along with the corporation. What is new is the new motive that is provided by the corporation. The possibility of acquiring prestige, and the further research support that prestige brings with it, have

---

6. Carl V. Patton, "Consulting by Faculty Members," *Academe* 66 (May 1980): 181–85.

been tempting enough to some errant faculty members; where large private profits can also be made, the temptation may greatly increase.

So far we have mentioned only the possibility of faculty members' finding themselves with conflicting interests; it would be at least as serious if the university itself had a similar conflict. Will the university be tempted to make preferential arrangements (in respect of promotions, tenure, salary, leaves, laboratory space, support for graduate students) for those faculty members whose research issues in inventions profitable to the university, or whose research enables the university to attract additional corporate funds for research?

It is arguable that the potential profits to the university from patents on the results of research carried out in its laboratories are not sufficiently great to constitute a serious source of concern. Harvard President Derek Bok writes:

> The normal rule of thumb is that it takes one thousand reported discoveries to produce one hundred patents; it takes one hundred patents to produce ten licenses; and only one license in ten will yield more than $25,000 per year.[7]

On the other hand, some universities have made sizable amounts from their patents: MIT, for example, is reported to have made $19 million from one patent (core memory for computers) and $10 million from another (synthetic penicillin).[8]

The university's conflict of interest would be greatly aggravated if it formed a for-profit corporation with one or more of its faculty members. With the best will in the world, university administrators could not fail to be affected, more or less subtly, by the university's direct financial involvement in the enterprise. As President Bok writes, the new role would shed "an aura of ambiguity and doubt on many decisions that the administration regularly makes."[9] And it would

> be harder still to convince the outside world, or even the rest of the faculty, that commercial considerations [had] not subtly begun to infect what have always been regarded as strictly academic decisions. Since the reputation for integrity is essential in matters such as appointments, and since the faculty's confidence in that integrity is important to its morale, even the appearance of impropriety could be extremely damaging.[10]

7. Bok, p. 156, n. 9.
8. *Business Week*, January 12, 1981.
9. Bok, p. 161.
10. *Ibid.*, p. 162.

Dissemination of Research Results

Some observers have expressed serious concern about the possibility that there has been a breakdown in normal familiar understandings governing the informal exchange of information and materials among academic scientists. It is widely reported, in fact, that academic scientists are now withholding information and materials with a view to making private profit from them.

Again, while much corporately supported research is funded by consortia of companies, with the research results then made available to all of them, much is funded by large individual corporations; and in those cases the funding source is likely to want to place restrictions on the publication of the research results. We know of no instances in which universities have agreed to more than short-term delays in publication, on the one hand to allow time for the filing of patents, on the other hand to allow the funding source to check the projected publication for the presence in it of proprietary information, owned by the corporation but furnished by it to the university's scientists in order to assist them in carrying out the research project. Obviously, however, the possibilities of excessive delay are worrisome. More obviously still, if a university agrees to more than this—if it grants a corporation the right to veto, or even to censor, the publication of the results of research it has funded—then the threat to academic freedom would be very serious indeed.

Choice of Research Topic

Much fear has been expressed that university scientists may be pressured into undertaking work on research problems that do not interest them by a university eager to acquire a profitable patent, or to please or attract a corporate associate. To some extent this source of concern overlaps one that we mentioned earlier, *viz.,* that the university might find itself in a conflict of interest vis-à-vis its own faculty. But it is perhaps worth singling out for special mention. The university which deflects its faculty members away from research in which they are interested, and in which they therefore do their best work, with a view to short-term financial gain, is compromising its own future.

A related fear is that a university may allow its corporate associate to interfere in a faculty member's choice of research topic. It is on any view certainly acceptable for a corporation to tell a university what area it wishes to support research in; but there are a great many different ways in which the research funds may be dispensed inside the university. As we saw earlier, some arrangements leave the dispensing of the corporation's funds entirely to the university. In the case of other arrangements, a faculty member interested in carrying out research in the relevant area submits a research proposal to a committee whose members are partly corporate, partly university. There is a potential for trouble in such an arrangement—very serious trouble if faculty members' continued employment at the university turns on their being able to obtain the committee's agreement to fund their research proposals. More troublesome still would be an arrangement under which the corporate funds are dispensed to one or more faculty members whose research for the duration of the grant is then entirely under the direction of the corporation—thereby in effect making them employees of the corporation. Fortunately we have seen no instances of this kind of research arrangement.

Part IV: Recommendations

Our impression is that, despite the small size of the corporate contribution to academic research (by comparison with the contribution made by the federal government), the concerns we surveyed in Part III are serious enough to call for closer attention by the AAUP. It seems to us that the Association should try to see if it can work out—preferably in conjunction with organizations representing university administrations—a statement on "Corporate Funding of Academic Research." We envisage such a statement as having two parts: (1) a suggested list of guidelines to be adopted by a faculty to minimize its own potential conflict of interest; and (2) a suggested list of principles that should govern corporate-university research arrangements.

An important preliminary is the acquisition of more information. This subcommittee examined a small sample of institutional "conflict-of-interest guidelines," and it looked at descriptions of some of the more widely publicized corporate-university research linkages. But it was not able to undertake a systematic study of these matters. The Association of American Universities has recently decided to gather information bearing on policy problems arising out of corporate-university relationships; the AAUP's own chapters are a source of information about conflict-of-interest guidelines and how they are viewed on the campuses which have them.

But discussion obviously cannot await the acquisition of more information. Many universities have long had conflict-of-interest guidelines, and on many campuses discussion is already under way about how they might be revised so as to speak to the concerns generated by the increasing availability of corporate funds; other universities have no such written guidelines, but discussion is under way about whether the institution should adopt a set of guidelines, and if so, what it should contain. Again, while we know of no university that has adopted a set of detailed principles governing the kinds of relationships with industry that the university will enter, discussion has already begun on a number of campuses.

The subcommittee thought it might be helpful to report its own impressions of some of the considerations which a faculty would do well to take into account.

Conflict-of-Interest Guidelines

In the subcommittee's view a university should have a written set of guidelines governing faculty conduct. The point of adopting such a set of guidelines is not that faculty members cannot be trusted to behave with propriety; the point is rather to arrive at an open, general agreement about what behaving with propriety on a particular campus requires.

The responsibility for determining standards affecting the academic community rests within that community. The first paragraph of the section entitled "Academic Freedom" of the 1940 *Statement of Principles on Academic Freedom and Tenure* reads as follows:

> The teacher is entitled to full freedom in research and in the publication of the results, subject to the adequate performance of his other academic duties; but research for pecuniary return should be based upon an understanding with the authorities of the institution.

We believe that the understandings to be reached should be guided by criteria set by the faculty of the institution: if guidelines covering what is incompatible with adequate performance of a faculty member's academic duties, and governing research or other activities engaged in for pecuniary return, are to be adopted on a campus, then it is the faculty itself that should formulate and adopt them.

We mention four kinds of consideration that we think call for attention.

Off-campus activities. As we said earlier, most universities do place limits on the time that a faculty member may devote to consulting: many now permit a maximum of the equivalent of one day a week. Academic institutions differ, and what is appropriate on one campus is not necessarily so on another; we think that a faculty should arrive at a considered position on the matter of whether to adopt a limit for itself, and if so, what the limit should be.

Some universities have recently adopted rules under which faculty members are prohibited from becoming executives of companies while still retaining their full-time academic positions. We think it likely that other universities will adopt similar rules; and we think that the question whether to do so is one a faculty would do well to consider.

We also think that a faculty should consider whether it wishes to permit its members to own a significant percentage of the stock of a corporation for which they consult, or of a corporation which does research in their area.

Disclosure. Disclosure requirements have generated a considerable amount of controversy and call for careful consideration: the right to privacy and the possible chilling effect of a disclosure requirement have to be kept in mind. Nevertheless, the subcommittee believes that a faculty ought to require that its members make regular written disclosure of the names of any companies in which they serve in a managerial capacity, if so serving is not itself prohibited. We also think that regular written disclosure ought to be made of the holding of substantial shares of stock in corporations for which the faculty member consults, or which do research in the faculty member's area. So also for arrangements under which a faculty member serves as a regular paid consultant to a corporation, and so also for all university personnel, materials, and facilities of which faculty members make significant use in furtherance of their private corporate relationships.

We say merely that regular written disclosure should be made; we do not say to whom. A faculty will wish to decide whether the disclosures it requires should be public or made only to an officer of the institution or to a faculty committee.[11] A faculty committee,

---

11. In several states, faculty members at public institutions are required by law or regulation to notify appropriate state agencies of all corporately funded research projects they are conducting, the terms of the research arrangement, and the amounts of money involved. The faculty at these institutions thus may not have the choice of deciding what faculty members should disclose and to whom.

charged with approving the relationships disclosed, has obvious advantages—not to be overlooked is its value in legitimating activities about which a faculty member might have been in doubt.

Last, if faculty members make use of university personnel in furtherance of their corporate relationships, we think it plain that such use ought to be disclosed to those involved.

Use of university personnel. It seems to us that any conflict-of-interest guidelines ought to contain an explicit statement to the effect that student research and training must be governed by the educational needs and benefits of the student.

Private profits. The possibility of private profit is the major source of concern about faculty involvement with industry. There is need for agreement about how it is to be dealt with.

Many universities operate under a policy according to which patents obtained for the products of research done in the university's laboratories are owned by the university itself. The university shares some of the royalties obtained from licensing the patented products or processes with the campus investigators; but in accordance with what rule should the royalties be shared? It is widely believed that an individual faculty member's share should not be large—some commentators believe that a ceiling should be placed on the total amount a faculty member may receive in any one year—in the thought that profits derived from research done at the university are made possible by the university and the university community at large.

The faculty that addresses itself to this question will want to keep in mind, however, that there are other potentialities for private profit on the campus. For example, it is standard for universities to impose no profit-sharing duty on the author of the successful textbook, despite the fact that it was written at the university and is often the product of years of experience with the university's students in the university's classrooms. Again, it is standard for universities to impose no profit-sharing duty on those who consult for industry, despite the fact that the opportunity to consult, and the size of the fee for doing so, may in part be due to the distinction of the faculty member's university.[12]

There presumably are differences in degree to be taken into consid-

---

12. A recent article argues that law schools should impose a profit-sharing duty on their faculty who consult: see Bruce A. Ackerman, "The Marketplace of Ideas," *The Yale Law Journal* 90 (April 1981): 1131–48.

eration. It is the rare textbook that earns its author any substantial sum of money; and the average consulting fee is not very large. More important, research done in the university's laboratories is research on which university funds have been expended. But these (and other) differences need to be thought through and weighed if a principled policy is to be adopted.

Corporate-University Research Arrangements

There are any number of possible corporate-university funding arrangements; we merely mention some of the general matters on which we think a faculty will wish assurance.[13]

In the first place, a faculty will wish it to be clear that its university will not be giving any appearance of endorsement of any corporate product or service, or in any other way compromising its independence.

The general features of any corporate-university funding arrangement should be openly disclosed—in particular, those details of the arrangement that concern the ways in which faculty members and students will be involved. A faculty may decide that there should be a faculty committee charged with examining and approving all research contracts before they are signed.

We think a faculty will wish that every such contract make explicit provision for open communication of the results of the research and that any provisions for delay in publication be short-term. A faculty may wish to stipulate that research projects that do not permit the publication, presentation, and open discussion of the research results will not be accepted.

We strongly believe that procedures governing decisions about faculty appointment, renewal, promotion, tenure, salary, apportionment of faculty time, and disposition of faculty grievances should be those standard within the university: more generally, that decisions bearing on the conditions of faculty service should be made within the university, by university personnel.

We have drawn attention to the dangers confronted by the university which forms a for-profit corporation to exploit the results of research

---

13. Faculty groups engaged in an examination of their institution's policies will wish to examine the report of the Pajaro Dunes Conference, which was held in March 1982, to discuss university-industry research relationships, particularly in the field of biotechnology.

done by its faculty. We believe that the risks outweigh the potential benefits to the university; faculties that are invited to approve such enterprises will certainly want to give close attention to the details before doing so.

One final, very general consideration. Our review of the literature inclines us to feel the need to express the hope that universities will not allow their current financial difficulties to skew their educational and research missions. We think it greatly to be hoped that universities will place a high value on the diverse research capabilities of their faculties, and that they will make every effort to encourage and assist their faculties, in whatever area of research, to make optimal use of those capabilities. We hope that no compromise will be made with the principles and goals of disinterested university teaching and research that might threaten the integrity of the academic enterprise.

Judith Jarvis Thomson (Philosophy)
Massachusetts Institute of Technology, *chairman*

Burton S. Dreben (Philosophy)
Harvard University

Eric Holtzman (Biology)
Columbia University

B. Robert Kreiser, Staff

3
The University of Minnesota: Disclosure of Conflict of Interest (1991)

Guide to Users:

This policy is intended to facilitate the widest possible interactions between faculty and industry, while at the same time satisfying the growing national concern over potential conflicts of interest in academia. This policy was a leader when it was first passed in 1988. The current revisions will keep it in the forefront of institutional policy in this area.

The underlying premise upon which this is based is disclosure. Effectively, in all cases in which knowledge of a relationship with an entity would be material, there must be disclosure. This includes, by way of example, disclosure of the relationship in the following cases:

a) when presenting material by scholarly publication; and/or
b) when applying for sponsorship from the entity; and/or
c) when applying for sponsorship from a third party: e.g., National Institute of Health (NIH) or National Science Foundation (NSF), where the outcome of the research would affect the entity; and/or
d) when transferring technology to the entity.

Examples of a relationship with an entity that must be disclosed include:

a) consultantship; and/or
b) equity position, including stock options; and/or
c) gifts or loans; and/or
d) official capacity such as serving on the board of directors or scientific board.

1. Preamble

The University of Minnesota actively encourages and participates in interaction with private companies as an important component of its

240

research, education, and public service missions. Research agreements between the University and private companies provide a valuable source of funds, equipment, and topics for University research. Consulting arrangements and other contacts between faculty and private companies advance the faculty's ability to provide a high quality research and educational experience for students and enhance employment opportunities for students. Licensing by the University to private companies, consulting services by faculty for private companies, assistance by faculty in new company starts, and other forms of technology transfer are critical to meeting society's needs. The University, therefore, clearly has a responsibility to foster the free flow of ideas and individuals between the University and the private sector.

The commitment of the University to this responsibility is reflected by its policies and guidelines relating to interaction with industry. The Patent and Technology Transfer Policy, Policy on Outside Consulting, and Guidelines on Interaction with Industry all recognize the value of various types of relationships with the private sector and provide the means to advance these relationships. These policies and guidelines are supported by the integrity of the faculty and by the adherence of the faculty to principles of good scholarly and professional practice. In view of the increased interaction between the University and the private sector, there is a need for a vehicle to safeguard the University's independence, credibility, primary missions, and the integrity of those University staff members involved in such interactions. Accordingly, this statement of principles is intended to facilitate and encourage interaction with the private sector by ensuring an environment in which University personnel are permitted the maximum freedom to enter into and continue various types of relationships outside of the University, while at the same time furthering the principal missions of the University and maintaining high standards of professional and ethical conduct.

2. Other Applicable Policies and Laws

This policy complements the provisions of other applicable policies, regulations, and laws, including the Policy on Outside Consulting, the Patent and Technology Transfer Policy, the statement on "Preventing Conflicts of Interest in Government-Sponsored Research at Universities," Guidelines on Interaction with Industry, the Tenure Code, and applicable state and federal law. This policy is intended to help implement and expand upon these other related requirements. It should be noted that this policy does not apply to Medical School consultation practices that are in accord with the Regents' Policy on Private Consultation Practice.

3. General Principles

With the acceptance of appointment or employment, an individual makes a commitment to the University and accords the University his or her primary professional loyalty according to the terms of appointment or employment. Every person is expected to arrange outside obligations, financial interests, and activities so as not to conflict or interfere with this overriding commitment to the University. At the same time, no one benefits from undue interference with the legitimate external activities of individuals who fulfill their primary full-time duties—teaching at the University, conducting scholarly research under its sponsorship, and meeting the other obligations to students and colleagues. Indeed, the involvement of individuals in outside professional activities, both public and private, often serves not only the participants but also the University as a whole. It has been, and continues to be, assumed that all individuals will be alert to the possible effects of outside activities on the objectivity of their decisions, their obligations to the University, and the University's responsibility to others.

The areas of potential conflict may be divided into two broad categories. The first relates to conventional conflicts of interest—situations in which individuals may have the opportunity to influence the University's decisions in ways that could lead to personal gain or give improper advantage to their associates. The second is concerned with conflicts of commitment—situations in which an individual's external activities, often valuable in themselves, interfere or appear to interfere with their paramount obligations to students, colleagues, and the University. Researchers and scholars are given great freedom in scheduling their activities with the understanding that their external activities will enhance the quality of their direct contributions to the University.

Currently, universities customarily use the term "industry" in the generic sense, to encompass their relations with all facets of the private sector. Throughout this policy, therefore, the term "industry" is not used in any restrictive sense, but rather applies generally to all private enterprise. This policy is intended to apply solely to sponsored research, technology transfer, and other written agreements as provided for in Section 5.f.

4. Definitions

a) PERSONNEL shall mean all persons appointed, employed and/or compensated by the University, including faculty, visiting faculty and researchers, professional and administrative staff, civil service employees, research and teaching assistants, residents, fellows, and trainees.

b) COMPANY shall mean any corporation, partnership, proprietorship, firm, association, or other legal entities worldwide, excluding government entities in the United States.

c) INTEREST shall mean any of the following interests in the aggregate held in a COMPANY, but not in a mutual fund whose investment policies are beyond the control of the individual, by PERSONNEL and/or PERSONNEL'S spouse and/or dependent children:

> (i) an investment comprising equity or options to purchase equity with a total current value of more than $1,000 or representing more than 5% of the total COMPANY equity; and/or
>
> (ii) personal payments (excluding consulting fees), gifts, and other benefits, including personal loans and services, received from a COMPANY to PERSONNEL within the previous twelve months with a total current value of more than $1,000; and/or
>
> (iii) a consulting arrangement with a COMPANY or other agreement to provide services to a COMPANY which is or should be disclosed in accordance with the Policy on Outside Consulting; and/or
>
> (iv) status as a director, scientific director or member of the scientific board of advisors, officer, partner, trustee, or employee (other than a consultant) of a COMPANY.

d) SPONSORED RESEARCH shall mean any research sponsored by the University or by any external entity including without limit a COMPANY, agencies of the U.S. federal and state governments, foundations, industry associations, and others.

5. Operating Principles

a) General. PERSONNEL may form relationships with COMPANIES, including acquiring an INTEREST in a COMPANY, provided that such relationships satisfy this policy and any other applicable policies and laws. The University encourages all PERSONNEL to form relationships with COMPANIES which further its education, research, and public service missions. For example, effective transfer of University technology may require that the PERSONNEL who originally developed the technology have a consulting agreement with or otherwise assist the COMPANY in acquiring rights in the technology. Under such circumstances, equity in the COMPANY may be an appropriate means to compensate the PERSONNEL. The COMPANY may also desire to fund further University research concerning the technology to be conducted by those PERSONNEL. These combination relationships and other relationships are permissible, and may indeed be very desirable to meeting University objectives, provided that the disclosure requirements in this policy are satisfied. Disclosure will allow the opportunity for review to ensure that the performance of PERSONNEL'S duties is not compromised.

b) Actual Conflicts. PERSONNEL shall not enter into or allow conflicts of interest or conflicts of commitment to the University, as those terms are annunciated in the General Principles. Determination whether an actual conflict exists shall be made by the appropriate vice president, or chancellor if a coordinate campus is involved. If PERSONNEL wish to initiate or continue such a conflicting relationship with a COMPANY and remain associated with the University, they shall seek a suitable leave of absence, reduction of appointment, or other arrangements with the University.

c) SPONSORED RESEARCH Proposals. PERSONNEL with an INTEREST in a COMPANY and who propose SPONSORED RESEARCH which may affect the COMPANY shall disclose the existence of the INTEREST. To the extent allowed by law, such disclosure shall be considered private until the project is awarded. The disclosure shall be public information after the project is awarded.

d) SPONSORED RESEARCH Participation. PERSONNEL, with an INTEREST in a COMPANY and who participated in SPONSORED RESEARCH which may affect the COMPANY shall disclose the existence of the INTEREST. Such disclosure shall be considered public information.

e) Technology Transfer. PERSONNEL with an INTEREST in a COMPANY shall disclose the existence of that INTEREST in the instance that the University is considering the transfer of rights, by license or otherwise, in technology developed by PERSONNEL to the

COMPANY. To the extent allowed by law, disclosure shall be considered private.

f) Other Written Agreements. In addition to restrictions in applicable law, PERSONNEL with an INTEREST in a COMPANY shall neither propose, negotiate, nor approve on behalf of the University a contract or other commitment concerning that COMPANY without full disclosure of the INTEREST. The disclosure shall be considered public information. This paragraph applies to all written agreements including, but not limited to, lease agreements, orders and requests for goods and services, or personnel from COMPANIES (including equipment, consulting services, and legal services). This provision does not cover research grants, contracts, and relationships otherwise covered by Section 5.c., 5.d. or 5.e. above.

g) Public Statements. PERSONNEL with an INTEREST in a COMPANY are expected to refrain from making public statements (statements for use by the press and/or to individuals with an interest in the stock of the COMPANY) regarding SPONSORED RESEARCH prior to publication of the results in recognized scientific literature or presentations at recognized scientific meetings. Whenever possible, the University shall include a clause reflecting this principle in each industry-sponsored grant, contract, or agreement.

h) PERSONNEL with an INTEREST in a COMPANY, or whose research was sponsored by a COMPANY, shall state such INTEREST or sponsorship when reporting research results and when providing expert commentary on a subject that may affect the COMPANY.

i) PERSONNEL with an INTEREST in a COMPANY who are proposing to perform research involving human subjects where the research may affect the COMPANY, shall disclose that INTEREST in the approved human subjects informed consent form.

6. Implementation

a) Compliance with this policy requires a three step determination:

(i) Does an INTEREST exist?[1]
(ii) When an INTEREST exists, must it be disclosed?[2]

---

1. The existence of an INTEREST is determined by applying Section 4.c. to the situation.

2. This is determined by applying Sections 5.c., 5.d., 5.e., and 5.f. to the situation.

246 University-Business Partnerships

(iii) When an INTEREST exists, must approval of a vice president, or chancellor if a coordinate campus is involved, be obtained?[3]

b) Disclosure under Sections 5.c. and 5.d. shall be made in the manner prescribed by the BA Form 23. These disclosures will be made as part of the proposal process. After acknowledgment by the appropriate department head and dean, the BA Form 23 and accompanying proposal shall be sent to the Office of Research and Technology Transfer Administration (ORTTA). ORTTA will forward the BA Form 23 to the appropriate vice president, or chancellor if a coordinate campus is involved, for approval when required.

It is the responsibility of all PERSONNEL to notify the appropriate department head and dean of any changes in the INTEREST originally reported on the BA Form 23. Such notification shall be made in a timely fashion (normally within a month) and in writing to permit reassessment by the appropriate officials.

It is required by University policy that all SPONSORED RESEARCH be covered by a BA Form 23. However, disclosures made during the term of the project and disclosures not made on a BA Form 23 shall be in the form of a memo to the appropriate department head and dean for their acknowledgment. The memo shall then be sent to ORTTA for consideration and for forwarding to the appropriate vice president, or chancellor if coordinate campus is involved, when approval is required.

The memo shall define the nature of the contract or other agreement and the COMPANY involved. Where possible, appropriate documentation from the COMPANY shall be attached. This memo shall be submitted in a timely manner so as to permit consideration by appropriate administration officials prior to consummation of the relationship.

c) Approval of the appropriate academic vice president, or chancellor if a coordinate campus is involved, must be obtained prior to submission of the SPONSORED RESEARCH proposal to the COMPANY or participation in SPONSORED RESEARCH, and approval of the senior vice president for finance and operations must be obtained prior to the transfer of rights in technology developed by PERSON-

---

3. This is determined by applying Section 6.b. to the situation or, when a BA Form 23 (Application for External Research or Training Support) is not involved, by the appropriate department head or dean after consultation with PERSONNEL involved.

NEL to the COMPANY, when PERSONNEL have an INTEREST in the COMPANY that is:

(i) an investment comprising equity or options to purchase equity with a total current value of more than $25,000 or representing more than 5% of the total COMPANY equity; and/or

(ii) personal payments (excluding consulting fees), gifts, and other benefits, including personal loans and services, received from a COMPANY to PERSONNEL within the previous twelve months with a total current value of more than $2,000; and/or

(iii) a consulting arrangement with a COMPANY or other agreement to provide services to a COMPANY which is or should be disclosed in accordance with the Policy on Outside Consulting and with annual compensation of more than $10,000; and/or

(iv) status as a director, scientific director or member of the scientific board of advisors, officer, partner, trustee, or employee (other than a consultant) of a COMPANY.

Faculty may wish to seek the above approval in appropriate cases where an INTEREST exists but does not meet the above definitions. Approval shall be granted or denied within two weeks of submission to the vice president, or chancellor if a coordinate campus is involved.

Factors that will be taken into account by the appropriate vice president, or chancellor if a coordinate campus is involved, determining approval include:

(i) THE PROMINENCE AND SIGNIFICANCE GIVEN THE UNIVERSITY AFFILIATION. Where the name and/or authority of the University (as opposed to that of the researcher) is more clearly being invoked, the University should institutionally examine research affiliations more carefully.

(ii) THE EFFECT OF THE OUTCOME OF THE PROJECT ON EXPECTED BEHAVIOR OF OTHERS. Where endorsement of a project or policy will result in people in significant numbers using a product or investing money or otherwise changing their lives, the University must bear responsibility to maintain objective evaluations. Where these first two factors combine to suggest the University, or a segment thereof, is acting as an independent evaluative laboratory, University responsibility is at a maximum.

(iii) DEGREE OF INVOLVEMENT AND DANGER OF OVER-COMMITMENT TO DETRIMENT OF UNIVERSITY MISSIONS. The University has the duty to scrutinize requests in the light of its own missions. High quality research should be encouraged. The extent of involvement of PERSONNEL in a project should not conflict with University activities.

d) Disclosure under section 5.e. shall be made in the form of a memo to the associate vice president for ORTTA. This memo shall be submitted in a timely manner so as to permit consideration by appropriate administration officials prior to consummation of the relationship.

e) Disclosure under Section 5.f. shall be made by memo to PERSONNEL with no INTEREST in the COMPANY who have final authority over negotiations and approval. The memo shall define the nature of the contract or other agreement and the COMPANY involved. Where possible, appropriate documentation from the COMPANY shall be detached. This memo shall be submitted in a timely manner so as to permit consideration by appropriate administration officials prior to consummation of the relationship.

f) The Senate Research Committee or, if the Committee so chooses, a subcommittee appointed by the Chair of the Senate Research Committee will deal with issues concerning this policy. It will perform the following functions when necessary:

(i) to assist in the implementation of this policy;

(ii) to answer questions concerning this policy (the identity of PERSONNEL asking questions and the specific facts of questions shall be kept private to the extent allowed by law);

(iii) to review and comment on any disciplinary action to be taken under this policy;

(iv) upon the request of affected faculty, to review a decision by an administration official that an INTEREST constitutes an actual conflict of interest. The results of this review shall be forwarded to the appropriate vice president or chancellor, if a coordinate campus is involved, and president of the University for final action; and

(v) to periodically review this policy, including the set financial thresholds established herein.

If a subcommittee is appointed, it should include representation from ORTTA, the Research Executive Council, and the Senate Research Committee. Additional appointments can reflect necessary expertise and concerns of the broader University community.

Appropriate disciplinary action may be taken by the University against PERSONNEL who violate this policy.

7. Discussion

By way of example, disclosure is required by this policy in the following situations. These situations are not the only situations requiring disclosure, but may be helpful in assessing the spirit of this policy.

a) The Principal Investigator must disclose on a BA Form 23 if a scientist working on the project has an INTEREST in the COMPANY funding the research.

b) The Principal Investigator must disclose on a BA Form 23 if the proposal is going to the National Institutes of Health (NIH) and if the research proposed may affect a COMPANY in which the Principal Investigator has an INTEREST.

c) The Principal Investigator must disclose in the Human Subjects Consent Form if the Principal Investigator has an INTEREST in a COMPANY that may be affected by the research.

d) The Principal Investigator must disclose to the editor of a journal, when submitting a paper for publication, the Principal Investigator's INTEREST in a COMPANY which may be affected by the publication.

e) An inventor must disclose by memo an INTEREST in a COMPANY to which the University is intending to license the inventor's technology.

f) If in the course of conducting research for a COMPANY the COMPANY grants an equity option to the Principal Investigator, the Principal Investigator must report that new INTEREST by memo to the Principal Investigator's department head and dean.

4
Guidelines for Technology Licensing to "Start-up" Companies in Which Stanford Faculty Are Involved (1991)

Introduction

Stanford is recognized for its innovative and entrepreneurial activities involving the transfer of knowledge and technology to the commercial area. The first start-up* company, formed in a garage on Channing Street in Palo Alto, involved investments by Stanford faculty, a dean and, some say, even the President of the University. Founded in 1909, the company successfully introduced radio technology to Santa Clara County long before it was to be known as Silicon Valley. It was the founding of another company thirty years later in 1939, again in a garage on Channing Street in Palo Alto, by two engineers encouraged by Stanford's Fred Terman, that set the tone for the successful interaction of a research university and surrounding companies. More than sixty companies have since been formed through actions of faculty, staff, and students associated with Stanford.

This record of technology transfer has taken place in an environment of trust in the integrity of the faculty. The region, the state, and the nation have benefited over time from the many spin offs of ideas and technologies. These spin offs have in turn benefited Stanford through access to modern technology, through direct support of the teaching and research programs and through contributions of individuals to the University mission of teaching and research. However, the less complex world of even twenty years ago has given way to one in which issues of conflict of interest, the appearance of conflicting situations

---

*"Start-up" or "spin off" companies are not rigidly defined for this purpose. Rather, considerations that would invoke these Guidelines include the age, size, and status of the company. For example, a company normally would be considered a "start-up" if it were not publicly traded, were less than five years old, had fewer than 100 employees and annual sales of less than $5 million.

250

and questions of conflict of commitment are part of the University and national environment.

These Guidelines are written to provide principles and procedures for the transfer of University-owned technology to companies through licensing arrangements where faculty members have interests or even may be founding members. The goal is to state the conflict of interest issues that are of concern, to provide an approach to manage these conflicts, and to provide a procedure for moving forward toward arranging licensing, both non-exclusive or exclusive where appropriate, as a means of assisting technology transfer into the commercial stream.

Principles

The underlying principle assumed in these Guidelines is that while Stanford faculty members are on active duty, they are fully committed to the teaching and research program of the University. It is up to the faculty member to manage his or her time to meet all obligations with regard to teaching, research and other University service. Involvement in technology transfer or with the activities of outside companies should be within the time constraints of Stanford's Faculty Consulting Policy as contained in the Faculty Handbook and the Research Policy Handbook.

Further, faculty should manage their outside activities such that they do not reduce scholarly openness with colleagues or impact the quality and direction of research activities or the supervision of students.

Even with the best intentions, involvement in technology transfer activities, especially with start-up companies in which faculty have an interest, raises real and potential conflict of interest issues. Of concern are conflicts of commitment, not only in time but in intellectual energy and direction of research activities; conflict of interest arising from financial decisions on behalf of the company or of the University; conflict of interest in research direction, especially as it may affect student training; and conflict of interest with regard to hiring as company employees or consultants, university students or staff. Interaction of more than one faculty member of a department with an outside company may raise questions about the independence of the departmental research and teaching program, or about the possibility of coercive influence over collegial relations.

The procedures presented below are designed to deal with these real and apparent conflict of interest issues in a manner that informs licensing decisions involving University-owned technology. Trust is placed in the faculty member, who is assumed to act with integrity on behalf of the University.

Procedures

Stanford's patent and copyright policies (see the Research Policy Handbook) explain who has rights to inventions and data created or discovered at the University. If Stanford has claim to the technology, or if faculty, staff or students choose to assign their rights to Stanford, a disclosure of the technology shall be made to the Office of Technology Licensing (OTL). OTL then determines whether to file a patent application and/or license the technology to outside entities for their use and/or commercialization on behalf of the University, based on marketability of the technology and its potential usefulness to the public. In those cases where a faculty member asks OTL to license the technology to a start-up company in which that faculty member is involved, the faculty member shall inform OTL of his or her involvement, if any, or the involvement of other Stanford faculty, staff, or students, in the outside enterprise. If OTL believes that the technology will be best transferred by the start-up company, OTL shall inform the involved faculty member, the department chair, and school dean of the terms of the proposed license. The faculty member must take the following steps to address the conflict of interest issues before OTL proceeds with licensing arrangements.

The faculty member assumes the responsibility to inform the department chair, in writing, of the request for licensing to the start-up company, why the request is appropriate, and how the issues of conflict of interest are to be managed. The written statement should provide information adequate for the chair to evaluate the licensing request in light of the real and potential conflict of interest issues. How conflicts are to be avoided and how University commitments are to be met are important elements of the written statement. If the involvement of the faculty member is extensive, the department chair may request more detailed information regarding general duties in the company, clarification of research responsibilities and directions in the company and at the University, equity and other financial arrangements with the company that may impact the licensing decision.

The chair shall review the written statements and consult with OTL and/or the faculty member further if more information is needed to fully inform the chair's response to the licensing proposal. If he/she is satisfied that the faculty member's involvement with the start-up will not create conflicts of interest that would adversely impact the faculty member's obligations to the University, and if he/she agrees that the technology transfer process is best achieved by the proposed licensing arrangements, the chair will recommend approval to the school dean.

Based on the chair's recommendation and with advice from the University's Dean of Research as appropriate, the school dean will make a decision. If a faculty member disagrees with the decision, it may be appealed to the Provost who in turn may choose to appoint an ad hoc faculty committee to advise him on the matter.

Ongoing Obligations of the Faculty Member

For those licensing arrangements that are approved, the involved faculty member shall have the ongoing obligation to keep the department chair and the school dean informed of any substantive changes in the outside involvement.

Licensing a company in which a faculty member is involved places additional responsibilities upon the faculty member to be vigilant in avoiding conflict of interest situations. For example, approval from the department chair and school dean should be obtained prior to accepting gifts from the company in support of the faculty member's University research. It is already the case that Stanford Investigators are obligated, under existing policy, to disclose on Proposal Routing Sheets any consulting or financial interests they may have in companies proposed as a sponsor, vendor, or subcontractor in any of their proposed sponsored project activities.

Further, the involved faculty member must obtain approval of the department chair and school dean if any students, staff or visiting scientists in the faculty member's lab are proposed to become involved as consultants or employees of the company. It is important to avoid the appearance that the University research laboratory is being used, in more than an incidental way, for product development or other business purposes.

Equity Royalty Payments

If the company being licensed by Stanford proposes to grant the University equity in the company as a form of royalty payment in lieu of cash, and if the involved faculty member also has equity holdings or stock options in the company, the equity may be accepted by Stanford after approval by the inventors, department chair, school dean, and the Provost, and with agreement of OTL. In such cases, the equity shares shall be transferred to the University Treasurer, who will distribute the "inventor's share" of the stock royalty income, as soon as feasible. The Treasurer shall act on behalf of the University with regard to the eventual sale of the stock. The inventor shall act on his own behalf with regard to the eventual distribution of stock received as royalty payment.

Review of these Guidelines

These Guidelines were approved by the Committee on Research on October 16, 1990, and reported to the Senate of the Academic Council on November 8, 1990. The Committee on Research shall review periodically these Guidelines and their implementation to ensure that they do not conflict with the University's primary missions of teaching and research.

Guidelines for University Investments in Start-up Companies Involving Stanford Faculty

Each year Stanford invests a small portion of its investment capital in "start-up" companies that are exploiting new technologies. Although many such companies do not succeed, those that do offer the potential for high returns to their investors.

On occasion Stanford may be faced with an opportunity to invest in a start-up company in which one or more Stanford faculty members also have equity interests. The University ordinarily will not invest in such companies if any of the involved faculty members also have line management responsibilities in them, given the potential for apparent or real conflicts of interest. However, Stanford may invest in start-ups in which the extent of its faculty involvement is limited to equity holdings (or rights to equity) and/or advisory roles under the following conditions:

1. Stanford will not act as a lead investor or syndicating agent. All investments will be as a "passive investor."

2. Stanford will not acquire an equity holding greater than 10% of the ownership of the company.

3. No Stanford officer is to be a member of the board, or be an officer of the company, or have a personal equity position in the company at the time of Stanford's investment in any of the equity rounds before the company goes public.

4. University investments in start-up companies in which Stanford faculty have equity interests are subject to the case-by-case approval of the Provost, based upon recommendations by the University Treasurer. If the involved faculty member(s) subsequently creates University-owned data or inventions for which the start-up company seeks a license for commercial use or development, the licensing request will be subject to the review and approval of the relevant department chair and school dean, in consultation with the Dean of Research.

5
Massachusetts Institute of Technology: Conflict of Interest

4.2.4 Licensing of M.I.T. Rights to Inventors

M.I.T. faculty, staff, or student inventors may also request a license to commercially develop their M.I.T.-owned inventions where such licensing would enhance the transfer of the technology, is consistent with M.I.T. obligations to third parties, and does not involve a conflict of interest.

4.2.5 Conflict of Interest or Commitment

Any of the following factors may signify a conflict of interest which will be taken into account prior to waiving or licensing M.I.T.'s rights to inventors under this Section 4.2 or to authors under Section 4.3:

(1) an adverse impact on M.I.T.'s educational responsibility to its students;

(2) an undue influence on the employment commitment of the inventor/author to M.I.T. in terms of time or direction of effort;

(3) a detrimental effect on M.I.T.'s obligation to serve the needs of the general public;

(4) potential conflict of interest as defined in M.I.T.'s Policies and Procedures.

If the inventor/author holds or will shortly acquire an equity or founder's stock position in a small, tightly controlled company, M.I.T. will accept equity in lieu of royalty only with the prior approval of the Vice President for Research. The inventor/author will be required to sign a Conflict Avoidance Statement (see p. 258) if a license is granted to the company in which the inventor/author has an equity position. If M.I.T. *does* acquire equity in lieu or partial lieu of royalties for intellectual property, it will require that the company distribute to the inventors/authors the percentages of equity that would have otherwise been distributed under the M.I.T. Policy if the payment had been made in cash.

From Guide to the Ownership and Commercial Development of M.I.T. Technology, May 24, 1989.

4.2.6 Research Funding/Equity

M.I.T. will not accept research funding from a license in which M.I.T., through the TLO, or an M.I.T. inventor has an equity interest (including stocks, options, warrants or other financial instruments convertible into equity) unless:

> (i) the research is not likely to result in inventions dominated by the claims of the licensed patent or in software that is a derivative work of the licensed software; and
> (ii) the research will not be conducted in the inventor's laboratory group; and
> (iii) the inventor's students will not participate in any project funded by the licensee.

When an inventor/author desires to avoid equity in order to obtain research funding from a small company, M.I.T. will also avoid taking equity through a license agreement so as to allow the sponsored research. In such cases, the TLO will require in its license agreements that the inventor not make any arrangements to obtain equity at a later date and avoid negotiating for equity until at least two years following the termination of the research agreement.

CONFLICT AVOIDANCE STATEMENT

Name:_____

Dept. or Lab.:_____

Company:_____

Address:_____

_____

Licensed Technology:_____

_____

_____

Because of the M.I.T. license granted to the above company and my equity* position and continuing relationship with this firm, I acknowledge the potential for a possible conflict of interest between the performance of research at M.I.T. and my contractual or other obligations to this firm. Therefore, I will not:

1) use students at M.I.T. for research and development projects for the company;

2) restrict or delay access to information from my M.I.T. research; or

3) take direct or indirect research support from the company in order to support my activities at M.I.T.

In addition, in order to avoid the appearance of a conflict, I will attempt to differentiate clearly between the intellectual directions of my M.I.T. research and my contributions to the firm. To that end, I will expressly inform my department head annually of the general nature of my activities on behalf of the firm.

Signed:_____

Date:_____

_____

*"Equity" includes stock, options, warrants or other financial instruments convertible into Equity, which are directly or indirectly controlled by the inventor.

Bibliography

35 US Code. Secs. 200–204. 1990.

Abe, Yoshiya, Hiroshi Inose, Tetsuji Nishikawa, Kotaro Shimo, and Akira Tezuka. "Policies and Practices of Government Support for Basic and Applied Science." *Science Policy Perspectives: USA-Japan*. Ed. Arthur Gerstenfeld. New York: Academic Press, 1982. Pp. 125–73.

Abelson, Philip H. "Academic-Industrial Interactions." Editorial. *Science* (15 April 1988): 265.

Abraham, E. P. "The Development of Penicillins and Cephalosporins—Similarities and Contrasts." *From Genetic Experimentation to Biotechnology— The Critical Transition*. Eds. William J. Whelan and Sandra Black. Chichester, Sussex: Wiley, 1982.

"Academic Elite." *Business Week,* 16 June 1989: 56–57.

Agurell, S. "Industry-University Cooperation." *Phamaceutisch Weekblad Scientific Edition* 7 (1985): 42–45.

American Association of University Professors. *Policy Documents and Reports*. Washington D.C.: American Association of University Professors, 1977.

Anderson, Richard E. "The Advantages and Risks of Entrepreneurship." *Academe* 76.5 (1990): 9–14.

Baldwin, Donald R. "Academia's New Role in Technology Transfer and Economic Development." *Research Management Review* 2.2 (1988): 1–16.

Baldwin, Donald R., and James W. Green. "University-Industry Relations: A Review of the Literature." *Journal of the Society of Research Administrators* 15.4 (1984): 5–17.

Barber, Albert A. "University-Industry Research Cooperation." *Journal of the Society of Research Administrators* 17.2 (1985): 19–30.

Barker, Robert. "Bringing Science into Industry from Universities." *Research Management* 28 (1985): 22–24.

259

Barlett, Joseph W., and James V. Siena. "Research and Development Limited Partnerships as a Device to Exploit University-Owned Technology." *Journal of College and University Law* 10.4 (1983/84): 435–54.

Barnes, Deborah M. "New University-Industry Pact Signed." *Science* 230 (1985): 1255–56.

Benda, Heike von, and F. J. Radermacher. "The Research Institute for Application-Oriented Knowledge Processing (FAW): Planning and Realizing a Higher-Technology Institute." *Interfaces* 20.6 (November–December 1990): 75–85.

Beauchamp, Tom L. "Ethical Issues in Funding and Monitoring University Research." *Business and Professional Ethics Journal* 11.1 (1992): 5–16.

Biddle, Wayne. "A Patent on Knowledge." *Harper's,* July 1981: 22–26.

Birnbaum, Jeffrey H. "Business Groups Uses Professors, Not Cash, To Influence Congress." *Wall Street Journal,* 25 June 1990.

Bitting, Robert K. "Observations from Japan: Lessons in Research and Technology Transfer." *Journal of the Society of Research Administrators* 19.4 (1988): 17–22.

Blevins, David E., and Sid R. Ewer. "University Research and Development Activities: Intrusion into Areas Untended? A Review of Recent Developments and Ethical Issues Raised." *Journal of Business Ethics* 7 (1988): 645–56.

Blumenthal, David, Sherrie Epstein, and James Maxwell. "Commercializing University Research." *New England Journal of Medicine* 314 (1986a): 1621–26.

Blumenthal, David, Michael Gluck, Karen Seashore Louis, Michael A. Stoto, and David Wise. "University-Industry Research Relationships in Biotechnology: Implications for the University." *Science* 232 (1986b): 1361–66.

Blumenthal, David, Michael Gluck, Karen Seashore Louis, and David Wise. "Industrial Support of University Research in Biotechnology." *Science* 231 (1986c): 242–46.

Bohrer, Robert A., ed. *From Research to Revolution.* Littleton, Col.: Rothman, 1987.

Bok, Derek. *Beyond the Ivory Tower.* Cambridge, Mass.: Harvard University Press, 1982.

Bok, Derek. "President's Report: Business and the Academy." *Harvard Magazine* 83 (May–June 1981): 23–35.

Bok, Derek. "Universities: Their Temptations and Tensions." *Journal of College and University Law* 18.1 (1991): 1–19.

Bourke, Jaron, and Robert Weissman. "Academics at Risk: The Temptations of Profit." *Academe* 76.5 (1990): 15–21.

Bowie, Norman E. "Business-University Partnerships." *Moral Responsibility And The University,* Ed., Steven M. Cahn. Philadelphia: Temple University Press, 1990.

Branscomb, Lewis M., Ed. *University-Industry Research Relationships: Myths, Realities and Potentials.* Washington, D.C.: National Science Foundation, 1982a.

Branscomb, Lewis M., Ed. *University-Industry Research Relationships: Selected Studies.* Washington, D.C.: National Science Foundation, 1982b.

Bray, David M. "Conflict of Interest: A Principle Business Officer's Perspective." *Journal of the Society of Research Administrators* 22.3 (1990): 13–18.

Bremer, Howard W. "University Technology Transfer—Publish or Perish." *Patent Policy.* Ed., Willard Marcy. Washington, D.C.: American Chemical Society, 1978.

Brown, Wayne S. "A Proposed Mechanism for Commercializing University Technology." *Technovation* 3 (1985): 19–25.

Browne, Rick. "The Tempest Raging Over Profit-Minded Professors." *Business Week,* 7 November 1983, 86 + .

Brust, Melvin F. "Technology Transfer and the University." *Journal of Applied Business Research* 7.1 (1990–91): 1–5.

Buchbinder, Howard, and Janice Newson. "Corporate-University Linkages in Canada: Transforming a Public Institution." *Higher Education* 20 (1990): 355–79.

Buchbinder, Howard, and Janice Newson. "The Service University and Market Forces." *Academe,* July–August 1992.

Buckey, Kim A. "A Tale of Three Cities." *World* 21 (1987): 32–41.

Bull, Alan T., Geoffrey Holt, and Malcolm D. Lilly. *Biotechnology: International Trends and Perspectives.* Paris: Organization for Economic Co-operation and Development, 1982.

Burke, April. "University Policies on Conflict of Interest and Delay of Publication: Report of the Clearinghouse on University-Industry Relations Association of American Universities." *Journal of College and University Law* 12 (1985): 175–200.

Burke, Joseph C. "The Academic-Business Partnership." *Vital Speeches of the Day* 52 (1985): 148–50.

"Business and Education: Forming New Partnerships." *I/S Analyzer* 27.4 (1984): 1–12.

Business-Higher Education Forum. *Beyond the Rhetoric: Evaluating University-Industry Cooperation in Research and Technology Exchange.* Washington, D.C.: Business-Higher Education Forum, 1988. Vol. 1, The Case. Vol. 2, A Handbook.

Buttel, Frederick H., J. Tadlock Cowan, Martin Kenney, and Jack Kloppenburg, Jr. "Biotechnology in Agriculture: The Political Economy of Agribusiness Reorganization and Industry-University Relationships." *Research in Rural Sociology and Development* 1 (1984): 315–48.

Carey, John. "Washington Inc.?" *Business Week,* 16 June 1989, 40–41.

Carey, N. H. "From Academic Information to Commercial Products: The Paths and Pitfalls." *From Genetic Experimentation to Biotechnology—The Critical Transition.* Eds., William J. Whelan and Sandra Black. Chichester, Sussex: Wiley, 1982.

Chernoff, Joel. "Duke Will Spin Off Subsidiary." *Pensions and Investments,* 14 May 1990, 1, 45.

Colton, Robert M. "University/Industrial Research Centers are Proving Themselves." *Research Management* 30 (1987): 34–37.

Cooper, Theodore. "Changing Patterns of Biomedical Research Funding: A View from Industry." *Clinical Research* 30 (1982): 300–301.

"Cooperative Research in Need of Improvement." *Chemical and Engineering News,* 25 January 1988, 13.

Cordes, Colleen. "Debate Flares Over Growing Pressures on Academe for Ties With Industry." *Chronicle of Higher Education,* 16 September 1992, A26–27, 29.

Cordes, Colleen. "More Partnerships to Boost Technology Sought for Academe." *Chronicle of Higher Education,* 19 April 1989, A21+.

Corsten, Hans. "Technology Transfer from Universities to Small and Medium-Sized Enterprises—An Empirical Survey from the Standpoint of Such Enterprises." *Technovation* 6 (1987): 57–68.

Culliton, Barbara J. "Biomedical Research Enters the Marketplace." *New England Journal of Medicine* 304 (1981): 1195–1201.

Culliton, Barbara J. "Drug Firm and UC Settle Interferon Suit." *Science* 219 (1983): 372.

Culliton, Barbara J. "Harvard and Monsanto: The $23-Million Alliance." *Science* 195 (1977): 759–63.

Culliton, Barbara J. "Pajaro Dunes: The Search for Consensus." *Science* 216 (1982a): 155–58.

Culliton, Barbara J. "The Hoechst Department at Mass General." *Science* 216 (1982b): 1200–1203.

Cutler, Robert S. "A Survey of High-Technology Transfer Practices in Japan and in the United States." *Interfaces* 19.6 (1989): 67–77.

Dagani, Ron. "Consortia Urged to Push Superconductors." *Chemical and Engineering News,* 9 January 1989, 6.

Dalton, L. G. "The Objectives and Development of the Heriot-Watt University Research Park." *Science Park and Innovation Centres: Their Economic and Social Impact*. Ed., John Michael Gibb. Amsterdam: Elsevier, 1985. Pp.231–36.

Davey, Jane. "Economic Developers as Critical Links Between Existing Industries and Federal Laboratories." *Economic Development Review* 9.1 (1991): 41–46.

David, E. E., Jr. "Striking a Bargain Between Company and Campus." *Environment* 24 (1982): 42–48.

Davis, Lance E., and Daniel J. Kevles. "The National Research Fund: A Case Study in the Industrial Support of Academic Science." *Minerva* 12.2 (1974): 207–20.

Davis, Michael. "University Research and the Wages of Commerce." *Journal of College and University Law* 18.1 (1991): 29–39.

Davis, Nancy. "Biotechnologists Create Nonprofit Clone." *Association Management* 41.8 (August 1989): 130–33.

Diamond *v.* Chakrabarty. 447 United States Reports 303–322. United States Supreme Ct. 1979.

Dickinson, Susan L-J. "Campus Science/Technology Officers Gain Stature." *The Scientist*, 26 November 1991: 1+.

Ditzel, Roger G. "Patent Rights at the University/Industry Interface." *Journal of the Society of Research Administrators* 20.1 (1988): 221–28.

Dreyfack, Kenneth, William J. Hampton, and John A. Byrne. "When Companies Tell B-Schools What to Teach." *Business Week*, 10 February 1986: 60–61, 65.

"Du Pont to Open Ames Lab for Grain Analysis." *Des Moines Register*, 9 March 1990.

Dunlop, R. H. "Facilitating University-Industry Relationships and Interactions." *Journal of Veterinary Medical Education* 9.2 (1983): 59–60.

Edsall, John T., and David Bearman. "Historical Records of Scientific Activity: The Survey of Sources for the History of Biochemistry and Molecular Biology." *Proceedings of the American Philosophical Society* 123 (1979): 279–92.

Emmert, Mark A., and Michael M. Crow. "The Cooperative University Research Laboratory." *Journal of Higher Education* 60 (1989): 408–22.

Eveland, J. D., William Hetzner, and Louis Tornatzky, Eds. *Development of University–Industry Cooperative Research Centers: Historical Profiles*. 2nd ed. Washington, D.C.: National Science Foundation, 1984.

Fairweather, James S. "Academic Research and Instruction." *Journal of Higher Education* 60 (1989): 388–407.

Fairweather, James S. "Education: The Forgotten Element in Industry-University Relationships." *The Review of Higher Education* 14. 1 (Fall 1990).

Fairweather, James S. "The University's Role in Economic Development: Lessons for Academic Leaders." *Journal of the Society of Research Administrators* 22.3 (1990): 5–11.

Fingeret, Arlene. "Who's in Control? A Case Study of University-Industry Collaboration." *New Directions for Continuing Education* 23 (1984): 39–63.

Foden, Harry, Pamela McNamar, and Robert Koepke. "Boosting Industry Competitiveness—Local-Level Technology Transfer." *Industrial Development* (March–April 1988): 17–26.

Forrest, Janet E. "Strategic Alliances and the Small Technology-Based Firm." *Journal of Small Business Management* 28.3 (1990): 37–45.

Fowler, Donald R. "University-Industry Research Relationships: The Research Agreement." *Journal of College and University Law* 9 (1982–83): 515–32.

Freundlich, Naomi. "Business Goes to College." *Business Week,* 16 June 1989: 50, 52.

Frye, Alva L., Ed. *From Source to Use: Bringing University Technology to the Marketplace.* New York: American Management Association, 1985.

Fuchsberg, Gilbert. "Boston U. Gambles on its Big Investment in Biotechnology Company." *Chronicle of Higher Education,* 12 April 1989a: A29.

Fuchsberg, Gilbert. "Notes on Technological Transfer." *Chronicle of Higher Education,* 7 June 1989b: A29 + .

Fuchsberg, Gilbert. "Universities Said to Go Too Fast in Quest of Profit from Research." *Chronicle of Higher Education,* 12 April 1989c: A28 + .

Fusfeld, Herbert I. "Overview of University-Industry Research." *Partners in the Research Enterprise: University-Corporate Relations in Science and Technology.* Eds., Thomas W. Langfitt, Sheldon Hackney, Alfred P. Fishman, and Albert V. Glowasky. Philadelphia: University of Pennsylvania Press, 1983. Pp. 10–19.

Fusfeld, Herbert I. *The Technical Enterprise: Present and Future Patterns.* Cambridge, Mass.: Ballinger, 1986.

Fusfeld, Herbert I., and Carmela S. Haklisch, Eds. *University-Industry Research Interactions.* New York: Pergamon, 1984.

Genetic Engineering: Commercial Opportunities in Australia. Canberra: Australian Government Publishing Service, 1982.

Gerstenfeld, Arthur, Ed. *Science Policy Perspectives: USA-Japan.* New York: Academic Press, 1982.

Giamatti, A. Bartlett. "Free Market and Free Industry: The University, Industry and Cooperative Research." *Partners in the Research Enterprise:*

University-Corporate Relations in Science and Technology. Eds., Thomas W. Langfitt, Sheldon Hackney, Alfred P. Fishman, and Albert V. Glowasky. Philadelphia: University of Pennsylvania Press, 1983. Pp. 3–9.

Gibb, J. M., Ed. *Science Parks and Innovation Centres: Their Economic and Social Impact.* Amsterdam: Elsevier, 1985.

Goldman, Alan H., "Ethical Issues in Proprietary Restrictions on Research Results." *Science, Technology, & Human Values* 12 (Winter 1987): 22–30.

Goodman, David. "A New Model for Federal-State-Industry Cooperation: Technology Transfer Lessons from the New Jersey Experience." *Journal of the Society of Research Administrators,* Spring 1990: 25–29.

Government-University-Industry Research Roundtable. *Industrial Perspectives on Innovation and Interactions with Universities* Washington, D.C.: Government-University-Industry Research Roundtable, 1991.

Government-University-Industry Research Roundtable. *New Alliances and Partnerships in American Science and Engineering.* Washington, D.C.: Government-University-Industry Research Roundtable, 1986.

Government-University-Industry Research Roundtable. *Perspectives on Financing Academic Research Facilities: A Resource for Policy Formulation.* Washington, D.C.: Government-University-Industry Research Roundtable, 1989a.

Government-University-Industry Research Roundtable. *Science and Technology in the Academic Enterprise: Status, Trends, and Issues.* Washington, D.C.: Government-University-Industry Research Roundtable, 1989b.

Government-University-Industry Research Roundtable. *Simplified and Standardized Model Agreements for University-Industry Cooperative Research.* Washington, D.C.: Government-University-Industry Research Roundtable, 1988.

Government-University-Industry Research Roundtable. *Survey to Assess the Usefulness of Two Model Agreements for University-Industry Cooperative Research.* Washington, D.C.: Government-University-Industry Research Roundtable, 1990a.

Government-University-Industry Research Roundtable. *The Academic Research Enterprise within the Industrialized Nations: Comparative Perspectives.* Washington, D.C.: Government-University-Industry Research Roundtable, 1990b.

Gray, Denis, Elmima C. Johnson, and Teresa R. Gidley. "Industry-University Projects and Centers." *Evaluation Review* 10 (1986): 776–93.

Gunsalus, C. K. "Considerations in Licensing Spin-off Technology." *Journal of the Society of Research Administrators* 21.1 (1989): 13–25.

Gupta, Udayan. "Turning University Research Into a Profitable Business." *Wall Street Journal,* 12 June 1990: B2 + .

Guterl, Fred V. "Technology Transfer Isn't Working." *Business Month* 130.3 (1987): 44–45, 48.

Guze, Samuel B. "The Monsanto–Washington University Biomedical Research Agreement." *Partners in the Research Enterprise: University-Corporate Relations in Science and Technology*. Eds., Thomas W. Langfitt, Sheldon Hackney, Alfred P. Fishman, and Albert V. Glowasky. Philadelphia: University of Pennsylvania Press, 1983. Pp. 53–58.

Hanson, David. "Academic R&D Gets Little Foreign Funding." *Chemical and Engineering News*, 25 April 1988: 18.

Harsanyi, Zsolt. "Issues in Industry—Research Interaction and Equity Considerations." *Genetic Engineering: Commercial Opportunities in Australia*. Canberra: Australian Government Publishing Service, 1982.

Haude, G. "The Role of Polytechnics in the Creation of Enterprises." *Science Park and Innovation Centres: Their Economic and Social Impact*. Ed., John Michael Gibb. Amsterdam: Elsevier, 1985. Pp.103–11.

Helwig, David. "The Profit-Minded Professors." *Canadian Business* 61 (1988): 46–49, 82–84.

Herbert, Evan. "Japanese R & D in the United States." *Research Technology Management* 32.6 (1989): 11–20.

Hill, Judith M. "The University and Industrial Research: Selling Out?" *Business and Professional Ethics Journal* 2 (Summer 1983): 27–35.

Hoornstra, Charles D., and Michael A. Liethen. "Academic Freedom and Civil Discovery." *Journal of College and University Law* 10.2 (1983–84): 113–28.

Hoppin, Margery E. "A University Perspective on Pharmaceutical and Industry Support of Research." *American Journal of Clinical Nutrition* 46 (1987): 226–28.

Hutt, Peter Barton. "University/Corporate Research Agreements." *Biotechnology in Society: Private Initiatives and Public Oversight*. Ed., Joseph G. Perpich. New York: Pergamon, 1986. Pp. 137–48.

Inose, Hiroshi, Tetsuju Nishikawa, and Michiyuki Uenohara. "Cooperation Between Universities and Industries in Basic and Applied Science." *Science Policy Perspectives: USA-Japan*. Ed., Arthur Gerstenfeld. New York: Academic Press, 1982. Pp. 43–61.

Isaacs, McAllister, III. "NCSU Textiles Moves to Better Serve Industry." *Textile World* 141.3 (1991): 57–59.

Israelsen, Ned. "Current Issues in Proprietary Rights to Biotechnology." *From Research to Revolution*. Ed., Robert Bohrer. Littleton, Colo.: Rothman, 1987.

Jacobs-Perkins, Andree. "Scientists Navigate Bermuda Triangle of Technology Transfer." *Journal of the National Cancer Institute* 82.7 (1990): 546–48.

Jaffe, Adam B. "Real Effects of Academic Research." *American Economic Review* 79.5 (1989): 957–70.

Johnson, Irving S. "Impact of Recombinant DNA Innovation on Academic-Industrial Relationships. II. The View from Industry—A Second Appraisal." *From Genetic Experimentation to Biotechnology—The Critical Transition*. Eds., William J. Whelan and Sandra Black. Chichester, Sussex: Wiley, 1982.

Johnson, Lynn G. *The High Technology Connection: Academic/Industrial Cooperation for Economic Growth*. Washington, D.C.: Association for Study of Higher Education, 1984. Report Number 6.

Johnston, Robert F., and Christopher G. Edwards. *Entrepreneurial Science: New Links Between Corporations, Universities and Government*. New York: Quorum, 1987.

Kenney, Martin. *Biotechnology: The University-Industrial Complex*. New Haven, Conn.: Yale University Press, 1986.

Kenney, Martin. "The Ethical Dilemmas of University-Industry Collaborations." *Journal of Business Ethics* 6 (1987): 127–35.

Kertz, Consuelo Lauda, and James K. Hasson, Jr. "University Research and Development Activities: The Federal Income Tax Consequences of Research Contracts, Research Subsidiaries and Joint Ventures." *Journal of College and University Law*, Vol. 13. No. 2.

Kiley, Thomas D. "Licensing Revenue for Universities: Impediments and Possibilities." *Partners in the Research Enterprise: University-Corporate Relations in Science and Technology*. Eds., Thomas W. Langfitt, Sheldon Hackney, Alfred P. Fishman, and Albert V. Glowasky. Philadelphia: University of Pennsylvania Press, 1983. Pp. 59–67.

Korn, David E. "Patent and Trade Secret Protection in University-Industry Research Relationships in Biotechnology." *Harvard Journal on Legislation* 24 (1987): 191–38.

Krimsky, Sheldon. "The University: Marketing Theories, Not Toothpaste." *Environment* 24 (1982): 46.

Kuhlman, James A. "Industry, Universities, and the Technological Imperative." *Business and Economic Review* 32.4 (1986): 15–19.

Kysiak, Ronald C. "The Impact of Research Parks on Regional Development." *Real Estate Finance Journal* 5.2 (1989): 64–69.

Lachs, Phyllis S. "University Patent Policy." *Journal of College and University Law* 10.3 (1983–84): 263–92.

Langfitt, Thomas W., Sheldon Hackney, Alfred P. Fishman, and Albert V. Glowasky, Eds. *Partners in the Research Enterprise: University-Corporate Relations in Science and Technology*. Philadelphia: University of Pennsylvania Press, 1983.

268   *University-Business Partnerships*

Lepkowski, Wil. "Corporate/University Ties Growing Stronger." *Chemical and Engineering News,* 3 January 1983: 32–33.

Lepkowski, Wil. "Debate Over Federal Funding of Academic Research Intensifies." *Chemical and Engineering News,* 14 January 1991: 20–21.

Lepkowski, Wil. "Lehigh: One University's Approach to Rejuvenating U.S. Industry." *Chemical and Engineering News,* 14 May 1984a: 37–41.

Lepkowski, Wil. "Research Universities Face New Fiscal Realities." *Chemical and Engineering News,* 23 November 1981: 23 + .

Lepkowski, Wil. "University/Industry Research Ties Still Viewed With Concern." *Chemical and Engineering News,* 25 June 1984b: 7–11.

Lerner, Maura and Joe Rigert. " 'U' Is Forced to Halt Sales of Drug ALG: FDA Cites Failures to Report Deaths, Adverse Reactions." *Star Tribune* 23 August 1992.

Lesch, William C., and Louis H. Peterson. "The Management of Discovery: Exploiting the Fruits of University Research." *Journal of Professional Services Marketing* 5.1 (1989): 71–85.

Leskovac, Helen. "Ties That Bind: Conflicts of Interest in University-Industry Links." *University of California–Davis Law Review* 17 (1984): 895–923.

Levine, Joe. "Technology Tales." *Johns Hopkins Magazine,* August 1990: 14–31.

Lilien, Gary L. "Industry-University Cooperation at Penn State's Institute for the Study of Business Markets." *Interfaces* 20.6 (1990): 94–98.

Linnell, Robert H., Ed. *Dollars and Scholars.* Los Angeles: University of Southern California Press, 1982.

Looker, Dan. "Genetics at Heart of Seed Fracas." *Des Moines Register,* February 25, 1990a: J1 + .

Looker, Dan. "Pioneer is Sued in Dispute Over Oil-Rich Corn." *Des Moines Register,* 17 February 1990b: 1A + .

Low, George M. "The Organization of Industrial Relationships in Universities." *Partners in the Research Enterprise: University-Corporate Relations in Science and Technology.* Eds., Thomas W. Langfitt, Sheldon Hackney, Alfred P. Fishman, and Albert V. Glowasky. Philadelphia: University of Pennsylvania Press, 1983. Pp. 68–80.

Lowe, Charles U. "The Triple Helix—NIH, Industry and the Academic World." *Yale Journal of Biology and Medicine* 55 (1982): 239–46.

Main, Jeremy. "Business Goes to College for a Brain Gain." *Fortune,* 16 March 1987: 80–86.

Maisel, Albert Q. "Combination in Restraint of Health." *Reader's Digest* 52.310 (February 1948): 42–45.

Marcy, Willard, Ed. *Patent Policy.* Washington, D.C.: American Chemical Society, 1978.

Marcy, Willard. "Patent Policies at Educational and Nonprofit Scientific Institutions." *Patent Policy.* Ed., Willard Marcy. Washington, D.C.: American Chemical Society, 1978.

Marshall, Eliot, "When Commerce and Academe Collide" *Science* 248 (April 13, 1990): 152–56.

Maurer, John E., Thomas I. O'Brien, Pauline Newman, and Donald M. Alstadt. "Toward Economic Recovery: University/Industry Cooperation." *Idea* 25 (1984): 63–82.

McDonald, David, and Scott M. Gieser. "Making Cooperative Research Relationships Work." *Research Management* 30 (1987): 38–42.

McDonald, Ellen. "University/Industry Partnerships: Premonitions for Academic Libraries." *Journal of Academic Librarianship* 11 (1985): 82–87.

McHenry, K. W. "University-Industry Research Cooperation: An Industrial View." *Journal of the Society of Research Administrators* 17.2 (1985): 31–43.

McHenry, Keith W. "Five Myths of Industry/University Cooperative Research—And the Realities." *Research Technology Management* 33.3 (1990): 40–42.

McQueen, Douglas H., and J. Torkel Wallmark. "Support for New Ventures at Chalmers University of Technology." *Science Park and Innovation Centres: Their Economic and Social Impact.* Ed., John Michael Gibb. Amsterdam: Elsevier, 1985. Pp. 153–61.

"Media Lab: An Innovative Business-Education Partnership." Editorial. *I/S Analyzer* 27.4 (1984): 13–14.

Melmon, Kenneth L. "Changing Patterns of Biomedical Research Funding: The Impact on the Clinical Investigator." *Clinical Research* 30 (1982): 308–15.

Mercier, D. "The Louvain-La-Neuve Science Park, Part of an Innovation Centre." *Science Park and Innovation Centres: Their Economic and Social Impact.* Ed. John Michael Gibb. Amsterdam: Elsevier, 1985. Pp. 98–102.

Merton, R. K. *The Sociology of Science.* Chicago: University of Chicago Press, 1973.

Meyerhoff, Albert H. "Ties That Bind: Conflicts of Interest in University-Industry Links—An Introduction." *University of California–Davis Law Review* 17 (1984): 891–94.

Milbank, Dana. "Research Setback: Scientists Have to Beat the Bushes to Stay in Business." *Wall Street Journal,* 7 November 1990: A1+.

Miller, Paul S. "Academia-Industry Collaborative Research Programs—A Legal Perspective." *Circulation* 72, suppl. 1 (1985): I-41-43.

Mitchell, Will. "Using Academic Technology: Transfer Methods and Licensing

Incidence in the Commercialization of American Diagnostic Imaging Equipment Research, 1954–1988." *Research Policy* 20 (1991): 203–16.

Moore, John H. "Knowledge Transfers in the United States." *European Economic Review* 32 (1988): 591–603.

Morgan, Henry M. "Pickled in Brine: The Possible Costs of Speculation." *Academe* 76.5 (1990): 22–26.

Morgenson, Gretchen. "In Pecunia Veritas?" *Forbes*, 28 November 1988: 204+.

Moylan, Martin J. "U of M[innesota] Research Efforts Paying Off in the Marketplace." *City Business*, 23 July 1990: 11+.

Mullins, Charles B. "A University Administrator's View of Academia-Industry Collaboration." *Circulation* 72, suppl. 1 (1985): I-8-12.

Nelkin, Dorothy, Richard Nelson, and Casey Kiernan. "Commentary: University-Industry Alliances." *Science, Technology and Human Values* 12.1 (1987): 65–74.

New York. Public Authorities Law. Book 42. Supplementary Pamphlet Covering Years 1981–1989. Article 10-A—New York State Science and Technology Foundation. 3100–3102a.

Nicklin, Julie L. "Ailing Italian Drug Company Reneges on $60-Million Deal with Georgetown U." *Chronicle of Higher Education*, 11 August 1993: A29+.

Nisbet, Robert. *The Degradation of the Academic Dogma: The University in America, 1945–1970*. New York: Basic Books, 1971.

Noble, David F. *America by Design*. New York: Knopf, 1977.

Noble, David F. "M.I.T.-Whitehead Merger: The Selling of the University." *Nation* 234,5 (1982): 129+.

Norcross, Phil. "We Patent Trees Now." *Research Review* (September 1992): 1, 10–12.

Office of Management and Budget. Circular No. A-124, Patents—Small Firms and Non-Profit Organizations. Federal Register 47 (1982): 7556–66.

Omenn, Gilbert. "Re-Energizing the Research University." *Environment* 24 (1982a): 49–51.

Omenn, Gilbert S. "Taking University Research into the Marketplace." *New England Journal of Medicine* 307 (1982b): 694–700.

Omenn, Gilbert S. "University-Corporate Relations in Science and Technology: An Analysis of Specific Models." *Partners in the Research Enterprise: University-Corporate Relations in Science and Technology*. Eds., Thomas W. Langfitt, Sheldon Hackney, Alfred P. Fishman, and Albert V. Glowasky. Philadelphia: University of Pennsylvania Press, 1983. Pp. 20–32.

Ostar, Allan W. "Partnerships Between the Interactive University and Its Constituencies." *Economic Development Review* 9.1 (1991): 56–57.

Owen, George M. "Interaction of the Infant Formula Industry with the Academic Community." *American Journal of Clinical Nutrition* 46 (1987): 221–25.

Owens, Mark, Jr. "Patent Program at the University of California." *Patent Policy*. Ed., Willard Marcy. Washington, D.C.: American Chemical Society, 1978.

Pajaro Dunes Conference Draft Statement." *Journal of College and University Law* 9 (1982–83): 533–39.

Pateman, J. "Industry-University Interactions: Centre for Recombinant DNA Research." *Genetic Engineering: Commercial Opportunities in Australia*. Canberra: Australian Government Publishing Service, 1982.

Patton, Carl V. "Consulting by Faculty Members." *Academe* 66 (1980): 181–85.

Pearson, John. "Technical and Management Assistance Through Research Universities: The Michigan Example." *Economic Development Review* 7.2 (1989): 22–24.

Pennsylvania. State Government. Title 71. Supplementary Pamphlet 1990 (Purdon's). Section 158, Administrative Boards and Commissions.

Pennsylvania. State Government. Title 71. Supplementary Pamphlet 1990 (Purdon's). Section 670.1, Duties and Powers of the Board of the Ben Franklin Partnership Fund.

Pennsylvania. Taxation and Fiscal Affairs. Title 72. Supplementary Pamphlet 1990 (Purdon's). Article XVII—Economic Revitalization Tax Credit.

Perpich, Joseph G. *Biotechnology in Society: Private Initiatives and Public Oversight*. New York: Pergamon, 1986.

Peterson, Ivars. "Academic Questions: Campus and Company Partnerships." *Science News*, 29 January 1983: 76–77.

Phillips, Phillip D. "A University Economic Development Approach: The Case of the University of Illinois at Urbana-Champaign." *Economic Development Review* 6.2 (1988): 16–19.

Pins, Kenneth. "Japanese Give New Life to College." *Des Moines Register*, 18 February 1990: 1A+.

Porter, David. "Technology Transfer Within the Electronics Industry in Witchita/Sedgwick County, Kansas." *Economic Development Review* 9:1 (1991): 38–40.

Prager, Denis J., and Gilbert S. Omenn. "Research, Innovation, and University-Industry Linkages." *Science* 201 (1980): 379–84.

Press, Frank. "Core Technologies and the National Economy." *Partners in the Research Enterprise: University-Corporate Relations in Science and Technology*. Eds., Thomas W. Langfitt, Sheldon Hackney, Alfred P. Fishman, and Albert V. Glowasky. Philadelphia: University of Pennsylvania Press, 1983. Pp. 40–48.

Rahm, Diane, Barry Bozeman, and Michael Crow. "Domestic Technology Transfer and Competitiveness: An Empirical Assessment of Roles of University and Governmental R & D Laboratories." *Public Administration Review* 48.6 (1988): 969–78.

Reams, Bernard D., Jr. *University-Industry Research Partnerships.* Westport, Conn.: Quorum, 1986.

Robbins, Frederick C. "Changing Patterns of Biomedical Research Funding: A View from the Medical School." *Clinical Research* 30 (1982): 302–7.

Roberts, E. B., and H. A. Wainer. "New Enterprises on Route 128." *Science Journal* 4 (1968): 78–83.

Rosenzweig, Robert M. "Research as Intellectual Property: Influences Within the University." *Science, Technology, and Human Values* 10.2 (1985): 41–48.

Ross, Richard S. "Academic Research and Industry Relationships." *Clinical and Investigative Medicine* 9 (1986): 269–72.

Saloom, Joseph A., and Charles A. Garber. "Taxing Debate: Is Nonprofit Research Fair?" *Association Management* 39.11 (November 1987): 41–43.

Sanders, John T., and Wade L. Robison. "Research Funding and the Value-Dependence of Science." *Business and Professional Ethics Journal* 11.1 (1992): 33–50.

Schimank, Uwe. "The Contribution of University Research to the Technological Innovation of the German Economy: Societal Auto-Dynamic and Political Guidance." *Research Policy* 17 (1988): 329–40.

Schlant, Robert C. "Principles of Partnership in Research." *Circulation* 72, suppl. 1 (1985): I-18–20.

Schweigert, Bernard S. "University-Industry Partnership in Research." *American Journal of Clinical Nutrition* 46 (1987): 229–31.

Segel, N. S., and R. E. Quince. "The Cambridge Phenomenon and the Role of the Cambridge Science Park." *Science Park and Innovation Centres: Their Economic and Social Impact.* Ed., John Michael Gibb. Amsterdam: Elsevier, 1985. Pp. 172–77.

Servos, John W. "The Industrial Relations of Science: Chemical Engineering at MIT, 1900–1939." *Isis* 71 (1980): 531–49.

Shrager, Carl A. "Corporate Growth Strategies in a Recession." *Corporate Growth Report,* February 1991: 4–5.

Siler, Julia Flynn. "Million-Dollar Professors: Should the Ivory Tower be a Gold Mine?" *Business Week,* 21 August 1989: 90–92.

Smith, Tim R., Mark Drabenstott, and Lynn Gibson. "The Role of Universities in Economic Development." *Economic Review* 72.9 (1987): 3–21.

Spalding, B. J. "Technology by Teamwork." *Chemical Week,* 11 March 1987: 14–15.

Sparks, Jack D. "The Creative Connection: University-Industrial Relations." *Research Management* 28 (1985): 19–21.

Steneck, Nicholas H. "Whose Academic Freedom Needs to Be Protected?: The Case for Classified Research." *Business and Professional Ethics Journal* 11.1 (1992): 17–32.

Stipp, David. "Schools Rein in Faculty Stakes in Biomedicine." *Wall Street Journal*, 12 March 1990.

"Study Updates Academe/Industry Research." *Chemical and Engineering News*, 28 November 1983: 21.

Susman, Marilyn, Judy Koenigsberg, and Beth Bongard. "The Business of Ivory Tower Research: Paradigms for University-Corporate Partnerships." *Journal of Business and Psychology* 4.2 (1989): 251–58.

Szybalski, W. "Benefits and Pitfalls of Patent Policies in Academic Research Employing Genetic Engineering Techniques." *From Genetic Experimentation to Biotechnology—The Critical Transition*. Eds., William J. Whelan and Sandra Black. Chichester, Sussex: Wiley, 1982.

Tasker, M. E., and D. E. Packham. "Freedom, Funding, and the Future of the Universities." *Studies in Higher Education* 15.2 (1990): 181–95.

Thayer, Ann. "University Sues Lilly Over Insulin Patent." *Chemical and Engineering News*, 19 February 1990: 6.

Thayer, Ann. "U.S. Firm, Chinese Set Up Biotech Venture." *Chemical and Engineering News*, 20 March 1989: 7.

Thither, Denis. "A Case Study of Technology Transfer and Funding Mechanisms in an Industrially Supported Multi-Centered University Research Initiative." *Technovation* 10.1 (1990): 39–46.

Thomas, Michael E. "The Manufacturing Research Center at the Georgia Institute of Technology." *Interfaces* 20.6 (1990): 69–74.

Thomson, Judith Jarvis, Burton S. Dreben, Eric Holtzman, and B. Robert Kreiser. "Corporate Funding of Academic Research." *Academe* 69 (November–December 1983): 18a–23a.

Thuente, John. "U of M Patenting and Licensing: A Growing Public Service." *University of Minnesota Research Review* 21 (March 1992): 1+.

Tolbert, T. L. "Industry/University Research Cooperation: Convenience or Necessity—The Industrial View." *Journal of the Society of Research Administrators*. 17.2 (1985): 45–52.

Turner, Judith Axler. "High Technology Companies Often Turn to Colleges for Confidential 'Beta Tests' of New Products." *Chronicle of Higher Education*, 12 October 1988: A13+.

U.S. Congress. House. Committee on Small Business. *Hearings on "The Future of the American Enterprise Economy."* 101st Cong., 1st sess. Washington, D.C.: Government Printing Office (GPO), 1989.

U.S. Congress. House. Human Resources and Intergovernmental Relations Subcommittee of the Committee on Government Operations. *Hearings on "Is Science for Sale? Conflicts of Interest vs. the Public Interest."* 101st Cong., 1st sess. Washington, D.C.: GPO, 1989.

U.S. Congress. House. Joint Committee on Taxation. *Descriptions of Tax Bills S. 1857 and S. 2165."* 98th Cong., 2nd sess. Washington, D.C.: GPO, 1984.

U.S. Congress. House. Subcommittee on Investigations and Oversight of the Committee on Science and Technology. *Hearings on "Biotechnology and Agriculture."* 99th Cong., 1st sess. Washington, D.C.: GPO, 1985.

U.S. Congress. House. Subcommittee on Investigations and Oversight and the Subcommittee on Science and Technology. *Hearings on "Joint Industry Cooperation with Federally Supported Research Facilities."* 98th Cong., 1st sess. Washington, D.C.: GPO, 1983.

U.S. Congress. House. *Hearings on "The Use of Human Biological Materials in the Development of Biomedical Products."* 99th Cong., 1st sess. Washington, D.C.: GPO, 1985.

U.S. Congress. House. Subcommittee on Investigations and Oversight and the Subcommittee on Science, Research, and Technology of the Committee on Science and Technology. *Hearing on "Commercialization of Academic Biomedical Research."* 97th Cong., 1st sess. Washington, D.C.: GPO, 1981.

U.S. Congress. House. Subcommittee on Investigations and Oversight and the Subcommittee on Science, Research, and Technology of the Committee on Science and Technology. *Hearings on "University/Industry Cooperation in Biotechnology."* 97th Cong., 2nd sess. Washington, D.C.: GPO, 1982.

U.S. Congress. House. Subcommittee on Science, Research and Technology of the Committee on Science and Technology. *Hearings on "Implementation of P.L. 96-480 Stevenson-Wydler Technology Innovation Act of 1980."* 97th Cong., 1st sess. Washington, D.C.: GPO, 1981.

U.S. Congress. House. Subcommittee on Science, Research and Technology of the Committee on Science, Space, and Technology. *Hearings on "University/Industry Alliances."* 100th Cong., 2nd sess. Washington, D.C.: GPO, 1988.

U.S. Congress. House. Subcommittee on Technology and Competitiveness of the Committee on Science, Space and Technology. *Hearings on "Biotechnology and Technology Transfer."* 102d Cong., 1st sess. Washington, D.C.: GPO, 1991.

U.S. Congress. Office of Technology Assessment. *Commercial Biotechnology: An International Analysis.* Washington, D.C.: GPO, 1984.

U.S. Congress. Senate. Committee on Finance. *Hearings on "Tax Reform Proposals IX."* 99th Cong., 1st sess. Washington, D.C.: GPO, 1985.

U.S. Congress. Senate. Subcommittee on Savings, Pensions, and Investment

Policy and the Subcommittee on Taxation and Debt Management of the Committee on Finance. *Hearings on "Proposals Relating to Foundations, High Technology, and Depreciation."* 98th Cong., 2nd sess. Washington, D.C.: GPO, 1984.

Varrin, Robert D., and Diane S. Kukich. "Guidelines for Industry-Sponsored Research at Universities." *Science* 227 (1985): 385–88.

Vleggaar, Jan. "Getting Research Off to a Fast Start—The University Route." *Research Technology Management* 34.3 (1991): 19–20.

Von Benda, Heike, and F. J. Radermacher. "The Research Institute for Application-Oriented Knowledge Processing (FAW): Planning and Realizing a High-Technology Institute." *Interfaces* 20.6 (1990): 75–82.

Wade, Nicholas. "The Role of God and Mammon in Molecular Biology." *From Genetic Experimentation to Biotechnology—The Critical Transition.* Eds., William J. Whelan and Sandra Black. Chichester, Sussex: Wiley, 1982.

Wade, Nicholas. *The Science Business.* Twentieth Century Fund Press, 1984.

Walker, William H. "The Technology Plan." *Science* 51 (1920): 357–59.

Waugaman, Paul G. "University-Industry Technology Transfer in Germany: Implications for U.S. Partners." *Journal of the Society of Research Administrators* 22.1 (1990): 7–15.

Weart, Spencer R. "The Rise of 'Prostituted' Physics." *Nature* 262, 1 July 1976: 13–17.

Weber, Kenneth A. "State Public Records Acts: The Need to Exempt Scientific Research Belonging to State Universities From Indiscriminate Public Disclosure." *Journal of College and University Law* 10.2 (1983–84): 129–46.

Weil Teresa. "Commentary—At the Industry-University Interface: Pajaro Dunes." *Idea* 23 (1982): 181–84.

Weinberg, Mark L., and Mary Ellen Mazey. "Government-University-Industry Partnerships in Technology Development: A Case Study." *Technovation* 7 (1988): 131–42.

Weiner, Charles. "Patenting and Academic Research: Historical Case Studies." *Science, Technology and Human Values* 12,1 (1987): 50–62.

Weiner, Charles. "Science in the Marketplace: Historical Precedents and Problems." *From Genetic Experimentation to Biotechnology—The Critical Transition.* Eds. William J. Whelan and Sandra Black. Chichester, Sussex: Wiley, 1982.

Wheeler, David L. "Pressure to Cash In on Research Stirs Conflict-of-Interest Issues." *Chronicle of Higher Education,* 12 April 1989: A29+.

Whelan, William J., and Sandra Black, Eds. *From Genetic Experimentation to Biotechnology—The Critical Transition.* Chichester, Sussex: Wiley, 1982.

Whitburn, Merrill D. "Freedom in the Research and Teaching of Rhetoric: University-Industry Cooperation." *ADE Bulletin* 79 (1984): 37–39.

Wiedhaup, K. "University-Industry: A Happy Match?" *Pharmaceutisch Weekblad Scientific Edition* 7 (1985): 46–50.

Wolfe, Robert J. "When a University Becomes a Developer." *Real Estate Finance Journal* 2.1 (1986): 56–61.

Worthy, Ward. "Purdue Program Enhances Academic/Industry Ties." *Chemical and Engineering News,* 29 July 1985: 24+.

Woutat, Donald. "College Goes Controversial as it Goes International." Minneapolis *Star Tribune,* 22 July 1990: A1.

Wroblewski, Rita. "The Pharmaceutical Industry and Academic Medicine in Collaboration." *Circulation* 72, suppl. 1 (1985): I-3-7.

Wroblewski, Rita, and Lawrence Sorel Cohen. "Cardiovascular Medicine: Opportunities for Enhanced University-Industry Collaboration. Introduction." *Circulation* 72, suppl. 1 (1985): I-1-2.

Wyckoff, Andrew W., and Louis G. Tornatzky. "State-Level Efforts to Transfer Manufacturing Technology: A Survey of Programs and Practices." *Management Science* 34.4 (1988): 469–81.

Yamamoto, Keith R. "Faculty Members as Corporate Officers: Does the Cost Outweigh Benefit?" *From Genetic Experimentation to Biotechnology—The Critical Transition.* Eds., William J. Whelan and Sandra Black. Chichester, Sussex: Wiley, 1982.

Index

About the Author

NORMAN E. BOWIE is the Elmer L. Andersen Chair of Corporate Responsibility and holds a joint appointment in the Departments of Strategic Management and Organization and Philosophy at the University of Minnesota. He currently serves as Chair of the Strategic Management and Organization Department.

Professor Bowie is co-author of *Business Ethics* (second edition) and the co-editor of *Ethical Theory and Business* (fourth edition). He is the author or co-editor of nine other books on professional ethics and political philosophy and is a frequent contributor to scholarly journals and conferences. His research interests include the morality of markets, stakeholder management and international business ethics. He is past president of the Society for Business Ethics, the American Society for Value Inquiry and the former Executive Secretary of the American Philosophical Association.